Honest
American Fare

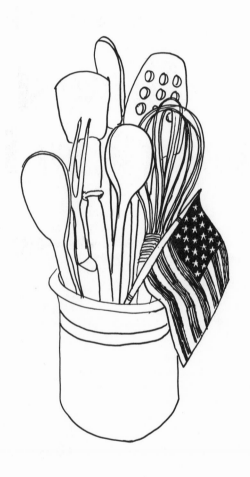

Honest
American Fare

Bert Greene

Contemporary Books, Inc.
Chicago

Library of Congress Cataloging in Publication Data

Greene, Bert, 1923–
   Honest American fare.

   Includes index.
   1. Cookery, American.   I. Title.
TX715.G8116   1981   641.5973   81-66083
ISBN 0-8092-5965-6   AACR2

Illustrations by the author

Copyright © 1981 by Bert Greene
All rights reserved
Published by Contemporary Books, Inc.
180 North Michigan Avenue, Chicago, Illinois 60601
Manufactured in the United States of America
Library of Congress Catalog Card Number: 81-66083
International Standard Book Number: 0-8092-5965-6

Published simultaneously in Canada by
Beaverbooks, Ltd.
150 Lesmill Road
Don Mills, Ontario M3B 2T5
Canada

This book is for

Phillip Stephen Schulz

with much gratitude.

Literally my right hand (in and out of the kitchen). He first helped sift through the thousands of yellowing recipes that were collected for this book. Later, he tested and logged the best of them—with the highest hopes—even when a dish went back to the burner five times or more for remedial seasoning. Where would a cookbook writer be without such good fellowship? Clearly, out of business!

Contents

Introduction

Talent, they say, skips a generation. In the kitchen, it probably takes even longer.

Like most of my middle-aged cooking contemporaries, I have done my share of public hankering after the vanished dishes I remember from childhood. Not because the state of our table is *so* lamentable today—it is not. But rather because American food has seemingly lost its natural character.

What, for instance, has become of the treasured larder of homemades (the natural soups and unwined stews . . . those incredible moist cakes . . . and loaves of true and wholesome substance) I grew up on? These dishes, once considered staples of the national diet, were the viands our grandmothers prepared three times a day as part of their normal household routines.

What has happened to that *honest American fare?*

It is mostly forgotten, I am sorry to say. Or at best, relegated to the limbo of food archives.

Our emancipated mothers outlawed all homely recipes from their kitchens not long after World War II because the earlier style of cooking simply required too much time to prepare. And, more importantly, it was not considered showy enough to compensate for the effort.

Almost forty years have passed since I can remember anyone taking true pride in native U.S.A. cookery. And the wondrous inheritance of that richly textured cuisine lies moldering still, while new generations of home cooks turn the art of food preparation into a cult performance: *French* yesterday; *Italian* today, and *Greek, Indonesian,* or *Coptic* tomorrow!

I am a self-professed lover of international cuisine (particularly in its land of origin), but if I have only one mission as a food writer it is to preserve the option of that bespoke "honest American fare."

The best of our native cookery was hand recorded. My own mother used to keep a worn, blue school notebook (inscribed, as I recall, in a rather florid scrawl) with all the recipes she considered worthy of being handed down. Mostly, these formulas were a record of the dishes she had seen prepared at my grandmother's elbow, for my maternal forebear was not a lady to mete or measure out as she stirred. But there were also mysterious appellations sprinkled through the pages, such as "Sylvia's Rich Cookies" or "Belle's Magnificent Spinach and Cheese Strudel," which whetted my appetite to the extreme. As I remember, my mother always kept this cookbook in her linen closet—so the yellowed pages retained a faint scent of crushed lavender mixed with laundry starch that made the recipes seem even more prodigal.

It was a volume that would have appeared insubstantial to most culinary bibliophiles, I suppose, but I always considered it a rightful family bequest. And deeply mourned the loss when my sister and I discovered that the ancient notebook had been misplaced or somehow gone astray during the cross-country migrations that studded the last years of my mother's life.

While many handsome cookbooks have been compiled in the name of our native cuisine, none seems to match the authority of a home-kept record to me. To render a dispassionate volume of what I deem "honest American fare," I logged more than a thousand of these family cookbooks—some dating back to the early nineteenth century—along with double that number of church pamphlets and Junior League bulletins. Some of these collections were from towns so miniscule they do not even have local post offices, but they *did* have chefs! I cannot accurately recall just how many rural food historians and simply good cooks assisted in this project (from one coast to another), but the number was prodigious.

The result—super good eating.

If there are better biscuits in this world than Kate Almand's mirific and tender Georgia concoctions, I cannot imagine where they would be found. The formula for Clara Armstrong's delectable ham loaf has won prizes at the Connecticut State Fair for more than three decades, but its devise has never seen the light of print before (unless it was reported in the *Stafford Springs Social Guide*). Johnny Reb oysters (from Laurel, Mississippi) may be only kissing kin to the better advertised oysters Rockefeller, Roffignac, or Bienville, but they are the best baked bivalves known to western man! California *cioppino*? For it I would gladly forswear bouillabaisse! Though, to tell the truth, they are both dishes with a common Mediterranean heritage. Kentucky burgoo is another kettle of fish entirely—compounded of no sea beast at all. Squirrel meat, rabbit, and wild fowl were this dish's chief ingredients originally, but pork, chicken, and beef are also-ran amendments—particularly on Derby Day. Pennsylvania's Chester County provided me with a winner of a different stripe, Funeral Pie. This dessert, concocted of dried raisins and orange peel was so named because it offered a full stomach after a spare burial. From Kansas Mennonites comes my favorite summer soup, fruity pfaumenüs, a tonic mix of plums, rhubarb, and soured cream, lightly thickened with sugar. Consider a glass yourself on the warmest June day—with a plate of homemade zwieback on the side. The collation is endless: ginger ice and gingersnaps and ginger cream pie; buttermilk brownies and buttermilk waffles with buttermilk fudge. But why belabor the point. This is simply the very best American food I know. Honestly!

APPETIZERS

Chapter One

An American of decidedly unsophisticated palate, I recall relishing no appetizer served to me as a child unless it was crowned with a bright red cherry. And, sad to relate, my first-course-consciousness was never raised a jot above the level of canned fruit salad or honeydew melon until I approached the very brink of adolescence.

From her European-born parents, my mother had inherited a mouth for tangy foods. She adored sturgeon, herring, anchovies, and (most of all) caviar as meal starters. On the rare occasions when I was offered a bite, I rejected all of these delicacies out of hand.

"Too fishy! Too salty!" I cried in revulsion. Pâté, when first tasted, was equally dismissed as mere chopped liver. Hor-ri-ble! was the evaluation.

I cannot rightly remember when my taste buds became internationalized, but surely the late French actress, Irene Bordoni, had something to do with the dietary change.

In the mid-1930s, before the picture tube was little more than a gleam in some electronic engineer's eye, Americans settled around radios for home entertainment. Our household was no exception. Of all the "sketches" (a name my father gave to all radio drama) we listened to, my favorite was called "Evenings in Paris." Aired on Sunday nights just before my bedtime, this program was the quintessential soap opera *bouffe*. The adventures of a beautiful and glamorous chanteuse (Miss Bordoni of course), it detailed her exploits in fabled places like Le Trocadéro and Casino de Paris—enthralling geography to a boy from Queens, New York.

I suppose I should not credit radio alone for my miscreant culinary allegiance, but overnight I developed into a hard-edged Francophile.

As family chef (my mother worked full-time at this point), I would ransack our small shelf of cookbooks, searching for any recipes that seemed even remotely "foreign" to my eye.

Haute cuisine was a phrase that I picked up somewhere, and I used it indiscriminately to garnish my conversation as other cooks might employ parsley. However, my infatuation with elegant cookery was total conjecture, as I had never tasted a forkful of the real thing.

By hook or by crook I made up my mind to repair that omission. For weeks prior to my thirteenth birthday, I nagged my mother to take me to a French restaurant for dinner. Such hostelries, I must note, were not common in Manhattan in those days and many maternal inquiries were made before my parent determined on the right establishment for our outing.

"A place where a woman alone can take a growing boy to eat!"

With great expectations (on my part at least), we met for this fateful dinner. The restaurant was a small bistro in the West Fifties. There were checkered tablecloths and aproned waiters—even a Dubonnet sign over the bar—but no dishes that truly whetted my appetite. Perhaps there were, but I could not read them as the menu was one long purplish blur of ink entirely in French! For an appetizer, my mother chose *canapé au anchois* and was not disappointed; I opted for *maquereau* and was—never expecting a whole silvery fish with its head still intact.

Later, my mother asked the waiter's advice and was directed to rack of lamb. I, eschewing assistance, ordered *boeuf Bourguignonne* by default and hated every winy mouthful of the stew.

The bitterest disappointment of the evening was dessert. Bypassing *meringue glacé* and *pot de crème au chocolat*, I ordered the grandest sounding item I could make out—*crème caramel renversée*. To my utter chagrin, it turned out to be that most loathsome nursery food, baked custard.

My mother was sanguine about the largely uneaten meal.

"Maybe you should switch languages from Latin to French

next term," she suggested as we took the subway home. "So next time you will be able to read the menu!"

I merely shrugged.

My interest in things *français* was never quite the same somehow.

When did I develop a latent passion for the food of my native land? After my first long tour of the Continent almost forty years later. Why? Too much of a good thing too late, I suppose!

Unlike the Greenes, early Americans (Pilgrims, Puritans, and that spartan crowd) never ate more than one dish at a meal, except for religious celebrations like tradition-heavy Thanksgiving dinners. Working folk, who took their main meal when the sun was high, they had very little time off from tending of crops and defending their homes for niceties of the table.

The arrangement of meals into multicoursed affairs came with the arrival of ethnic groups (the French, Italians, Germans, Scandinavians, Irish, Russians, and Jews) in the nineteenth century. These early immigrants brought their table customs, like their culinary prejudices and prides, with them from the Old Country. Their menus however, suffered a sea change, and most dishes were soon judiciously adapted to suit the raw ingredients available on the new turf.

The names of American appetizers are curiously artless—reflecting a mirror of history, religion, war, geographical location, and even a state of mind. Take fritters, for instance. These airy batter cakes may have some marginal connection to *frittata* (a northern Italian mix of cooked leftovers and eggs), as some food snoops imply. Personally, I doubt it strongly, preferring to believe that the name merely describes some early housewife's lassitude. After a day misspent in dalliance, the lady throws together eggs, flour, and whatever fruit or vegetable she has on hand and her *frittered* time is not only assuaged but actually celebrated!

Appetizer names are sometimes descriptive. Frazzled green

onions certainly hints at the harried condition of some midwestern frau. *Eggplant lagniappes* (from the Cajun country), on the other hand, are plainly named for kitchen surplus. From two familiar ingredients, an uncommon-tasting third was concocted—and dubbed with the Louisiana handle for all such bonuses. If a dish has a moniker like "Smack Good," the suspicion arises that a wife beater is lurking near the stove. Not a bit of it. This tonic relish (a Norwegian transplant of green and red peppers is a mustardy vinaigrette) was known as *smake godt* in the land of fjords. The translation—"goodie," and it is too!

Johnny Reb Oysters were so called not for the army of prodigal young soldiers but rather for the scapegrace kitchen invention that celebrated their unvictorious return. A thin strip of ham or a handful of stale bread was usually all that could be scrounged up in the way of banquet provender. But added to a harvest of young Atlantic oysters, these ingredients were the basis of a great American dish, because of an overlooked seasoning perhaps—purest love.

My personal feeling for the appetizers presented here is very strong. Aside from any historical or national ties, they all hold a favored place at my dinner table because, frankly, they taste so good!

But why speak of it any longer? The first course most definitely awaits.

I came upon the following prescription for Frazzled Green Onions in a turn-of-the-century farm journal, printed in Illinois. The author (anonymous) allowed that "scallions should be picked when they are no bigger in circumference than a plump baby's finger." Having no tot of my own around for instant comparison, I simply make do with the firmest, fattest bulbs I can find—picking them most often at the supermarket and *not* the garden.

The dish is easy, economical, and very satisfying before a roast. Best of all, it may be prepared in advance and merely topped with cheese before it goes into the oven. *A note about cheese:* This recipe originally specified no variety. A devotee of Parmesan, I therefore amended it to suit my taste. Parmesan cheese (and particularly Parmigiano-Reggiano imported from Italy) may not be a 100 percent Yankee ingredient but it surely gives our native cuisine a touch of class.

FRAZZLED GREEN ONIONS

4 *bunches green onions (about ¾ pound)*
3½ *tablespoons butter*
2 *tablespoons all-purpose flour*
1 *cup hot strong Chicken Stock (see Index)*
½ *cup whipping cream*
¼ *teaspoon freshly grated nutmeg*
Dash of hot pepper sauce
Salt and freshly ground pepper
¼ *cup Parmesan cheese*
¼ *cup fine bread crumbs*
Pinch of crushed dried hot red peppers

I.   Heat oven to 350°. Trim tops of onions, leaving about 1½ inches green stems. Trim roots. Drop into boiling salted water. Return to boiling over high heat; cook 1 minute. Rinse briefly under cold water; drain thoroughly. Place in a shallow baking dish.

II.   Melt 2 tablespoons butter in a medium saucepan; stir in the flour. Cook, stirring constantly, 2 minutes. Beat in chicken stock; cook over medium heat until very thick, about 5 minutes. Stir in cream. Add nutmeg, hot pepper sauce, salt and pepper to taste, and 2 tablespoons cheese. Cook 5 minutes. Spoon over onions.

III. Melt remaining 1½ tablespoons butter in a small saucepan; stir in bread crumbs. Cook over medium-high heat, stirring constantly, until crumbs become golden. Stir in hot peppers; spoon mixture over onions. Top with remaining 2 tablespoons Parmesan cheese. Bake until bubbly, about 15 minutes.

Serves 4 to 6.

Having unburdened myself earlier on the subject of the fritter's origins, I will skip all prefatory remarks except to note that these delicious fried morsels dot family recipe books from Maine to Mississippi. The following is a Moravian version from Pennsylvania. The Lemon Cream Gravy accompaniment is merely a table option. For years, hearty folk have eaten the fritters with syrup, and even confectioners' sugar, mated with a thick cut of ham or bacon. I find the carrot fritter makes a particularly satisfying preliminary to a dinner on the spare side, like unadorned broiled chicken or fish.

CARROT FRITTERS

1 *cup all-purpose flour*
1 *teaspoon baking powder*
½ *teaspoon salt*
¼ *teaspoon freshly grated nutmeg*
⅛ *teaspoon ground allspice*
½ *teaspoon beef bouillon powder*
1 *egg, lightly beaten*
½ *cup whipping cream*
Juice of 1 lemon
1 *cup cooked carrots, mashed*
1 *tablespoon finely chopped chives*
Oil
Lemon Cream Gravy (recipe follows)

I.   Heat oven to 250°. Combine the flour, baking powder, salt, nutmeg, allspice, and bouillon powder in a large bowl; mix thoroughly. Add beaten egg, cream, lemon juice, carrots, and chives. Beat batter with a wooden spoon until smooth.

II.   Heat 1½ inches oil in a large saucepan until very hot. Spoon up a generous teaspoon of fritter batter and drop into the oil. (Spoon out no more than six fritters at a time). Fry until deep golden on both sides. Drain on paper toweling. Place fritters in a shallow baking dish; keep warm in the oven until serving. Serve with Lemon Cream Gravy.

Serves 4 to 6.

LEMON CREAM GRAVY

2 *tablespoons unsalted butter*
1 *large shallot, minced*
2 *tablespoons all-purpose flour*
1½ *cups hot strong chicken broth*
3 *tablespoons lemon juice*
Dash of hot pepper sauce
½ *cup whipping cream*
Pinch of freshly grated nutmeg
1 *teaspoon finely grated lemon rind*

I.   Melt butter in a medium saucepan over medium-low heat. Stir in shallot; cook until soft, about 5 minutes. Stir in flour; cook, stirring constantly, 2 minutes. Slowly add chicken broth and lemon juice. Simmer 5 minutes.

II.   Add hot pepper sauce and cream to chicken broth mixture. Cook until slightly thickened. (Gravy should be the consistency of light cream.) Add nutmeg and lemon rind. Serve with Carrot Fritters.

Makes about 1½ cups.

Some of the most tonic fare served in this country was annexed from our good neighbor Mexico, without so much as a tip of the hat. Bastardized by generations of *gringo* chuck-wagon chefs, this borrowed cuisine is now an entity unto itself, dubbed *Tex-Mex* cookery most of the time. The following formula for a runny cheese hors d'oeuvre (like a pyromaniacal version of rarebit eaten on flour tortillas) comes intact from San Diego—a classic example of what I suspect will be tagged *Cal-Mex* cookery from now on.

CHILI CON QUESO

Flour Tortillas (recipe follows)
1 *pound Monterey Jack, or any white melting cheese, grated*
3 *tablespoons olive oil*
1 *large onion, finely chopped*
1 *clove garlic, minced*
½ *cup chopped green bell pepper*
1 *tablespoon chili powder*
1 *can (10 ounces) mixed tomatoes and green chiles (I use Ortega brand)*
2 *tablespoons chopped, canned jalapeño peppers*
⅔ *cup whipping cream*

I.   Make tortillas. Keep warm.

II.   Heat oven to 200°. Place the cheese in a large, heatproof bowl. Heat in oven for 10 minutes. (Do not let cheese become too hot. It should melt, but not be stringy.)

III.   Meanwhile, heat the oil in a large sauté pan over medium heat. Add onion, garlic, and green pepper; cook 5 minutes. Add chili powder, mixed tomatoes and chiles, and jalapeño peppers. Cook 3 to 4 minutes longer.

IV.   Remove cheese from oven. Slowly beat in the whipping cream. Stir in tomato-peppers mixture. Mix thoroughly. Serve with tortillas.

Fills 18 to 20 tortillas.

The ritual for eating *chili con queso* requires the diner to spread a healthy dab of the stuff on the edge of a tortilla, then roll it up like a fat cigar and chomp away, using fingers only—never, never forks!

The following unorthodox tortillas substitute all-purpose flour for traditional *masa harina.*

FLOUR TORTILLAS

4 *cups all-purpose flour*
½ *cup cold vegetable shortening*
2 *teaspoons salt*
1 *cup warm water (115°)*

I.   Sift the flour into a large bowl. Cut in the shortening; blend with a pastry blender until the texture of coarse crumbs.

II.   Dissolve the salt in the warm water. Add to flour mixture in a steady stream while working the two together with your fingers. (The warm water causes a rapid expansion of the flour particles, giving the tortillas a chewy texture.) Knead the ingredients in the large bowl until a solid mass is formed. Transfer to a floured board; knead 3 minutes. (The dough will be quite rough.)

III.   Cover dough with a towel and let stand 1 hour. Knead 1 minute. Re-cover; let stand 10 minutes longer.

IV.   Pinch off 1½-inch-long pieces of dough. Roll out on a lightly floured board into 7-inch circles. Roll from the center outward, being careful not to taper the edges by rolling over them. Stack tortillas on top of each other.

V.   Heat a heavy, cast-iron griddle or skillet over medium-high heat until very hot. Cook the tortillas, one at a time, in the griddle, 20 seconds on one side, 10 seconds on the other. Tortillas should be white with a light brown, spotty surface. Stack on a platter. Wipe pan occasionally with paper toweling to keep flour from burning. Cover with a towel to keep warm. Just before serving, cover loosely with aluminum foil and reheat in a low oven.

Makes 20 tortillas.

The next recipe (as noted early on) is of strictly Norwegian descent. The original version actually made its way to Minnesota by Conestoga wagon. In its seminal renderings, the dish was prepared by burning off the skins of the peppers over an open fire. But time and technology took care of that practice some while back. Reclaimed from an old family cookbook in Chaska, this dish has been part and parcel of my party food repertoire for almost two decades. I have served it at balls and picnics alike. Nowadays I portion it out only as an opening to a meal when a burnished roast (lamb, pork, or veal) is to follow tableside.

SMACK GOOD PEPPERS

4 *green bell peppers*
4 *red bell peppers*
¼ *cup chopped shallots*
2 *tablespoons Dijon mustard*
2 *tablespoons red wine vinegar*

2 *teaspoons soy sauce*
⅓ to ½ cup olive oil
Salt and freshly ground pepper
¼ cup chopped fresh parsley

I.   Heat oven to 350°. Cook the peppers in boiling salted water 2 minutes; drain. Place peppers in a shallow, aluminum foil-lined baking dish. Bake until lightly roasted and the skins peel easily, about 50 minutes.

II.   Cool peppers slightly; peel and remove seeds. Cut into thin strips. Combine pepper strips and shallots in a large bowl.

III. Combine mustard, vinegar, and soy sauce in a medium bowl. Slowly beat in the oil, a few drops at a time. (The mixture should be quite thick.) Season to taste with salt and pepper. Pour mixture over pepper strips and shallots; mix well. Transfer to a serving dish. Sprinkle with parsley. Chill well before serving.

Serves 6.

The following is another expatriate dish that has found its way into American cuisine. The canon came into my hot hands recently from a good friend, Mary Surina (of Yugoslavian forebears), who was born in Washington and lived most of her long life in San Pedro, California. Mary never exactly prepared this recipe for me. Instead, she recited the steps after dinner, like a digestive! *Zelje*, appropriately enough, means greens in Yugoslavian.

ZELJE

3 *cups strong Chicken Stock (see Index)*
1 *medium potato, pared, cubed*
1 *bunch kale (about 12 ounces), trimmed, chopped*
1 *bunch broccoli (about 18 ounces), chopped*
1 *bunch Swiss chard (about 10 ounces), trimmed, chopped*
1 *bunch spinach (about 6 ounces), trimmed, chopped*
⅓ *cup olive oil*
3 *cloves garlic, minced*
¼ *cup freshly grated Parmesan cheese*

I.   Heat oven to 350°. Heat Chicken Stock to boiling in a
        large saucepan; reduce heat. Add potato and kale;
        simmer 10 minutes. Add broccoli and chard; simmer 8
        minutes. Add spinach; simmer 3 minutes longer. Drain,
        reserving stock for use at another time.

II.   Heat oil in a large, heavy saucepan over medium heat.
        Add garlic; cook until golden, about 3 minutes. Stir in
        vegetables; cook 2 minutes. Transfer to a buttered,
        shallow baking dish. Sprinkle with cheese. Bake until
        bubbly, about 20 minutes.

                                                Serves 4 to 6.

Oysters, like the taste buds of their devoted fanciers, are a
national tradition. The earliest English settlers in New York
found the Indians eating oysters when they arrived. And, what
is more, the native Americans were rather discerning in their
allegiance to one variety as opposed to another. Hastily, the
colonists adopted this gastronomic elitism. Today, oyster selec-
tion is still a pretty snobby business; the cognoscenti only slurp
oysters of distinguished place of origin. The favorites are Blue-
points, Lynnhavens, Cotuits, Cape Cods, and Chincoteagues in

the East, and nothing but Olympias in the West. My favored oyster, however, is found off Grand Isle, Louisiana, where the next recipe just might have originated. It didn't. This version is from Laurel, Mississippi!

JOHNNY REB OYSTERS

¼ *cup unsalted butter*
3 *tablespoons finely chopped shallots*
1½ *cups cracker crumbs*
¼ *cup chopped fresh parsley*
24 *shucked oysters (about 1½ pints), drained*
Juice of 1 lemon
Hot pepper sauce
Soy sauce
Freshly ground pepper
¼ *cup finely chopped, cooked ham*
½ *cup whipping cream*
Chopped fresh parsley

I. Heat oven to 375°. Melt butter in a medium sauté pan over medium-low heat. Add shallots; cook until soft, about 5 minutes.

II. Combine cracker crumbs, fresh parsley, and cooked shallots (including all butter left in the pan) in large bowl. Stir with a fork until well mixed.

III. Place half the cracker mixture on the bottom of a shallow baking dish. Place the oysters on top of the crackers. Season oysters to taste with lemon juice, hot pepper sauce, soy sauce, and freshly ground pepper.

IV.   Sprinkle oysters lightly with half the remaining cracker mixture and then the chopped ham. Spoon the cream evenly over the top. Add remaining cracker mixture. Bake until nicely browned, 25 to 30 minutes. Garnish with chopped parsley.

Serves 4 to 6.

More Southern exposures. A Sunday night summer "slaw" of green beans and bacon (from Tennessee) meant to be consumed "as fast as the pot can be got from the stove to the table" is the way I took down this recipe. I prefer the dish as a wintry treat—a prelude to a hearty dinner. If tastes have changed a mite, string bean crops are not far behind. That once seasonal treat now makes a year-round appearance in kitchens all over the U.S. So let us celebrate them, please!

GREEN BEANS WITH CRACKLINGS

½ pound fresh green beans, cut in the French style
1 clove garlic, bruised
½ cup watercress leaves
2 teaspoons Dijon mustard
1 tablespoon red wine vinegar
¼ cup olive oil
2 tablespoons hot enriched beef bouillon
2 tablespoons Clabbered Cream (recipe follows)
Salt and freshly ground pepper
4 strips cooked bacon, crumbled

I.   Drop the beans in boiling salted water. Return to a rolling boil; remove from heat. Drain immediately under cold running water. Drain again.

II.   Rub a wooden salad bowl well with the bruised garlic. Discard garlic. Combine the beans and watercress in the bowl.

III.   Combine the mustard and vinegar in a small bowl. Slowly add the oil, bouillon, cream, and salt and freshly ground pepper to taste. Pour over the beans and watercress. Toss well. Sprinkle with bacon.

Serves 4.

The Clabbered Cream that makes such a taste difference in the foregoing slaw is actually kin to France's fabled *crème fraîche.* This American cousin, enormously popular in Southern kitchens until the twentieth century, lost favor for half a century before I got to taste it. Like a yogurt-scented cream, it is a food definitely due for revival! I must confess that I make up a pint twice a month for kitchen utility (such as instant dessert with berries when an unexpected guest pops up) or to enrich a pound cake, thin the soup, or mash the potatoes! Like me, I predict you will clamor for clabber!

CLABBERED CREAM

1 *cup whipping cream*
1 *teaspoon buttermilk (do not use ultrapasteurized)*

I.   Combine cream and buttermilk in a small saucepan. Heat slowly until lukewarm (90°). Pour mixture into a sterilized, screw-top jar. Screw on the top loosely. Wrap jar in a towel; let stand in a warm place until cream begins to thicken, 10 to 12 hours in warm weather, 20 or more hours in cold weather. Store cream, tightly covered, in refrigerator. Cream will thicken as it chills. Chilled Clabbered Cream will keep for about two weeks.

Makes 1 cup.

Quiffle is a New England invention—from Truro, on Cape Cod, Massachusetts. I named the savory custard and ham tart thusly because the finished recipe seemed so ambivalently half quiche-half soufflé!

QUIFFLE

1 *shallot, minced*
1 *teaspoon butter*
1 *pound cooked ham, ground*
1 *cup cold mashed cooked potatoes*
2 *teaspooons Dijon mustard*
¼ *teaspoon freshly ground pepper*
3 *egg yolks*
1 *cup whipping cream*
1 *tablespoon cognac*
1 *tablespoon Madeira*
⅛ *teaspoon freshly grated nutmeg*
⅛ *teaspoon ground white pepper*
⅛ *teaspoon ground allspice*
½ *teaspoon salt*
1 *cup grated Swiss or Jarlsberg cheese*
¼ *cup freshly grated Parmesan cheese*
4 *egg whites*

I.   Heat oven to 375°. Sauté shallot in butter until golden, about 4 minutes. Combine shallot, ham, potatoes, mustard, and freshly ground pepper in a large bowl. Press mixture into a buttered, 10-inch ceramic quiche pan, covering sides and bottom. Bake 15 minutes. Cool slightly on a rack.

II.   Beat the egg yolks in another large bowl until light. Beat in cream, cognac, Madeira, nutmeg, white pepper, allspice, and salt. Stir in Swiss cheese and 2 tablespoons Parmesan cheese.

III.   Beat egg whites until stiff. Fold into yolk-cheese mixture. Pour mixture into baked shell. Sprinkle remaining 2 tablespoons Parmesan cheese over the top. Bake until golden brown and set, 45 to 50 minutes.

Serves 6 to 8.

Despite any rumors you may have heard to the contrary, our neighbor Canada's cookery is extremely colorful: a cuisine which celebrates that country's ethnic differences in a multitude of ways. And just to keep the record straight, the national dish is most definitely *not* Eskimo Pie!

French Canadians have contributed a remarkably tasty meat pie they call *tourtière* that has managed to immigrate into the U.S. only as far as Brunswick, Maine. But that is our loss. Originally this double-crusted tart was prepared with passenger pigeons, or *tourtes* as they were known to the Bretons living in Nova Scotia. But the birds (an early endangered species) vanished from Acadian skies shortly after those hapless French were expelled themselves. The tradition of pigeon pie remains, but nowadays, fresh pork or a mixture of several different kinds of meat are combined to produce the dish. Tourtière is always set out on Christmas Eve or to denote some special occasion like weddings or christenings. More to the point, it is never served hot (room temperature only) and eaten, I must attest greedily, only with the fingers!

TOURTIÈRE

FOR THE PASTRY:
2 *cups all-purpose flour*
½ *teaspoon salt*
⅛ *teaspoon granulated sugar*
¼ *cup chilled unsalted butter*
3 *tablespoons chilled vegetable shortening*
5 *tablespoons cold water (approximately)*

FOR THE FILLING:
1 *tablespoon butter*
1 *tablespoon vegetable oil*
1 *large onion, finely chopped*
1 *large clove garlic, minced*
1 *pound lean uncooked veal, diced*
1 *pound lean uncooked pork, diced*
½ *teaspoon ground cloves*
¼ *teaspoon ground cinnamon*
½ *teaspoon ground savory*
1 *bay leaf, crumbled*
3 *tablespoons sherry*
1⅓ *cups chicken broth*
3 *medium potatoes, pared, diced, rinsed in cold water, drained*
2 *tablespoons butter, softened*
3 *tablespoons all-purpose flour*
⅛ *teaspoon ground allspice*
Salt and freshly ground pepper

I. To make the pastry: Combine the flour, salt, and sugar in a large bowl. Mix well. Cut in butter and shortening. Blend with a pastry blender until the texture of coarse crumbs. Blend in the water with a fork; mix to make a soft dough. Knead briefly on a floured board; chill dough 1 hour.

II.   Divide the chilled dough in half; refrigerate one half. Roll out the other half; line an 11-to-12-inch pie plate. Chill.

III.   To make the filling: Heat 1 tablespoon butter and the oil in a large saute pan over medium heat. Add onion and garlic; cook 5 minutes.

IV.   Increase heat slightly; stir in meats. Sauté until meats lose pink color. Reduce heat to medium low; add cloves, cinnamon, savory, bay leaf, sherry, and broth. Cook, stirring occasionally, 25 minutes. Stir in potatoes; cook 20 minutes. Drain the meat and potatoes reserving the liquid. Let meat mixture cool.

V.   Heat oven to 425°. Heat reserved liquid to boiling in a small saucepan. Reduce heat. Mix softened butter and the flour until smooth. Stir into liquid. Add allspice, and salt and pepper to taste. Cook until thickened, about 5 minutes.

VI.   Roll out remaining dough to an approximate 13-inch circle. Fill the chilled pie shell with meat and potato mixture. Spoon sauce over the top. Cover with pastry; crimp edges to seal. Cut a hole in the center to allow steam to escape. Bake until golden brown, about 35 minutes. Serve chilled or at room temperature.

Serves 6 to 8.

From Missouri comes a very old-time dish. Named "cleats," these little underpinnings of cornmeal take on an upholstery of melted cheese in the formula I originally discovered. Recently, however, I was informed that these delicate nubbins made an appearance at the White House—dabbed with Clabbered Cream and a speck of American caviar.

CORNMEAL CLEATS

2½ cups milk
¾ cup yellow cornmeal
½ teaspoon salt
¼ cup melted butter
3 tablespoons grated Swiss or Jarlsberg cheese
3 tablespoons freshly grated Parmesan cheese

I.   Heat the milk slowly to boiling in a medium saucepan over medium-low heat. (Do not allow to scorch.) Slowly beat in the cornmeal with a wire whisk. Continue to beat until smooth and thick. Remove from heat; stir in salt. Pour into a lightly buttered 8-inch square or 9-inch round cake pan. Cool on a wire rack.

II.   Heat oven to 375°. Cut the cooked mixture into 1½-inch rounds. Arrange, slightly overlapping, in a shallow baking dish. Pour melted butter over the top and sprinkle with Swiss and Parmesan cheeses. Bake until tops are lightly browned, about 15 minutes.

Serves 6 to 8.

Gunk is a purely American phenomenon invented for the rapacious dippers and scrapers who appear at the sideboard during a cocktail party. The following canon for a most exemplary hot version was produced by the wife of one of New York's most distinguished psychiatrists. I begged her for the recipe—she afforded it kindly—and then being a typical Libra I stuffed tomatoes with it for a first course instead of offering it to you with toast fingers. You may make your own dictums on the matter. Millie Steven's original baked formula (sans tomatoes) serves about ten hungry topers.

MILLIE STEVEN'S HOT ARTICHOKE GUNK

8 *medium tomatoes*
1 *can (14 ounces) water-packed artichoke hearts*
1 *clove garlic, minced*
1 *cup mayonnaise*
1 *cup freshly grated Parmesan cheese*
¼ *teaspoon soy sauce*
Dash of hot pepper sauce
Freshly ground pepper

I.   Heat oven to 350°. Cut tops off tomatoes. Scoop out insides with a spoon (reserve pulp for use at another time); turn tomatoes upside down on paper toweling.

II. Drain artichokes; coarsely chop. Combine with garlic, mayonnaise, ¾ cup cheese, the soy sauce, hot pepper sauce, and fresh pepper to taste. Spoon mixture into tomatoes. Place in a shallow baking dish. Sprinkle with remaining ¼ cup cheese. Bake until golden brown, about 20 minutes.

Serves 8.

From the Southwest (New Mexico to be exact) comes a kitchen inheritance. From the Spanish? Well, not quite. This dish is more cowboy than conquistador material. These poached eggs are decidedly at home on the range—wherever that stove top happens to be!

HUEVOS RANCHEROS

¼ *pound bacon, coarsely chopped*
1 *onion, chopped*
2 *large cloves garlic, thinly sliced*
1 *medium potato, diced*
2 *medium jalapeños or hot green peppers, seeded, minced*
1 *can (1 pound, 12 ounces) plum tomatoes*
3 *large fresh basil leaves, chopped or a pinch of dried*
⅛ *teaspoon chopped fresh thyme or a pinch of dried*
½ *teaspoon salt*
¼ *teaspoon freshly ground pepper*
4 *to 6 eggs*
Chopped fresh parsley

I.   Fry the bacon in a large, heavy skillet over medium heat until almost crisp. Drain all but 2 tablespoons grease from skillet. Add onion and garlic. Sauté until golden, about 4 minutes.

II.   Stir potato, jalapeños, tomatoes, basil, thyme, salt, and pepper into skillet. Cook, stirring occasionally, over medium-low heat until fairly thick and smooth, about 1 hour.

III.   Break each egg into individual bowl. Place eggs, one at a time, on top of tomato mixture. Cook eggs, covered, until consistency of poached eggs, 3 to 5 minutes. Sprinkle with salt and pepper; dust with parsley. Serve with hot crusty bread, preferably sourdough.

Serves 4 to 6.

Last, but still *lagniappe,* is one of the Cajun country's best (and for some curious reason, unsung) table delights.

CAJUN EGGPLANT LAGNIAPPE

8 *or* 10 *small eggplants*
2 *shallots, minced*
1 *small Italian green pepper, minced*
½ *cup plus* 3 *tablespoons freshly grated Parmesan cheese*
½ *cup chopped fresh parsley*
1 *clove garlic, minced*
2 *egg yolks*
1 *teaspoon salt*
¼ *teaspoon freshly ground pepper*
¾ *cup crumbled white bread*
¼ *cup milk*
1 *pound small shrimps, shelled, deveined*
6 *tablespoons butter*

I.   Heat oven to 375°. Wrap eggplants in aluminum foil.
        Bake until soft, about 45 minutes. Cut eggplants length-
        wise in half. Scoop out pulp; chop pulp. Reserve shells.
        Combine chopped pulp, shallots, green pepper, ½ cup
        cheese, the parsley, garlic, egg yolks, salt, and pepper
        in a large bowl. Soak bread in milk; stir into eggplant
        mixture.

II.   Sauté shrimps in butter in a medium saucepan until
        pink, about 3 minutes. Chop three-fourths of the
        shrimps; reserve remainder for garnish. Stir chopped
        shrimps into eggplant mixture. Spoon stuffing into
        shells. Garnish with reserved shrimps; sprinkle with
        remaining 3 tablespoons cheese. Bake until tops are
        golden, about 20 minutes. Serve hot (or at room temper-
        ature sprinkled with olive oil and vinegar).

Serves 8 to 10.

SOUPS

Chapter Two

The most seductive phrase in the lexicon of American cookery is indubitably "Soup's on!"

Having been brought up cloistered between Campbell and Heinz, I never heard that magical locution uttered by anyone who actually stirred up a potful from scratch—until I was well into maturity.

My maternal grandmother had a wondrous hand with chicken soup, of course. I also recall steaming bowls of mushroom and barley (well dappled with carrots and beef) as standard convalescent fare whenever I was lucky enough to be felled by an ailment on her territory. But my forebear was no earth mother. She cooked with pride and joy for more than fifty years, but I am certain that the notion of food as "fleshly pleasure" never once entered her mind in all that time.

My induction into hedonism, as you may have suspected, began with a totally alien soup.

The downfall took place over a bowl of pale, leafy-colored froth—a cream of Swiss chard or spinach, ladled icy cold from a milk jug by a farmer's wife. If I ever knew the name of this miraculous emollient, I have long forgotten it, but never the flavor! The meal took place the year that I turned twelve. My parents had sequestered me for the month of August at a working dairy in the upper Catskill Mountains, to escape a particularly torpid and enervating summer.

The dairyman and his wife let the upstairs rooms of their commodious farmhouse to summer people on weekends. I, however, as a slightly more permanent guest became part of the family unit.

Austro-Hungarians, in America for less than twenty years, these kindly people spoke practically no English aside from the colloquial expressions taught them by their children.

"Okey-dokey," they would repeat happily, or "Hiya, keed" and the aforementioned "Soup's on!" The lady of the house in particular would shout this latter phrase from a small kitchen window, three times a day in rain or shine, whether soup was on the menu or not.

A large, well-upholstered lady, blessed with bright blue eyes and hair the color of lightning bugs, she wore Hoover aprons from morning till night. And she allowed me to sit in her kitchen helping her stretch strudel dough or pit cherries, even though she faithfully promised my mother to keep me outdoors.

Her husband, the farmer, had tried to live up to that commitment, attempting to interest me in hay mowing or milking the cows. But I was clumsy at the performance of these chores, and too inhibited to ask for proper instruction.

Instead, I became the charge of his four sons (of varying ages) who became my tour guides in the facts of life.

In retrospect, the mysterious business of sex, learned in the barnyard, has become irrevocably intertwined for me with an aura of kitchen perfumes: the pungence of dill, the dull fire of dried peppers, and the searing sting of golden onions shattered by a knife. Was that truly the bouquet that kept my young eyes watering and knees weak with fear that fateful August? Or was it simply the enormity of life, waiting just beyond the pantry door?

I will never know. But, oddly, it no longer matters. Soup's on, you see!

My version of that bespoke Catskill farm soup is dependent, I regret to say, on freshly made chicken stock for its potency. I have cheated at times and used various canned broths, but the results have lacked gustative savor. A formula for an excellent, aromatic stock composed of poultry odds and ends and soup greens follows the soup recipe. The stock can be kept frozen for months and months. Unfrozen, it will remain fresh at least three weeks in the refrigerator.

FARMER'S SOUP

2 *tablespoons butter*
1 *large onion, chopped*
2 *tablespoons all-purpose flour*
1½ *cups Chicken Stock (recipe follows)*
1½ *cups water*
¾ *pound Swiss chard, rinsed, chopped*
½ *teaspoon salt*
¼ *teaspoon freshly ground pepper*
Pinch of ground allspice
Pinch of freshly grated nutmeg
Dash of hot pepper sauce
1 *cup sour cream*

I.   Melt butter in a medium saucepan over low heat. Add onion; cook 5 minutes. Stir in flour; cook, stirring constantly, 2 minutes. Add Chicken Stock and water. Heat to boiling; reduce heat. Add Swiss chard, salt, pepper, allspice, and nutmeg. Simmer 30 minutes. Cool slightly.

II.   Place soup in a blender container or food processor. Blend until smooth. Transfer to a large bowl. Cover and refrigerate until cold. Season with hot pepper sauce. Stir in sour cream.

Serves 4 to 6.

CHICKEN STOCK

---

4 *pounds chicken pieces (backs, necks, wings)*
Cold water
1 *onion*
1 *clove garlic*
2 *carrots, cut into quarters*
2 *stalks celery, broken*
8 *sprigs parsley*
4 *whole cloves*
10 *peppercorns*
1 *teaspoon salt*
1 *bay leaf*
½ *teaspoon dried thyme*

I. Place the chicken pieces in a large, heavy pot; cover with cold water. Heat to boiling; boil 5 minutes. Drain.

II. Return chicken to pot; cover with 4 quarts cold water. Add remaining ingredients. Heat to boiling; reduce heat. Cook, barely simmering, until stock is reduced by half, about 3 hours. Strain stock.

Makes 2 quarts.

I have sung the praises of my grandmother's kitchen prowess in so many books and publications, that a playful friend accused me of "living off the annuity for years!" But her culinary bequests to this book are not merely familial.

Though untraditionally Jewish, her kitchen output certainly bears the imprint of middle-European origin. What is so fascinating to me is how that cookery altered after a sea change to America.

Never a religious woman, she eschewed all the tenets of a kosher kitchen, except in her choice of freshly killed chicken, the basis for many of her nourishing soups. The pottage here, enriched with *knaidlach* (matzo meal dumplings) was made solely for the celebration of Passover. Matzo balls, as they are known in Jewish communities all over this country, are often heavy and sometimes indigestible table treats. My grandparent's were lighter than air. The secret? A judicious supplement of purely American club soda to the batter of eggs, chicken fat, and matzo meal. For hers, my grandmother always chose bottled seltzer. I, poor, unbenighted follower, make do with Perrier.

GRANDMOTHERLY CHICKEN SOUP WITH MATZO BALLS

1 *chicken (about 3½ to 4 pounds)*
Water
Matzo Balls (recipe follows)
1 *clove garlic*
1 *whole onion with skin*
2 *whole cloves*
1 *large carrot, cut into quarters*
1 *stalk celery with leaves, broken*
1 *medium white turnip, quartered*
1 *large parsnip, quartered*
2 *sprigs parsley*
2 *tablespoons chopped fresh dill*
1 *slice lemon*
Salt
10 *peppercorns*
3½ *cups chicken broth*

VEGETABLE GARNISH:
Optional: 1 chopped onion, 1 chopped medium turnip, 1 chopped parsnip, 1 chopped carrot
Freshly ground pepper
Chopped fresh dill

I.   With a sharp scissors, remove all fat and excess skin from cavity and neck area of chicken. Cut off tips of each wing. Peel the neck and scrape off fat. (You should have about ⅔ cup fat all together.) Wrap chicken; refrigerate until ready to use. Place chicken fat, skin fat, and wing tips in a small saucepan. Add ⅓ cup water. Heat to simmering; simmer slowly over low heat for about 30 minutes. As the water is absorbed by the chicken, it will be replaced by chicken fat in the pan. When it begins to sizzle, the fat is rendered. Remove the fat by spoonfuls until you have 3 tablespoons. Chill for 30 minutes.

II.   Make Matzo Balls.

III.   To make the soup: Place chicken in a large, heavy pot. Add garlic, whole onion, cloves, carrot, celery, turnip, parsnip, parsley, 2 tablespoons dill, the lemon slice, 2 teaspoons salt, the peppercorns, chicken broth, and water to cover. Heat to boiling; reduce heat. Simmer over medium-low heat until tender, about 1 hour. Remove scum and fat with a spoon as they rise to the surface. When chicken is tender, remove from pot. Increase heat and boil liquid 10 minutes. (Reserve chicken for use at another time. See *Note.*)

IV.   Strain soup; return to heat. Add optional vegetables; reduce heat. Simmer until tender, about 15 minutes. Add salt and freshly ground pepper to taste. Add Matzo Balls; cook 10 minutes. Garnish with chopped dill; ladle soup into bowls and add one Matzo Ball to each bowl.

Note: To reheat chicken, place covered in a low oven to warm, about 15 minutes. Then, place skin side up under a broiler until skin crackles, about 5 minutes.

Serves 8 to 10.

MATZO BALLS

3 *eggs*
6 *tablespoons cold club soda*
3 *tablespoons rendered chicken fat (see preceding recipe)*
Salt
Pinch of ground white pepper
⅔ *cup matzo meal (approximately)*
3 *quarts water*

I.   Lightly beat the eggs in a medium bowl. Beat in the club soda, chicken fat, and the salt and white pepper to taste. Slowly beat in ¼ cup matzo meal. Add more matzo meal, 2 tablespoons at a time, until mixture is the consistency of soft mashed potatoes. Cover; chill 5 hours.

II.   Heat the water to boiling. With wet hands, shape the matzo mixture into balls about 1½ inches in diameter. Drop into the boiling water; reduce heat to medium. Simmer 25 minutes. Remove balls with a slotted spoon; let cool. Refrigerate until ready to use. Remove from refrigerator 30 minutes before heating in soup.

Makes 10 matzo balls.

From the rich Pennsylvania Dutch country, a chicken soup of yet another color. Divine inspiration obviously caused some Amish housewife to fuse slices of cooked chicken, raw vegetables, and newly rolled noodle dough into her soup pot. For there is no other logical explanation to this dish, aside from culinary boredom. But why belabor the point? Chicken Pŭt Pie is a classic "honest American" treasure.

CHICKEN PÜT PIE

1 *chicken (about 3½ to 4 pounds)*
1 *can (1 quart, 14 ounces) chicken broth*
2 *whole onions*
1 *clove garlic*
1 *sprig fresh thyme or ⅛ teaspoon dried*
3 *sprigs parsley*
2 *tablespoons chopped fresh dill*
1 *bay leaf*
1 *teaspoon salt*
½ *teaspoon freshly ground pepper*
Water
Egg Noodles (recipe follows)
2 *onions, chopped*
3 *stalks celery, diced*
3 *carrots, diced*
1 *parsnip, diced*
2 *white turnips, diced*
3 *tablespoons finely chopped fresh dill*

I.   Place the chicken in a large pot. Add chicken broth, whole onions, garlic, thyme, parsley, 2 tablespoons chopped dill, the bay leaf, salt, and pepper; cover with water. Heat to boiling; reduce heat. Simmer, partially covered, 1 hour.

II. Remove chicken from pot; let cool. Strain broth; reserve broth.

III. Make Egg Noodles.

IV. Remove chicken meat from bones in bite-size pieces; reserve. Heat strained broth in large saucepan, keeping just below simmering.

V.   Place a third each of the chopped onions, the diced celery, the diced carrots, the diced parsnip, the diced turnips, and the chicken pieces in a 5-quart, heavy pot or Dutch oven. Mix lightly; top with a layer of noodles. Repeat procedure until there are three layers in the pot. Add heated chicken broth to cover, tilting pot to distribute broth evenly.

VI.   Heat layered mixture over medium heat until liquid begins to boil; reduce heat. Cook, covered, over medium-low heat 1 hour. Sprinkle with chopped dill; serve in soup bowls.

Serves 4 to 6.

Note: A word of kitchen counsel. In the foregoing recipe the ingredient list calls for chicken broth rather than stock. *Broth* is a culinary option when the essential flavor of a dish (in this case chicken) is intensified by other strong flavors. *Stock* is demanded, in every case, when the other flavors tend to be bland.

There are no hard and fast rules for noodle-making. I learned to do it by hand, using a long wooden rolling pin and as much backbone as I could muster. Culinary plutocrats, with pasta machines as part of their kitchen equipment, are most definitely advised to make use of them here!

EGG NOODLES

1¼ *cups all-purpose flour (approximately)*
½ *teaspoon salt*
2 *large eggs, lightly beaten*

I.   Mix flour and salt in a large bowl. Add eggs; blend with a fork until a soft dough is formed. Scrape dough onto a floured board; knead 10 minutes, adding more flour if necessary. Cover with a towel. Let stand 30 minutes.

II.   Roll out dough as thin as possible; cut into 4-inch squares. Place on lightly greased waxed paper until ready to use.

Makes about ½ pound.

A word or two would seem to be in order here about how the recipes for this book were chosen. The foods I sought, though honest and certainly American, were not necessarily the famed specialties of any geographic area. Long ago, in another book, I logged the best recipe for New England clam chowder I could find. Why bother to print it again? Rather, I chose to uncover the hidden, and often unsung, ethnic donations that give our native cuisine—for surely it *is* a cuisine—its greatness.

Speaking of ethnic, a fabled pot of Jewish-Polish-Rumanian-Russian and very much American origins follows: mushroom and barley soup! This too, is a family inheritance. My grandmother, Minna Cohn, is the only woman I ever knew who put tomatoes in barley soup. Perhaps because her kitchen garden bloomed scarlet one summer. Whatever the reason, the version is unique and eminently worth noting.

MUSHROOM, BARLEY, AND TOMATO SOUP

2 *tablespoons vegetable oil*
1¼ *pounds stewing beef, cut into 1-inch cubes*
1 *clove garlic*

5 *cups water*
½ *cup boiling water*
½ *ounce dried, sliced mushrooms*
1 *small onion, chopped*
1 *carrot, chopped*
¾ *cup chopped celery, including root end*
1 *cup chopped, seeded, peeled tomatoes*
½ *teaspoon granulated sugar*
1 *small parsnip, chopped*
1 *small white turnip, chopped*
Pinch of dried thyme
¼ *cup barley*
4 *cups beef broth (approximately)*
Salt and freshly ground pepper
Chopped fresh parsley

I.   Heat oil in a large, heavy pot or Dutch oven over high heat. Sauté meat until well browned on all sides. Add garlic and 4 cups water. Stir, scraping bottom and sides of pot. Heat to boiling; reduce heat. Simmer, partially covered, 1 hour. Remove scum with spoon as it rises to the surface. Discard garlic.

II.   Pour ½ cup boiling water over mushrooms in a small bowl. Let stand at least 20 minutes.

III. Add mushrooms with liquid to the soup. Add onion, carrot, celery, tomatoes, sugar, parsnip, turnip, thyme, barley, beef broth, and remaining 1 cup water. Simmer, partially covered, until meat is tender, about 1¼ hours. If soup becomes too thick, thin with more beef broth. Season to taste with salt and pepper. Sprinkle with parsley.

Serves 6 to 8.

Prospectors came to Colorado in droves in the early nineteenth century, searching not for provender, but gold. Some of the more sharp-witted, however, quickly discovered that a bumper crop of wheat or a few bushels of fruit brought them far greater riches than any frantic panning or digging. Which, I suppose, was the basis for Colorado's enormous agrarian economy.

The soil and climate of that state proved particularly felicitous for growing sugar beets, and today most western sugar bowls are still filled with Colorado's finest.

Beet-top consumption is another legacy entirely. A peculiarly soothing prescription for a local beet-top soup (made of tenderest green leaves, potatoes, and cream) comes to this collection from the kitchen of Mildred Schulz of Golden, Colorado. Mrs. Schulz has been cooking up this equally golden elixir every spring as long as her family can remember. But beet-top soup is never on the menu after the beets in her garden yield a leaf that is over four inches high. For tenderness is the soup's secret ingredient!

MILDRED SCHULZ'S BEET-TOP SOUP

Beet tops from 8 beets (about 2½ cups chopped)
3 medium potatoes, pared and diced
1 cup strong Chicken Stock (see Index)
1 cup light cream
2 tablespoons butter, softened
1 tablespoon cornstarch
⅛ teaspoon ground allspice
Dash of hot pepper sauce
Salt and freshly ground pepper

I.   Wash beet tops; remove stems, including tough veins down centers of leaves. (If beet tops are not young and tender, parboil 5 minutes. Rinse under cold running water; drain. This step removes the bitterness from the leaves.) Coarsely chop beet tops.

II.   Combine the chopped beet tops and potatoes in a medium saucepan. Add Chicken Stock. Heat to boiling; reduce heat. Simmer until potatoes are tender, about 20 minutes. Stir in the cream; simmer 5 minutes.

III.   Mash the butter with the cornstarch in a small bowl until smooth. Stir into the soup. Cook until soup thickens, about 5 minutes. Season with allspice, hot pepper sauce, and salt and freshly ground pepper to taste.

Serves 4.

Like *les Acadiens*, the original settlers of southwest Louisiana, the food of that area was transplanted from Brittany via Canada. But so many other ethnic spoons have dipped into the "Cajun" pot over the past two centuries that no dish bears any resemblance to true French cookery.

Take gumbo, for instance. This soup-stew is such a catholic devise that it may be made of practically anything. In Cajun legend there are said to be more gumbos "in ze pot" than fish in the bayou, birds in the sky, or *chatwe* (raccoons) under the live oaks. After a little sleuthing in gumbo country, I racked up a record number of formulas based on such odd pot mates as chicken and oysters, shrimp and okra, not to mention gamier twosomes like wild duck and squirrel.

If gumbo was originally a French Canadian *pot-au-feu* that suffered a sea change in the bayou, African slaves certainly enriched the broth with okra, which they called *guingômbo*. Filé powder, however, was a Choctaw bestowal. This powder of dried, crushed, wild sassafras imparts a truly distinctive bite (like the taste of pine needles) to any gumbo adjudged to be "of

middlin' flavor." Go easy on the filé powder if it is an untried
seasoning, however! Even Cajuns sprinkle it *lightly* at the table
side, for cooked file turns stringy in the pot.

CHICKEN AND OYSTER GUMBO

3 *pounds chicken pieces*
½ *teaspoon salt*
¾ *teaspoon freshly ground pepper*
3 *tablespoons butter*
1 *tablespoon vegetable oil*
3 *tablespoons all-purpose flour*
2 *large onions, chopped*
2 *stalks celery, chopped*
1 *green pepper, seeded, chopped*
3 *cloves garlic, minced*
3 *cups hot Chicken Stock (see Index)*
1 *cup water*
1 *tablespoon Worcestershire sauce*
1 *tablespoon crushed dried hot red peppers*
1 *bay leaf, crumbled*
1 *teaspoon chopped fresh thyme or ½ teaspoon dried*
¼ *teaspoon ground allspice*
⅛ *teaspoon ground cloves*
18 *oysters, shucked*
¼ *cup chopped fresh parsley*
4 *green onion tops, minced*
Steamed rice (see Index)
Filé powder
Hot pepper sauce

I.   Sprinkle chicken with salt and ¼ teaspoon ground
        pepper. Sauté chicken in butter and oil in a heavy
        Dutch oven until dark golden brown on all sides, about
        20 minutes. Remove chicken from pan; reserve. Stir
        flour into drippings to make a roux. Reduce heat to low;
        cook, stirring frequently, until roux turns the color of

dark mahogany, about 45 minutes. (Roux must turn very dark but should not burn; do not undercook.)

II. Add onions, celery, green pepper, and garlic to roux. Cook, stirring constantly, 5 minutes. Stir in stock, water, Worcestershire sauce, dried red peppers, bay leaf, thyme, remaining ½ teaspoon ground pepper, the allspice, cloves, and reserved chicken. Heat to boiling; reduce heat. Simmer uncovered 1½ hours. Skim any fat that rises to the surface.

III. Add oysters, parsley, and green onion tops to gumbo; cook uncovered 5 minutes. Serve with rice. Pass filé powder and hot pepper sauce.

Serves 6 to 8.

SHRIMP AND OKRA GUMBO

¼ *cup vegetable oil*
¼ *cup all-purpose flour*
2 *large onions, chopped*
5 *tablespoons butter*
4 *cups coarsely chopped fresh okra*
2⅔ *cups chopped, seeded tomatoes*
2 *large green peppers, seeded, chopped*
4 *cloves garlic, minced*
2½ *pounds shrimps, shelled, deveined*
1½ *quarts Chicken Stock (see Index)*
2 *cups water*
2 *tablespoons crushed dried hot red peppers*
Salt
2 *bay leaves, crumbled*
2 *teaspoons Worcestershire sauce*
1 *teaspoon ground allspice*
¼ *teaspoon dried thyme*
Freshly ground pepper
Steamed rice (see Index)
Filé powder
Hot pepper sauce

I.   Mix oil and flour in a small, heavy saucepan to make a roux; cook over low heat, stirring frequently, until roux is the color of dark mahogany, about 45 minutes. (Roux must turn very dark brown, but should not burn; do not undercook.) Reserve.

II.   Sauté onions in 3 tablespoons butter in a large, heavy Dutch oven until soft, about 3 minutes. Stir in okra. Cook until tender, about 3 minutes. Stir in tomatoes; cook 30 minutes.

III. Sauté green peppers and garlic in remaining 2 tablespoons butter in a large skillet, about 5 minutes. Add shrimps. Cook until shrimps turn pink, about 3 minutes. Add shrimp mixture, Chicken Stock, water, dried red peppers, 2 teaspoons salt, the bay leaves, Worcestershire sauce, allspice, thyme, and reserved roux to okra mixture. Simmer covered 1½ hours. Season to taste with salt and pepper.

IV.   Ladle gumbo into soup bowls; top each with a scoop of rice. Pass filé powder and hot pepper sauce.

Serves 8.

Tall tales are inexplicably part and parcel of southern California's heritage. In 1682, a monk named Francisco de Escobar noted in his diary that a tribe of local Indians seemed to live "wholly on the odor of fruit trees . . . sniffing often but eating nothing at all!"

One would hope that olive groves abounded in the territory for there is no sweeter, more revivifying scent in the world than an olive tree in blossom. Unless it is the smell of an olive itself (at its ripest) cured in brine, garlic, and sweet oil.

Spanish conquistadors brought olives to the Southwest, and

their beneficence is still happily in harvest along the San Diego freeways. I can attest to that fact from my sense of smell!

A most unusual soup comes from the same scented baili-wick (Coronado del Mar, to be specific). A remarkably tasty dish served up warm, it is pure velvet, chilled and blended, topped with a crescent of scarlet pimiento.

SOUTHWESTERN BLACK OLIVE SOUP

2 *tablespoons butter*
1 *small clove garlic, minced*
2 *tablespoons all-purpose flour*
3 *cups hot Chicken Stock (see Index)*
½ *cup finely chopped black olives*
1 *cup whipping cream*
2 *egg yolks*
Chopped fresh parsley

I.   Melt butter in a medium saucepan over medium-low heat. Add garlic; cook 5 minutes. Stir in flour; cook, stirring constantly, 2 minutes. Slowly whisk in chicken stock. Beat until smooth. Stir in olives; simmer 20 minutes. Add ½ cup cream; cook 5 minutes. Remove from heat.

II.   Beat remaining ½ cup cream with egg yolks. Slowly stir into soup. Heat soup over low heat until thickened. Do not boil. Sprinkle with parsley.

Serves 4 to 6.

The earliest recipe for black bean soup that I could find was printed in a slim little volume entitled *American Cookery* (adapted to this country and all grades of life). This 1796 work, credited anonymously to "An American Orphan," presents the following formula in toto:

> Soak one pint beans (black) overnight. Then parboil in two and a half quarts of water till soft. To four quarts of stock add the beans (strained through a cloth), one teaspoon cloves, a half teaspoon cinnamon, one teaspoon pepper, a whole lemon sliced and four boiled eggs. Just before serving add one glass of port wine and a half glass of brandy to every three quarts of soup.

Curiously, the recipe works. But for a less tipsy pottage, I am indebted to Puerto Rico—where I came upon the following dark devise at the fabled Su Casa restaurant of Dorado Beach.

PUERTO RICO BLACK BEAN SOUP

1 *pound black turtle beans*
⅓ *cup diced salt pork*
2 *tablespoons olive oil*
½ *cup diced cooked ham*
2 *medium onions, chopped*
2 *cloves garlic, minced*
8 *cups beef stock or broth*
8 *cups water*
1 *large bay leaf*
1 *small onion, studded with 2 cloves*
1 *small sprig fresh oregano or a pinch of dried*
Pinch of cayenne pepper
2 *teaspoons wine vinegar*
2 *tablespoons sherry*
Salt and freshly ground pepper

FOR GARNISH:
¼ *cup finely chopped cooked ham*
¼ *cup chopped green onions*

1 *hard-cooked egg, chopped*
½ *lime, thinly sliced*
1 *cup cooked rice*

I.   Sort through the beans; soak in cold water overnight.
         Drain.

II.   Drop the salt pork into boiling water; boil 5 minutes.
         Drain and pat dry with paper toweling.

III.   Heat oil in a large, heavy pot over medium heat; add
         the salt pork and diced ham. Cook, stirring constantly,
         8 minutes. Add chopped onions and garlic; cook 5
         minutes longer.

IV.   Stir in the beans, beef stock, 4 cups water, the bay leaf,
         onion studded with cloves, and oregano. Heat to boiling;
         reduce heat. Cook over medium heat, stirring occasion-
         ally, 1½ hours. Add the remaining water as the liquid
         begins to reduce.

V.   When the beans are tender, remove three-fifths of them
         with a slotted spoon. Place, in two batches, in a blender
         container or food processor. Add some soup liquid;
         blend until smooth. Stir back into the soup. Discard
         whole onion and bay leaf.

VI.   Add cayenne pepper, vinegar, sherry, and salt and
         pepper to taste. Cook until soup becomes quite thick,
         about 30 minutes. Serve with the garnishes passed
         individually on the side.

Serves 8.

In the Pacific Northwest, fish dinners are legendary. Take
Seattle's barbecue for instance: whole Chinook salmon, cooked on

stone slabs over an applewood fire, served with drawn butter, lemon chunks, and Tabasco sauce—lots of it. If you are thinking that he-man fare alone is a mandate in the tall tree country, think again. The following chowder (of salmon too, by coincidence) gives lie to that notion. This pearly soup is a triumph of local imagination over ingredient!

PUGET SOUND SALMON CHOWDER

3 *cups Fish Stock (recipe follows)*
1 *tablespoon olive oil*
1 *tablespoon unsalted butter*
1 *large onion, finely chopped*
1 *clove garlic, minced*
1 *cup chicken broth*
1 *can (8 ounces) plum tomatoes*
½ *teaspoon granulated sugar*
⅛ *teaspoon chopped fresh thyme or a pinch of dried*
1 *large potato, pared, cubed, rinsed in cold water*
1 *teaspoon lemon juice*
Salt and freshly ground pepper
10 *ounces fresh salmon, cut into 1-inch cubes*
3 *tablespoons chopped fresh dill*

I.   Make Fish Stock. Keep hot.

II.   Heat oil and butter in a medium saucepan over medium-low heat. Add onion and garlic; cook 5 minutes. Add Fish Stock, chicken broth, and tomatoes. Sprinkle with sugar and thyme. Heat to boiling; reduce heat. Simmer 5 minutes. Add potato, lemon juice, and salt and pepper to taste. Simmer until potato is tender, about 12 minutes. Stir in salmon cubes; cook until fish flakes easily with a fork, about 7 minutes. Sprinkle with dill; serve.

Serves 4 to 6.

FISH STOCK

1½ *pounds fish bones, including heads*
1½ *cups water*
1 *cup dry white wine*
1½ *cups clam juice*
1 *onion, studded with 2 cloves*
1 *bay leaf*
3 *sprigs parsley*
½ *stalk celery*
10 *peppercorns*
1 *teaspoon salt*
½ *lemon*

I.   Combine all ingredients in a large, heavy pot. Heat to
         boiling; reduce heat. Simmer 15 minutes. Strain stock.
                                        Makes 3 cups stock.

The slavic people of New England (latter day pilgrims to be
sure) brought some hearty native recipes to their adoptive soil.
Consider the following version of *borscht* (New Hampshire-style).
Wonderfully comforting winter food, it is easy on the pocketbook
too!

NEW HAMPSHIRE BORSCHT

2 *tablespoons unsalted butter*
1 *large onion, chopped*
1 *clove garlic, minced*
1 *tablespoon vegetable oil*
1 *pound lamb riblets (shoulder ends), cut into 1½-inch pieces*
1 *quart water*
1 *can (13¾ ounces) beef broth*
1 *can (17 ounces) plum tomatoes*
¼ *cup chopped, fresh dill*
Salt and freshly ground pepper

1 *large potato, peeled, diced*
1 *large white turnip, peeled, diced*
1 *small cabbage (2 pounds), trimmed, shredded*
1 *tablespoon chili sauce*
¼ *teaspoon ground allspice*
⅛ *teaspoon ground ginger*
Chopped fresh dill

I.   Melt 1 tablespoon butter in a large heavy pot over medium-low heat. Add onion and garlic; cook, stirring occasionally, 5 minutes.

II.   Meanwhile, heat remaining 1 tablespoon butter with oil in a large heavy skillet over medium heat. Saute lamb riblets, a few pieces at a time, until well browned. Add to onion in pot as meat is done.

III.   Add the water, beef broth, tomatoes, the ¼ cup dill, ¼ teaspoon salt, and ¼ teaspoon pepper to onion-lamb mixture. Heat to boiling; reduce heat. Simmer covered until lamb is tender, about 1 hour and 15 minutes. Add potato, turnip, cabbage, chili sauce, allspice, and ginger. Simmer covered ½ hour longer. Add more salt and pepper to taste. Sprinkle with more dill before serving.

Serves 6 to 8.

Pfaumenüs (out of Kansas circa 1850) is a fruit soup that marries the best of two seasons. Made originally from September's yield of home-canned plums and May's first sprouted rhubarb, it is an object lesson in American pragmatism at work.

Proper Mennonites imbibed this soup from a bowl—dabbed with sour cream and sugar cookies on the side. I suggest it for your next brunch, in lieu of screwdrivers and the inevitable Bloody Mary. A splash of vodka does not hurt the original recipe in the slightest. Though Pfaumenüs surely started life as a teetotal beverage entirely, the version I acquired is intemperate as all hell. But a delectable quaff despite the spikes!

PFAUMENÜS

---

2 *cans (16 ounces each) purple plums in heavy syrup*
½ *cup finely chopped rhubarb*
⅔ *cup granulated sugar*
1 *cup water*
½ *cup dry red wine*
¼ *teaspoon ground white pepper*
Pinch of salt
½ *teaspoon grated lemon peel*
1 *tablespoon lemon juice*
1 *cinnamon stick*
½ *cup whipping cream*
1 *tablespoon cornstarch*
3 *tablespoons brandy*
1 *cup sour cream*
Sour cream
Ground cinnamon

I.   Drain plums; reserve syrup. Remove pits; chop plums into small pieces. Place chopped plums in a medium saucepan. Add reserved syrup, the rhubarb, sugar, water, wine, white pepper, salt, lemon peel, lemon juice, and cinnamon stick. Heat to boiling; reduce heat. Simmer 15 minutes. Add whipping cream. Simmer 5 minutes. Discard cinnamon stick.

II.   Mix the cornstarch and brandy until smooth. Slowly stir into soup. Cook until slightly thickened. Remove soup from heat.

III.   Combine 1 cup sour cream with 1 cup soup in a small bowl; mix thoroughly. Slowly stir this mixture back into soup; mix well. Let soup cool. Chill thoroughly before serving. Serve in bowls, each topped with a teaspoon of sour cream and a dusting of ground cinnamon.

Serves 6 to 8.

BREADS

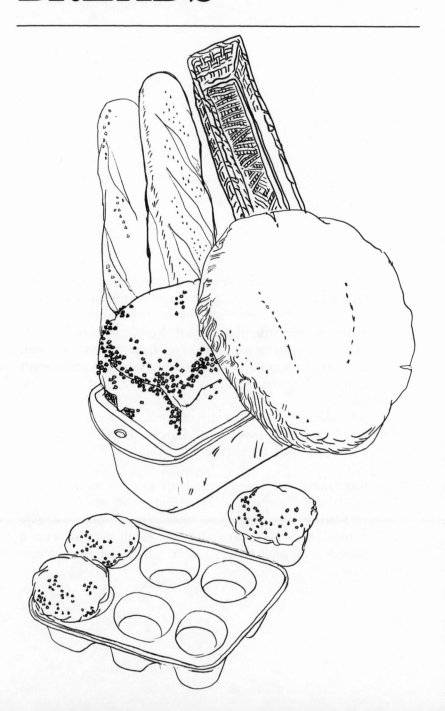

Chapter Three

A misheard phrase can certainly alter one's perception for life.

When I was a youngster growing up in the suburbs outside New York, I had a grade school teacher with a penchant for making ringing declarative statements. To my mind, Mrs. Zenner was the all-American Athena. A striking goddess of the classroom, possessed of deadly aim with blackboard chalk to stem pupils' misconduct, she also was gifted with a set of compelling vocal chords.

Unfortunately, her *glissando* rhetoric had a tendency to blur in my tender ear. I went through half of my childhood, for instance, certain that "time and tide wait for nomads."

Another of her aphorisms affected me even more viscerally.

"Bread," she pronounced grandly in civics class one day, ". . . is the *stab* of life!"

That statement came as a particular body blow. For I was a kid (almost six feet tall at age twelve) who lived on a guilty diet of superhigh carbohydrates. My midday meal was inevitably composed of three sandwiches—"stabs" of pale, packaged white bread alternately upholstered with peanut butter, fried bologna, or merely mayonnaise with no other embellishment except salt and pepper. Small wonder that for years I harbored the notion that a lunch break was the most secret vice of all!

As I grew older, the sandwich lost its sex appeal.

In 1861, a cookbook, published in Boston (entitled *Christianity in the Kitchen)* first seriously questioned bread's "purported health giving property." This fierce tome, penned by Mrs. Horace Mann, likewise condemned drinking, soft living, and unnatural ingredients found in every American larder.

"There is death in the pot, . . ." this lady warned, proscribing an entire pantry shelf of foods for being (1) un-Christian and (2) indigestible. A glance at her list is like a week at Weight Watchers!

No piecrust made with butter or lard.

No wedding cake.

No plum pudding.

No mince pie.

No butter generally. But never butter melted, since it contained butyric acid.

No lard.

No suet.

No pork products.

No fruit (when picked green).

No wheat flour. (It was rumored to be adulterated with plaster of Paris.)

No refined sugar.

No confectionery.

And no commercial bread whatsoever! *Christianity in the Kitchen* granted a housewife the option to make her own bread, only "if the occasion absolutely demands," with admonition that saleratus or baking powder must *never* be substituted for yeast!

Happily, home bakery survived.

Early nineteenth-century bread was usually made of unrefined flour, water, salt, and yeast and flavored with molasses, honey, or nothing at all—depending on the condition of the baker's purse strings.

It may sound like heresy, but that antique formula was remarkably close to the pricey, rough-textured creations found only in health food shops today.

One of the most *honest* loaves I have ever tasted was improvised by a young Greenville, Mississippi, lawyer named Charles Sherman, who makes bread for a hobby. Now transplanted to Glen Cove, Long Island, Charles bakes his bread once a week, and freely credits the late Adelle Davis as the inspiration for his superb, sesame seed-dusted loaf.

"But like all good things in this world," he amends, "this bread simply evolved!"

Whatever the genesis, Charles' Bread is a loaf that little children (and aging cookbook authors) literally cry for!

CHARLES' BREAD

2 *tablespoons granulated yeast*
2 *cups warm water*
3 *tablespoons blackstrap molasses*
5 *tablespoons honey*
5⅓ *cups stone-ground whole wheat flour (available in health food stores)*
1½ *teaspoons salt*
3 *tablespoons unsalted butter, softened*
1 *egg white*
⅔ *cup sesame seeds (approximately)*
2 *tablespoons butter, melted*

I. Dissolve the yeast in warm water in a large bowl. Add molasses and honey. Let stand 10 minutes.

II. Stir in 3 cups whole wheat flour. Add the salt and 3 tablespoons butter. Beat with a wooden spoon until smooth. Slowly add more flour, ½ cup at a time, until a stiff dough is formed. Turn onto a floured board; knead 10 minutes.

III. Place the dough in a large, greased bowl. Cover; let rise in a warm place until doubled in bulk, about 1½ hours.

IV. Punch down dough. Knead 5 minutes; return to bowl. Cover; let rise until doubled in bulk, about 1 hour.

V. Punch down dough. Knead 5 minutes. Divide dough in half. Roll each half lengthwise into sausage shapes, about 10 inches long each. Beat flat with your hands; fold dough into thirds. Brush each loaf with egg white; roll in sesame seeds to completely coat. Place in two buttered 10- × 5- × 3-inch bread pans. Cover; let rise 50 minutes.

VI.   Heat oven to 350°. Bake bread until loaves sound hollow when tapped, about 45 minutes. Turn out on a wire rack. Brush top with melted butter to give the bread sheen.

Makes 2 loaves.

Dedicated bread lovers insist that no other slice on earth has the uniquely astringent taste or the resilient texture of true sourdough. In our national heritage, sourdough's invention is usually traced directly to the Gold Rush of California. Diet-deprived forty-niners, it is reported, carried lumps of fermenting flour with them on their westward trek so they could bake a loaf or two betwixt grizzlies and Indian shoot-outs.

That *yeasty* prototype might surprise some West Coast cognoscenti 150 years later. Today, they claim their local output outstrips even the famed *petitpains* of Paris, crunch for crunch!

I try to stay neutral in all such bread wars. Though I did notice with mild stupefaction recently that some baker is now selling beribboned loaves of sourdough as souvenirs at San Francisco's International Airport. And, I must add, the consumers who buy them up most eagerly all seem to be French!

The following recipe is for a compromise loaf. Half *old*–half *new*!

PROSPECTOR'S SOURDOUGH BREAD

FOR THE STARTER:
1 *tablespoon granulated yeast*
2 *cups unbleached all-purpose flour*
2 *cups warm water*

FOR THE BREAD:
2 *cups starter*
2 *tablespoons granulated sugar*

1 *teaspoon salt*
3 *tablespoons melted butter, cooled*
3½ *to* 4 *cups unbleached all-purpose flour*
Cornmeal
2 *tablespoons melted butter*

I.   To make the starter: Combine the yeast, flour, and warm water in a medium bowl. Mix well. Cover; let stand at room temperature 2 to 3 days, depending on degree of "sourness" desired.

II.   Before making bread, remove ½ cup starter from bowl. Keep in refrigerator for use at another time. There should be about 2 cups starter left.

III.   To make the bread: Place starter in a large bowl. Add sugar, salt, and 3 tablespoons melted butter. Stir in just enough flour to make a stiff dough. Turn onto a floured board; knead 15 minutes, adding more flour as needed. Place dough in a large greased bowl. Cover; let rise until doubled in bulk, about 1½ hours.

IV.   Punch down dough; knead briefly. Form into 2 French- or Italian-style loaves. Place on a baking sheet sprinkled with cornmeal. Cover; let rise until doubled in bulk, about 1 hour.

V.   Heat oven to 375°. Brush bread with 2 tablespoons melted butter. Bake until loaves sound hollow when tapped, about 25 minutes.

Makes 2 loaves.

To my mind, the best use a fresh-baked sourdough bread can be put to is breakfast, when the still-warm loaf is torn hastily apart, buttered, and absolutely slathered with homemade strawberry jam. The finest jam-maker of my acquaintance, Linda Herbert of Morrison, Colorado, claims there is no special trick to the homely art. Her strawberries, picked straight from the Herbert garden, are merely drizzled with sugar, boiled for twenty minutes, and funneled into sterilized, Ball-type jars— sans paraffin wax. While I have no strawberry patch to speak of, I do have a produce counter at the supermarket, and the Herbert method makes for pluperfect preserves all year round.

LINDA HERBERT'S QUICK STRAWBERRY JAM

4 *pints strawberries, washed, hulled*
6 *cups granulated sugar (approximately)*

I.   Cut large strawberries in half. (You should have about 6 cups.) Place strawberries in a large, heavy pot. Add sugar to berries (1 cup sugar for each 1 cup fruit). Heat quickly to boiling. Boil rapidly 20 minutes. Cool slightly.

II.   Pour jam into sterilized jars; seal.

Makes about 4½ pints.

The Swedish always bake their bread in perfect rounds. Each loaf is meant to be cut down the middle by the head of the household before any other dish is placed on the table. Then, tradition decrees that the female who baked the bread take over. She carves the entire loaf into slices of equal size, making it manifest that God intended no favoritism at her table, and that all persons taking nourishment together are due neither more nor less than one another.

Happily, this ritual of *Gödt bröd* followed Sweden's immigrants to the New World as well, where the same impartiality was observed for a century. Or at least until 1910 when the Ward Baking Company of Chicago turned out packaged white and rye!

The perfect round bread of Sweden (or Minnesota as the case may be) is called *limpa*. Flavored with cardamom and slivers of orange and lemon peel, this loaf is no mere adjunct to *smörgåsbord* but is a wonderfully edible addition to the non-Scandinavian's diet as well. The following recipe (one of a dozen tested) is adapted from James Beard's collection.

SWEDISH LIMPA

1 *tablespoon granulated yeast*
1 *teaspoon light brown sugar*
¼ *cup warm water*
2 *cups lukewarm beer*
½ *cup honey*
¼ *cup melted butter*
1 *cardamom seed, shelled, crushed*
2 *teaspoons salt*
1 *tablespoon caraway seeds*
2 *tablespoons grated orange peel*
1 *tablespoon grated lemon peel*
2½ *cups rye flour*
3 *cups all-purpose flour*
Cornmeal

I.   Dissolve the yeast and sugar in warm water in a large bowl. Add beer, honey, 2 tablespoons melted butter, the cardamom, salt, caraway seeds, orange peel, and lemon peel. Stir in rye flour; mix with a wooden spoon until smooth. Add 1½ cups all-purpose flour; stir until smooth. Add remaining all-purpose flour, ½ cup at a time, until a stiff dough is formed. Turn onto a floured board; knead 10 minutes, adding more flour as necessary.

II.   Place the dough in a large greased bowl. Cover; let rise in a warm place until doubled in bulk, about 1½ hours.

III.   Punch down dough. Divide in half. Roll each half into a ball. Place on a baking sheet sprinkled with cornmeal. Brush well with remaining 2 tablespoons melted butter. Cover loosely with waxed paper. Refrigerate 3 hours.

IV.   Heat oven to 375°. Remove bread from refrigerator. Let stand at room temperature 15 minutes. Bake until loaves sound hollow when tapped, about 40 minutes.

Makes 2 loaves.

Hot home-baked biscuits are a culinary penchant of mine, acquired during a late adolescence spent slightly below the Mason-Dixon line. I was seventeen a long, long time ago but I still remember the Southern admonition: "Honey, there are biscuits and BISCUITS in this world."

Here are a trio of the latter variety to whet the rest of the country's appetite. The first (Kate Almand's heirloom treasures) are undoubtedly the best I ever chomped. Kate prepares them (at Nathalie Dupree's cooking school in Atlanta) the way an experienced Italian lady makes pasta: scooping out a well of flour and working in the shortening and milk as it is needed. Her recipe is amended here for bakers with less expertise. And while we are on the subject of shortening, a caveat: Never, never substitute butter in Kate Almand's biscuits. It will not work.

KATE ALMAND'S GEORGIA-STYLE DROP BISCUITS

2½ cups self-rising cake flour
½ cup cold Crisco shortening
1 cup milk

I.   Heat oven to 500°. Place 2 cups flour in a large bowl. Add shortening; blend with a pastry blender until the texture of coarse crumbs. Stir in milk to form a very soft dough. Beat with a wooden spoon until smooth, about 4 minutes.

II.   Place remaining flour in a small bowl. With a spoon, scoop up dough, about the size of a large egg. Roll in flour to coat; place on a lightly greased baking sheet. Repeat procedure with all of the remaining dough.

III.   Bake biscuits in top third of hot oven 10 minutes. Biscuits should be almost white, not golden brown.

Makes 12 to 15 biscuits.

Everyone who is anyone in New Iberia ("doctors, nurses, undertakers, business folks, and pink ladies") goes to Helen's Restaurant, next door to the Episcopal Church on Main Street, for breakfast. And with good reason, for Helen Johnson is plainly the best biscuit maker in the state of Louisiana. Her buttermilk biscuits are the biggest, fattest skyscraper buns you have ever seen or digested. Here's the recipe!

HELEN JOHNSON'S BUTTERMILK BISCUITS

4 *cups all-purpose flour*
2 *tablespoons baking powder*
1 *tablespoon plus 1 teaspoon granulated sugar*
1 *teaspoon baking soda*
1 *teaspoon salt*
⅔ *cup chilled unsalted butter*
1½ *cups buttermilk*
¼ *cup melted butter*

I.   Heat oven to 450°. Sift flour, baking powder, sugar, baking soda, and salt into a large bowl. Cut in ⅔ cup butter; blend with a pastry blender until the texture of coarse crumbs. Stir in buttermilk to form a soft dough.

II.   Turn onto a floured board. Knead lightly, about 1 minute. Roll dough 1¼ inches thick. Cut into 3-inch circles. Arrange biscuits with sides touching in buttered 9-inch square cake pan. Brush tops lightly with melted butter. Bake until golden, about 25 minutes.

Makes 8 biscuits.

Miss Sarah (or Miz Sarey as she was called) was the venerable grandmother of a girl I courted once in Richmond, Virginia. Miss Sarah was rumored to be nearing eighty when I first met her. Still, she cleaned the house on Franklin Street each morning and made a batch of "Tennessee prides" every single afternoon at four exactly. The prides were her legacy—a melting cream biscuit whose recipe she obdurately refused to reveal.

"No . . . no," Miss Sarah would sigh. "That is my inheritance and must be passed down to a proper family member. Along with the Wedgwood salad plates and the good silver . . . ."

After I left Virginia (and my lady ultimately married someone else) I sent Miss Sarah a card every Christmas. But never received a reply. One Easter, however, fully ten years after I had last seen the matriarch, a pale pink envelope arrived in my mail. There was at first glance, nothing inside; then a flimsy scrap dropped to the floor. It contained the following recipe in an equally pale, penciled scrawl. With two words printed above: "My Pride."

MISS SARAH'S SOUTHERN CREAM BISCUITS

2 *cups sifted all-purpose flour*
2½ *teaspoons baking powder*
1 *teaspoon salt*
3 *tablespoons butter*
2 *tablespoons lard*
¾ *cup whipping cream*
Cornmeal

I.   Heat oven to 450°. Sift flour with baking powder and salt in a large bowl. Cut in butter and lard; blend with a pastry blender until the texture of coarse crumbs.

II.   Add cream gradually to form a soft dough. Roll out on a floured board ½ inch thick. Cut into 2½-inch circles. Place biscuits on a baking sheet sprinkled with cornmeal. Bake until golden brown, 12 to 15 minutes.

Makes about 12 biscuits.

It must be obvious by this time that in the best of all possible worlds, my heavenly reward would be an eternal sabbatical down South. And why not? The land of grits and gravy is just my kind of gastronomic geography.

For further evidence, see the following family version of skillet corn bread, passed along from a fan in Charlotte, North Carolina. In my kitchen this dish goes to brunch rather than dinner—mated with a creamy Rhode Island fish stew and no apologies whatsoever! See Newport Fish Shortcake, and try it yourself.

CAROLINA CRACKLIN' BREAD

4 *strips bacon*
1½ *cups yellow cornmeal*
½ *cup sifted all-purpose flour*
3 *teaspoons baking powder*
½ *teaspoon baking soda*
¾ *teaspoon salt*
1½ *cups buttermilk*
1 *egg, lightly beaten*

I.   Heat oven to 425°. Fry bacon in a 10-inch cast-iron skillet until crisp. Remove bacon with a slotted spoon. Drain on paper toweling. Crumble bacon; reserve. Reserve pan with drippings.

II.   Combine cornmeal, flour, baking powder, baking soda, and salt in a large bowl. Mix well. Beat in buttermilk and egg.

III.   Add all but 1 tablespoon bacon drippings from skillet to the cornmeal mixture. Beat until smooth. Heat skillet over low heat 3 to 4 minutes; remove from heat. Spoon cornmeal mixture evenly into skillet. Sprinkle crumbled bacon over top. Bake until golden and firm, 15 to 20 minutes.

Serves 8.

The notion that bread is the "staff" of life is probably prebiblical. Leavened loaves, however, date back to mere Egyptian times. In primitive cultures, bread (or some form of grain porridge) often was used as currency. Curiously, most Americans make some illicit connection between the bread box and the wallet. We either have enough *bread* or we are *stony*! And life is a toss-up between breadwinners and breadlines, one might say. But not in Virginia.

This state was the first culinary home of our nation's brick ovens. But the concoction they produced was like no other bread in the world: slow baked in a deep dish until the crust rose so high that it colored with embarrassment. Beneath that monumental exterior there was still another treasure—soft drifts of custard so fragile the contents have to be carefully *spooned* on a plate before it could be buttered.

That is bread too, my friends, in the old Virginia style!

OLD VIRGINIA SPOON BREAD

2⅓ *cups light cream*
¼ *cup unsalted butter*
3 *teaspoons granulated sugar*
1 *tablespoon honey*
½ *teaspoon salt*
1 *cup white cornmeal*
4 *eggs, separated*
1 *teaspoon baking powder*
Pinch of ground white pepper

I. Heat oven to 375°. Combine cream, butter, sugar, honey, and salt in a medium saucepan over low heat. Cook until the butter melts. Do not boil. Slowly add cornmeal. Cook, stirring constantly, over low heat until thick. (Do not boil.)

II. Transfer cornmeal mixture to a large bowl. Beat in egg yolks, one at a time, beating well after each addition. Add baking powder and white pepper.

III. Beat egg whites until stiff. Fold into mixture. Pour into a buttered 2-quart casserole or soufflé dish. Bake until puffed and golden, about 35 minutes. Serve with plenty of butter, syrup, honey, or just salt and pepper.

Serves 6 to 8.

In a slim, spiral-bound volume (the color of fresh curry) are published the recipes of the women of Christ Episcopal Church in Savannah, Georgia.

I learned about this little cookbook in Rome from a Georgian expatriate named Jo Bettoja. Jo runs Lo Scaldavivande, a cooking school that is practically in the fountains of Trevi.

"The recipes in this book are darlin'," Jo assured me. "Authentic, very home timey . . . and I don't know, just darlin'!"

I took her at her word—and they are darling!

From the book that I now keep on my kitchen cabinet for instant thumbing comes a final *Southern* bread, one that is neither loaf, biscuit, nor wafer. Actually, it is a fraud, you see— the transformation of common soda crackers into *pappadum* (spicy Indian bread puffs). I suppose you could call it *dishonest* American fare, but it tastes good!

CHRIST CHURCH INDIA BREAD

4 *ounces Premium soda crackers*
6 *tablespoons butter, melted*
1 *tablespoon curry powder*
¼ *teaspoon ground turmeric*
Salt and freshly ground pepper

I.   Soak the soda crackers in a large bowl of ice water 10 minutes.

II.   Line two baking sheets, or any work surface, with paper towling. Transfer the soaked crackers, one at a time, with a spatula and place on paper toweling. Cover with more paper toweling. Press lightly. Let stand until almost dry, about 6 hours. (*Note:* The crackers never completely dry. Do not worry if they seem damp.)

III.   Heat oven to 500°. Combine butter, curry powder, and turmeric in a small bowl. Brush two baking sheets lightly with the mixture. Carefully transfer crackers. Brush each cracker generously with curry mixture. Bake 10 minutes. Reduce heat to 350°; bake until crisp and brown, about 15 minutes. Sprinkle with salt and pepper. Transfer to a wire rack. For the best results, serve within 10 minutes. However, crackers can be stored in an airtight container and reheated on a rack in the oven at 500° for 5 minutes.

Makes about 40 crackers.

The final bread recipe is actually for a delectable muffin made of bran, named "heavenly" by the donor, Mrs. Anna Teel Barlow, of Lemon Grove, California. A lady of some purpose, Mrs. Barlow came to a session of cooking lessons that I taught in San Diego last year. After class, she presented me with her family treasure, instead of an apple.

I reprint it, herewith, with all her notes and baking secrets virtually intact, including the following afterthought:

I have never seen this in print before.

Given to me by my Grandmother, Anna Dixie Teel,

El Paso, Texas, pioneer.

ANNA TEEL BARLOW'S HEAVENLY MUFFINS

2 *ounces dates, chopped*
½ *cup walnuts, chopped*
2 *tablespoons all-purpose flour*
¼ *cup vegetable oil*
1 *egg*
6 *tablespoons granulated sugar*
1 *cup buttermilk*
½ *cup boiling water*
1 *cup Kellogg's All-Bran cereal*
1 *cup all-purpose flour, sifted*
1¼ *teaspoons baking soda*
½ *teaspoon salt*
½ *cup Nabisco 100% Bran cereal*
Bakers' Secret (see Note)

I.   Heat oven to 400°. Sprinkle the dates and walnuts with 2 tablespoons flour; reserve.

II.   Combine oil, egg, and sugar in a large bowl. Beat well; add buttermilk. Pour boiling water over *Kellogg's All-Bran.* Stir into buttermilk mixture.

III.   Sift 1 cup flour with baking soda and salt. Stir into batter. Add *Nabisco 100% Bran,* and the reserved dates and walnuts. Mix well.

IV.   Spoon batter into muffin tins that have been greased with Bakers' Secret. Bake until golden brown, about 25 minutes.

Note: To make Bakers' Secret, combine ¼ cup Crisco shortening, ¼ cup vegetable oil, and ¼ cup all-purpose flour. Beat until creamy. Store in a jar in the refrigerator. Use Bakers' Secret to grease cake pans, bread pans, etc.

Makes 15 to 16 muffins.

Technically no bread at all, Vermont Fried Cheddar Cakes are noted as "church supper pannycakes" in my log. Originally inscribed (in pencil) on the back of a *Farmer's Almanac*, this 1930 formula makes a fine brunch dish dabbed with sour cream or tomato sauce.

VERMONT FRIED CHEDDAR CAKES

¾ *cup roughly grated Vermont Cheddar cheese*
2 *tablespoons all-purpose flour*
½ *teaspoon baking powder*
⅛ *teaspoon freshly grated nutmeg*
½ *teaspoon finely grated lemon rind*
¼ *teaspoon salt*
Pinch of freshly ground pepper
½ *cup sour cream*
2 *egg yolks*
Creamy Tomato Gravy (see Index), optional

I. Combine the cheese, flour, baking powder, nutmeg, lemon rind, salt, and pepper in a medium bowl. Toss well. Beat in sour cream and egg yolks until smooth.

II. Heat a lightly greased cast iron griddle or skillet over medium-high heat until hot, but not smoking. Drop batter on hot griddle by large teaspoonfuls. Do no more than four at a time. When surface bubbles, carefully turn over with a spatula. Let cook about ½ minute to lighly brown bottoms. Transfer to a serving platter and keep warm while frying remaining cakes. Serve hot with Creamy Tomato Gravy, if desired.

Serves 4.

FISH AND SEAFOOD

Chapter Four

A prejudiced fish lover, I neither angle, cast, nor trawl. But having spent the better part of my life in beach houses along the broad Atlantic, I learned a long time back that fish may be *bought* even if they cannot always be caught!

At the risk of sounding even smugger, I would venture the opinion that there is *no* variety of sea creature from Maine to Florida that has not ended belly-up in my skillet, stewpot, or poacher, at one time or another.

I did say I was prejudiced, didn't I?

Of foreign fish (from the waters of the West Coast and the limpid Gulf) I had scant knowledge and to tell the terrible truth, supreme indifference, until I began my travels for this book.

I dread to think what banquets of the soul might have gone untasted if I had never visited Louisiana's Atchafalaya Basin or Mississippi's Yazoo Bottoms, not to mention San Francisco Bay and the crystal Puget Sound. The tall tales of unctuous oyster gumbos and "po' boys" melting with an overload of shrimp, fried the color of Fort Knox gold—are definitely not wild exaggerations. And, I defy any man with appetite left in his body to pass up a platter of Olympia oysters. These tender bivalves (faintly copper-colored at the shell) are such a remarkable restorative, it is rumored that denizens of the Pacific Northwest get drunk on Saturday night just so they may indulge in an Olympian hangover cure on Sunday morning!

When I first came to San Francisco, I ate *cioppino* (the justly famed local bouillabaisse) three days in a row, without any ostensible compulsion. There were so many noteworthy varieties of this pungent fish stew available on Fisherman's Wharf that I might have consumed a week's worth before all the differences were logged. Later, I discovered at least five other versions in San Pedro, down the coast. Both San Franciscans and San Pedrovians are obdurate about only one aspect of their very special chowder. They always make it with Dungeness crab.

And rightly so, if one wishes to duplicate the utter sense of anesthesia that overtakes the palate when a tongue meets this remarkable crustacean head on!

I, however, living 3,000 miles away from the habitat of *Cancer magister*, have inevitably made do with local crabs (like Atlantic "Jimmies" or "Blues"), added a touch of fennel seeds and saffron, and shamed the devil as they say.

Last year when I was invited to teach a cooking class of "All-American Foods" in Sonoma, California, my good friend M.F.K. Fisher warned me against the culinary temper of the populace.

"You're a brave man if you plan to tell San Franciscans about *cioppino!!!!!* (five exclamation points)" she wrote. "Watch out!"

Always treading where angels fear to, I took a quick course in how to crack a live Dungeness crab, from a sanguine San Franciscan chef, before setting forth across the bay to confront the cognoscenti on their own turf.

To my surprise (and shock) the Dungeness crab supply turned out to be frozen—no expertise required. The requested saffron was also mislaid, so it never got in the soup at all. And the feared critical tongues? Curiously amenable to any alien ingredients that might be lurking in the kettle.

They pronounced my version of their soup a delight. You will too, I hope!

SAN FRANCISCO BAY CIOPPINO

3 *cups hot Fish Stock (see Index)*
24 *clams or mussels*
3 *fresh Dungeness crabs or 2 small lobsters*
½ *cup olive oil*
2 *cloves garlic, minced*
2 *onions, finely chopped*
6 *green onions, finely chopped*

2 *stalks celery, finely chopped*
1 *green pepper, chopped*
1 *teaspoon chopped fresh thyme or ½ teaspoon dried*
1 *bay leaf, crumbled*
2 *cups finely chopped, seeded, peeled tomatoes*
1 *can (17 ounces) plum tomatoes*
2 *cups red wine (a dry white wine may be substituted)*
1 *teaspoon fennel seeds, crushed*
Good pinch of saffron
¼ *cup chopped fresh parsley*
Salt and freshly ground pepper
32 *small shrimp, shelled, deveined*
2 *pounds red snapper, cut into pieces (heads used for stock)*
1 *clove garlic*
1 *teaspoon anchovy paste*

I.   Make Fish Stock. Keep warm.

II.   If using clams, scrub well. If using mussels, scrub and remove beards; place in a large pot of cold water with 1 tablespoon cornstarch. Let stand 30 minutes; wash well under cold running water. (This procedure cleans the bivalves effectively.) If using crab, lay each on its back and place a sharp knife along the midline. Hit the knife hard with a mallet. Twist off claws and legs. Scrub well. Pry off the shell and scrape out the spongy gills. Cut the body in half; crack each leg and claw. If using lobsters, insert a sharp knife where the tail and body meet. Turn lobster over and cut undershells lengthwise with a scissors. Remove dark veins, sacs near the head, and any spongy tissue. Cut lobsters into pieces, slicing tails in half. Crack the claws and any hard pieces.

III.   Heat the oil in a large, heavy pot or Dutch oven. Add the minced garlic, onions, and green onions. Cook over low heat 5 minutes. Add celery, green pepper, thyme, bay leaf, tomatoes, stock, wine, fennel seeds, saffron, parsley, and salt and pepper to taste. Simmer uncovered 30 minutes.

IV.   Add the crab or lobster to the tomato mixture. Cover and cook 5 minutes. Add remaining seafood; cover. Cook 5 minutes, stirring once. Mash 1 clove garlic with the anchovy paste and 1 tablespoon cooking liquid. Stir into pot; simmer 5 minutes.

Serves 8.

I never tasted swordfish until the summer of 1945. The event, I well recall, took place in a restaurant in Provincetown, Massachusetts. In retrospect it was a mighty memorable August evening. Not only did I have a signal bite of that moist and incredibly toothsome saltwater treat but the Second World War came to a close at the very next minute. I must confess, the twin celebrations have always become inexplicably entwined!

Provincetown (indeed all of Cape Cod) is much changed from the clapboard-fronted, slightly rural-raffish summer place it was back then. Cars, for one thing, were a decided rarity in '45. A crazy, antique open-air bus was the only means of transportation for visitors, aside from shanks' mare. The bus rattled up Bradford and down Commercial streets, making no formal stops whatsoever; one simply shouted it to a halt. The busman (an antiquarian himself) allowed passengers with the loudest voices on or off.

Good food was to be found everywhere in P-town: at one-man beach shacks and glossily appointed cantinas alike. Today, the fare is quite different, I am sorry to report. Often a dish is so overlaid with foreign refinements one half expects the province to be Mediterranean rather than Atlantic.

There is, however, some honest fare to be found in the precinct. But one must search hard for it. The recipe I include for broiled swordfish was given to me by a native short-order chef. He performed this striking dish in ten minutes flat and served it up unadorned, except for an old-fashioned baked potato (sans foil or sour cream and chives).

PROVINCETOWN BROILED SWORDFISH

1 *tablespoon olive oil*
1 *small clove garlic, minced*
2 *teaspoons lemon juice*
¼ *teaspoon dried oregano*
¼ *teaspoon dry mustard*
⅛ *teaspoon freshly ground pepper*
1 *tablespoon finely chopped fresh parsley*
1½ *teaspoons anchovy paste*
3 *tablespoons butter, softened*
2 *swordfish steaks (about 2 pounds), 1 inch thick each*
Chopped fresh dill
Lemon or lime wedges

I.   Heat oil in a small saute pan. Saute garlic until golden. Transfer to a small bowl. Cool.

II.   Add lemon juice, oregano, mustard, pepper, parsley, and anchovy paste to the sauteed garlic. Mix well. Stir in softened butter with a spoon. Mix until smooth. Coat both sides of swordfish steaks with mixture. Let stand 30 minutes.

III.   Heat broiling unit. Broil fish until it flakes when pierced with a fork, about 5 minutes on each side. Sprinkle with fresh dill; garnish with lemon wedges.

Serves 4.

My experience with Maryland crab cakes is recent history. I sampled these gilded morsels *on demand* during a trip to our nation's capital not too long ago. William Rice, then the food editor of the *Washington Post,* insisted I try the dish at once. Declaring with some passion that he would gladly "kill" for a platter, the way they were served at Duke Zeibert's fabled restaurant on L Street North West.

I took his forswearal to heart and tried the crab cakes at once. And, if not actually prepared to kill for a repeat order, I am certainly ready to *wound* at the very least.

Unfortunately, Duke Zeibert shuttered its notewrothy doors some short while ago so there is no test of mettle required. The following recipe was passed along from another crab-cake maker par excellence, Chef Robert P. Reilly of Angelina's Restaurant in Baltimore, Maryland.

Mr. Reilly submits his formula with a caveat:

If you are using Chesapeake Bay crab meat it is *not* necessary to pick over or finger. The meat is good! The more you handle crab meat the more it gets busted up . . . the idea is to keep the meat in lumps. (Don't be misled by other recipes calling for removal of cartilage, etc. If you buy *good* Chesapeake crabs, this is totally unnecessary!)

CRAB CAKES MARYLAND

1 *pound lump crab meat*
1 *cup fresh bread crumbs*
⅓ *cup milk (approximately)*
1 *egg, lightly beaten*
¼ *cup mayonnaise*

½ *teaspoon baking powder*
2 *tablespoons finely chopped fresh parsley*
2 *tablespoons minced green onions (optional)*
½ *teaspoon salt*
¼ *teaspoon ground white pepper*
Flour
Butter or vegetable oil
Tartar Sauce or Creamy Tomato Gravy (see Index)

I.   Place crab meat in a large bowl. Cover with bread crumbs. Moisten crumbs with the milk.

II.   Combine beaten egg and mayonnaise in a small bowl. Add baking powder, parsley, green onions, salt, and white pepper. Pour over crab meat mixture. Toss lightly until well mixed. Form into ten large crab cakes, adding more milk if needed. Place on a plate. Refrigerate at least 1 hour.

III.   Dust the cakes lightly with flour. Heat butter in skillet until hot. Fry cakes in hot butter or oil until golden. Drain on paper toweling. Serve with Tartar Sauce or Creamy Tomato Gravy.

Serves 4 to 5.

Mr. Reilly may be a bit prejudiced about Chesapeake Bay crab. For my part, I feel remarkably opinionated on the subject of tartar sauce! Most versions found at seafood establishments across the country are far too tame. Mine is devised for a wild palate!

TARTAR SAUCE

1 *cup mayonnaise*
½ *cup sour cream*
½ *teaspoon Dijon mustard*
1 *small shallot, minced*
1 *sour gherkin, chopped*
1 *teaspoon finely chopped fresh parsley*
1 *tablespoon finely chopped fresh dill*
¼ *teaspoon finely chopped fresh tarragon or a pinch of dried*
Dash of hot pepper sauce
Salt and freshly ground pepper to taste

I.   Whisk the mayonnaise with the sour cream and mus-
        tard in a medium bowl. Stir in remaining ingredients;
        mix well. Refrigerate until cold.

                                        Makes about 1½ cups.

Forty years ago, nobody but Greenes and Catholics ate fish
every Friday—or so it seems today. My parents were devoted
fish lovers who took any excuse to indulge their piscine appe-
tites. I, however, detested all manner of seafood with utter
impartiality.

In every household some compromise is usually effected.
They ate salmon, sole, smelts, or whatever scaled object seemed
freshest on the fish man's glittering ice tray. *I* settled for codfish
cakes (well disguised with mashed potatoes and slivered bits of
silvery onion) from Lorenzen's, our corner "deli."

At that long-ago time, a half pound of upstanding fish cakes
might be purchased (breaded but uncooked) straight from the
counter on Friday afternoons. The pale patties to be fried to
amber splendor in a skillet at your very own kitchen stove. They
were utterly delicious, too, although I must confess that I never
ate one unless it was well slathered with rosy ketchup—to
further the disguise, you see.

I hadn't consumed a fish cake in years (since I became a proper fish lover myself, I guess) until I found myself thinking on honest American sea fare. The recipe here is donated by a lady friend who chooses anonymity here. She claims to have learned the homely art of fish cakes shortly after mud pies—at her mother's elbow, in Cape May, New Jersey.

CAPE MAY FISH CAKES

1 *large shallot, minced*
1 *small clove garlic, minced*
1 *teaspoon butter*
1½ *cups cold, mashed, cooked potatoes*
¼ *cup all-purpose flour*
1 *egg, lightly beaten*
1 *teaspoon Dijon mustard*
1 *tablespoon wine vinegar*
1 *teaspoon grated lemon rind*
1 *tablespoon finely chopped fresh parsley*
Pinch of dried thyme
½ *teaspoon ground ginger*
¼ *teaspoon salt*
¼ *teaspoon freshly ground pepper*
Dash of hot pepper sauce
1½ *cups flaked, cooked scrod*
Flour
⅓ *cup milk*
1 *cup fine bread crumbs*
6 *tablespoons butter*
1 *tablespoon vegetable oil*
Creamy Tomato Gravy (recipe follows)

I.   Cook shallot and garlic in 1 teaspoon butter over low heat until soft, about 4 minutes.

II.   Place the mashed potatoes in a large bowl. Add cooked shallot and garlic, ¼ cup flour, the egg, mustard, vinegar, lemon rind, parsley, thyme, ginger, salt, pepper, and hot pepper sauce. Mix well. Stir in cooked scrod. Form into small fish cakes.

III.   Roll the fish cakes in flour to lightly coat. Dip in milk; roll in bread crumbs. Sauté fish cakes in a 10- or 12-inch skillet in 6 tablespoons butter and the oil, a few at a time, until golden on both sides. Drain on paper toweling. Keep warm. Serve with Creamy Tomato Gravy.

Serves 4 to 6.

The following gravy is the only upholstery worthy of a sapid, scrod fish cake. Purists may substitute cod for the scrod in the preceding recipe, however, or even haddock, since each of these fish appears to be merely varieties of the same sea beast at different stages of development. And all take kindly to a *creamy* tomato sauce.

CREAMY TOMATO GRAVY

½ *cup unsalted butter*
1 *medium onion, finely chopped*
1 *clove garlic, minced*
1 *stalk celery, finely chopped*
4 *large ripe tomatoes, peeled, seeded, chopped*
1 *teaspoon fresh basil or ½ teaspoon dried*
1 *teaspoon fresh oregano or ½ teaspoon dried*
Pinch of dried thyme
1 *teaspoon granulated sugar*
¼ *teaspoon grated orange peel*
½ *cup whipping cream (approximately)*

I.   Melt 4 tablespoons butter in a large, heavy saucepan.
        Add onion and garlic; cook over low heat 5 minutes. Do
        not brown. Add celery; cook 4 minutes.

II.   Add tomatoes, basil, oregano, thyme, sugar, and orange
        peel to the saucepan. Cook over medium heat, stirring
        frequently, 20 minutes. Cut in remaining butter; stir in
        cream. Cook until smooth and creamy, about 5 minutes.

Makes 1½ cups.

Hangtown Fry in my opinion, is an epitaph more than an actual recipe—since no plateful is ever served up without an accompanying legend.

The best Hangtown Fry comes from Placerville, California, a town that purports to be the dish's place of origin.

It seems that men were hanged easily in lawless Gold Rush communities like Placerville 100 years ago. One poor soul, accused of stealing a prospector's poke, bargained for his life right up to the foot of the hanging tree. For a reprieve, this fellow proposed a gastronomic trade-off. A cook by profession, he offered to prepare the best dish the miners had ever tasted.

Obviously, a hungry jury gave his skillet a chance. From a secret cache (he really was a thief, you see) he produced oysters, butter, bacon, ham, and even a few precious eggs. With great dexterity, under the circumstances, he sautéed the meat and oysters together and at precisely the correct moment beat the eggs to a froth and folded them over the sizzling contents of his pan. The result? A most unusual omelet that happily served twelve.

They never did hang him. How could they? He brought culinary refinement to the neighborhood!

WEST COAST HANGTOWN FRY

4 *strips bacon*
½ *cup smoked ham, cut into strips*
4 *eggs*
¼ *cup whipping cream*
2 *tablespoons water*
¼ *cup chopped fresh parsley*
3 *tablespoons freshly grated Parmesan cheese*
8 *to* 10 *oysters, shucked*
2 *eggs, beaten*
1 *cup bread crumbs (approximately)*
2 *tablespoons butter*
1 *shallot or small onion, minced*
Salt and freshly ground pepper
Chopped fresh parsley

I.   Heat broiling unit. Fry bacon in a large, heavy skillet until crisp. Remove with a slotted spoon. Drain on paper toweling. Crumble bacon; reserve.

II.   Increase heat slightly. Sauté ham strips in bacon drippings until lightly browned. Drain on paper toweling. Reserve.

III. Beat 4 eggs in a medium bowl until light. Add cream, water, ¼ cup parsley, and the cheese. Set aside.

IV.   Dip oysters in the two beaten eggs. Roll in bread crumbs.

V.   Heat the butter in the skillet over medium heat. Stir in shallot. Add oysters, sauté until golden, about 1 minute on each side. Stir in reserved bacon and ham.

VI.   Pour the egg-cream mixture over the oyster mixture in the skillet; do not stir. Let stand a few minutes. As the eggs begin to set, lift up bottom with a spatula to prevent burning and to let uncooked egg mixture run underneath. Cook until almost set. Season to taste with salt and pepper. Place under broiler to lightly brown. Sprinkle with parsley.

Serves 6.

Spiritually, my home is in Amagansett—at the almost end of Long Island—where the best bay scallops in the world have their habitat as well. I say *spiritual* because, despite good intentions, my corporeal presence is usually in some kitchen elsewhere across the nation these days.

When I get to the family homestead, however, the first meal taken is most often a platter of scallops fresh from Gardiners Bay. The following recipe is most likely a favorite because it is a product of the famed Long Island inertia. This dish may be completed in less than a half hour—perfect on a hot beach day.

Bay Scallop Hash is more work but eminently satisfying to the tongue. This piece of culinary handiwork is my own mix entirely, produced after a steady diet of high-blown cookery I was testing for a magazine article. When you make it, be certain that the potatoes do not overcook. The hash must have a bite, or it simply becomes bay scallop mush.

GARLICKY GARDINERS BAY SCALLOPS

1¼ *pounds bay scallops*
3 *tablespoons all-purpose flour*
6 *tablespoons butter*
1 *tablespoon olive oil*
2 *cloves garlic, minced*
¼ *cup dry white wine*
2 *tablespoons lemon juice*
2 *tablespoons chopped fresh parsley*
Salt and freshly ground pepper
Hot cooked rice

I.   Dust scallops lightly with the flour.

II.   Heat butter and oil in a large, heavy sauté pan over low
        heat. Add garlic; cook 2 minutes.

III.   Increase heat slightly; sauté scallops, a few at a time,
        until golden. Transfer to a plate as they are done.

IV.   Add wine and lemon juice to the pan. Heat to boiling;
        boil, scraping sides and bottom of pan, until syrupy,
        about 5 minutes. Return scallops to the pan. Add
        parsley; toss until warmed through. Add salt and
        pepper to taste. Serve over rice.

Serves 2 to 3.

BAY SCALLOP HASH

2 *cloves garlic, minced*
6 *tablespoons butter*
1 *tablespoon olive oil*
2 *large baking potatoes, pared, cubed*
1 *pound bay scallops*
3 *tablespoons all-purpose flour*
4 *green onions, chopped*
1 *tablespoon lemon juice*
1 *teaspoon lemon rind*
½ *cup chopped fresh parsley*
1 *teaspoon crushed dried hot red peppers*
Salt and freshly ground pepper

I.   Sauté garlic in butter and oil in a large skillet over
        medium heat until golden. Stir in potatoes. Cook, stir-
        ring constantly, until potatoes are light golden in color,
        about 10 minutes.

II.   Coat scallops lightly with the flour. Stir into potatoes. Add green onions, lemon juice, and lemon rind. Cook, stirring frequently, until potatoes are tender, about 6 minutes. Add parsley, red peppers, and salt and pepper to taste.

Serves 4.

One of the most savory fish snacks ever chomped is undoubtedly the Michigan lake smelt. True aficionados of this treat can put away a dozen or so at one sitting, skin, bones and all!

For untried smelt palates, I recommend a starter course, beginning with a platter of finger food—these tiny migrating coastal fish, well pickled in brine.

The average smelt is about six or seven inches long and produces a herring of unforgettable savor that may also be eaten in one mouthful. I had my first bite not too long ago myself at a dinner party that was composed of only dishes indigenous to the Michigan area. Who served it up? Andrea Wojack and Sandra Silfven, two extremely pretty and no-nonsense cooks, who also happen to be food editors at the *Detroit News*.

Andrea's recipe (it came from an old and treasured Michigan cookbook) follows.

UPPER MICHIGAN PICKLED SMELTS

2 *quarts smelts, heads removed, cleaned*
½ *cup kosher or pickling salt*
2 *medium onions, sliced*
2 *teaspoons pickling spices*
2 *small bay leaves*
¾ *cup granulated sugar*
2 *cups distilled white vinegar*

I.   Sprinkle the smelts with the salt. Let stand 10 hours. Rinse fish six times in cold water; drain. Cut fish into pieces.

II.   Place fish in 2 sterilized 1-quart jars. Add 1 sliced onion, 1 teaspoon pickling spices, and 1 small bay leaf to each jar.

III.   Combine sugar and vinegar in a small saucepan. Heat to boiling; boil 5 minutes. Pour over fish. Cover and refrigerate at least 3 days before tasting. Pickled smelts must be stored in refrigerator.

Makes 2 quarts.

From the Swedish denizens of the Northeast, comes a little known (but highly economical) version of standard Scandinavian smorgasbord fare: *Grav Lax*. This rendering is dependent upon Atlantic bluefish, hence the curious cognomen. *Gravad* means marinated; *Blå Fisk* means a fish that is blue in color. But forget the hue and cry; the dish is best served icy cold with boiled, unbuttered new potatoes on the side. Not bad for hors d'oeuvres accompanied with toothpicks either!

GRAVAD BLÅ FISK

1 *fresh bluefish filet (about 2 pounds), boned, skinned*
3 *tablespoons plus ¾ cup olive oil*
2 *tablespoons granulated sugar*
1 *tablespoon salt*
½ *teaspoon crushed craway seeds*
½ *teaspoon ground white pepper*
1¼ *cups chopped fresh dill*
¼ *cup dry gin or Akavit*
2 *tablespoons Dijon mustard*
3 *tablespoons tarragon vinegar*
1 *teaspoon lemon juice*
Salt and freshly ground pepper

I.   Pat bluefish dry with paper toweling. Dip a clean cloth into 3 tablespoons oil and rub fish well on both sides. Combine 1 tablespoon sugar, 1 tablespoon salt, the crushed caraway seeds, and white pepper in a small bowl; rub into fish on both sides.

II.   Use a shallow dish in which bluefish fits snugly and sprinkle bottom with ½ cup dill. Place the fish over dill; pour gin over. Sprinkle top with ½ cup dill.

III. Cover fish with aluminum foil and place a wood plank or heavy dish on top. Place a heavy weight on top of that. Refrigerate 6 days, turning fish over daily.

IV.   Before serving, combine 1 tablespoon sugar, the mustard, and vinegar in a small bowl. Gradually whisk in remaining ¾ cup oil, 1 tablespoon at a time, until thick. Add lemon juice and salt and pepper to taste.

V.   To serve: slice the marinated bluefish on the diagonal. Place on a serving platter; spoon mustard sauce over. Sprinkle with remaining ¼ cup dill.
      Serves 6 as a main course, more as an appetizer.

Fish shortcake is a Rhode Island bestowal composed of freshly caught haddock, scalded milk and a mite of Cheddar for tang. I consumed this dish on my way to sight-see the pleasure domes of stately Newport Beach not too long ago. The prescription for the shortcake was curiously circumscribed by the social station of the diner, I discovered in my travels. Plain fare (like this) was only served in the great houses as part of "the help's breakfast," while grander folks, like Mrs. Vanderbilt, took kippers and grilled kidneys on the terrace!

NEWPORT FISH SHORTCAKE

3 *tablespoons finely chopped onion*
4 *tablespoons butter*
3 *tablespoons all-purpose flour*
2 *cups hot milk*
Pinch of ground allspice
Pinch of cayenne pepper
⅛ *teaspoon freshly grated nutmeg*
Salt and ground white pepper
⅓ *cup grated, medium-sharp Cheddar cheese*
1½ *cups flaked, cooked haddock*
Chopped fresh parsley
Carolina Cracklin' Bread or Helen Johnson's Buttermilk Biscuits
    (see Index)

I.   Cook the onions in butter in a medium saucepan over
        low heat until tender, about 5 minutes. Stir in flour;
        cook, stirring constantly, 2 minutes. Whisk in hot milk.
        Simmer until thickened, about 10 minutes.

II.   Season sauce with allspice, cayenne pepper, nutmeg,
        and salt and white pepper to taste. Stir in cheese and
        haddock. Cook until warmed through, about 3 minutes.
        Sprinkle with parsley. Serve over Carolina Cracklin'
        Bread or Helen Johnson's Buttermilk Biscuits.

Serves 6.

Petrale is a succulent Pacific flounder (slightly stronger in
flavor) which, like its cousins the lemon and grey sole, is
eminently suitable to any mirific fillet. The recipe for a crumb-
dusted, sautéed petrale, anointed with red wine vinegar, comes
from a cooking friend who lives in Carmel. She insists no other
flounder makes the grade in this devise. I lovingly disagree. Use
whatever fresh flat fish you can find!

DUSTY PETRALE MONTEREY

4 *large petrale fillets, cut in half*
¼ *cup all-purpose flour*
½ *cup milk*
1¼ *cups soft bread crumbs (approximately)*
½ *cup butter*
2 *tablespoons olive oil*
1½ *tablespoons red wine vinegar*
Lemon slices
Chopped fresh parsley

I.   Heat oven to 350°. Roll fillets in the flour; shake off excess. Dip fillets in milk; roll in bread crumbs.

II.   Melt ¼ cup butter with 1 tablespoon oil in a large, heavy skillet. Sauté fish until golden, about 2 minutes on each side. (Add remaining butter and oil as needed.) Transfer fish to heatproof serving platter.

III.   Sprinkle vinegar over the fish. Transfer platter to the oven. Bake until fish flakes easily when pierced with a fork, about 8 minutes. Garnish with lemon slices and chopped parsley.

Serves 4.

The Cajun country of Louisiana is a repository of fine food—particularly between the months of September and May when the shrimp in the basin are ripe for harvest and the crayfish run in every bayou mud stream. My pet restaurant of this region is the most unpretentious you will ever find. Black's Topless Oyster Bar in Abbeville is spare on decor, but the best fried shrimp in the country passes across its zinc counter top. Most often these treats are piled into a hollowed-out loaf of French bread that is absolutely slathered with melting butter, making it a disaster area for the diner, but "to die," as they say down South.

One may attempt reconstruction of a "po' boy" on alien turf, I suppose. The shrimp recipe below will help mightily but nothing in the world can duplicate the flavor of a Dixie beer (in a goblet thick with ice after a day in the freezer!). That's nonpareil nourishment!

ABBEVILLE FRIED SHRIMP

1 *pound shrimp, shelled, deveined*
1½ *to 2 cups Homemade Mayonnaise (recipe follows)*
2½ *cups bread crumbs (approximately)*
¾ *cup unsalted butter*
2 *tablespoons vegetable oil*
Salt
Lemon wedges

I.   Heat oven to 200°. Dip shrimp in mayonnaise; coat thickly with bread crumbs.

II.   Melt ½ cup butter with oil in a large, heavy sauté pan over medium heat. Sauté the shrimp, a few at a time, until golden brown on both sides. Drain on paper toweling. Sprinkle with salt. Keep warm in oven until all shrimp are done. Add more butter to sauté pan as needed. Serve with lemon wedges.

Serves 2 to 4.

The following mayonnaise will coat a shrimp munificently and is not bad on a sandwich, either. But never make it unless all the ingredients are at room temperature.

HOMEMADE MAYONNAISE

3 *egg yolks*
1 *tablespoon wine vinegar*
Juice of 1 lemon
½ *teaspon salt*
Pinch of ground white pepper
½ *teaspoon Dijon mustard*
2 *cups vegetable oil combined with* ½ *cup olive oil*
Dash of hot pepper sauce
2 *tablespoons boiling water*

I. Beat the egg yolks in a large bowl until thick. Slowly beat in vinegar, lemon juice, salt, white pepper, and mustard.

II. Beat in the oil, a few drops at a time, until ½ cup has been incorporated. (Mayonnaise should be very thick at this point.) Continue to beat in oil, 2 tablespoons at a time. Season with hot pepper sauce and more salt or lemon juice to taste. Thin with boiling water. Store tightly covered in refrigerator.

Makes about 2½ cups.

The last fish recipe in this collation is a quintessential deep-dish pie from Connecticut.

"Actually a chowder that got so creamy it just naturally put on airs!" is the way I heard the formula first described by the ample Mystic housewife who made it for me.

Cloaked in a mouth-watering, rich buttery crust, this is scallop's, flounder's, and clam's finest hour!

MYSTIC DEEP-DISH CHOWDER PIE

FOR THE PASTRY:
1½ *cups all-purpose flour*
¼ *teaspoon salt*
Pinch of granulated sugar
6 *tablespoons cold butter*
2¼ *tablespoons cold vegetable shortening*
4 to 4½ *tablespoons cold water*

FOR THE FILLING:
¼ *cup finely diced salt pork*
2 *tablespoons butter*
1 *large onion, finely chopped*
1 *clove garlic, minced*
4 *tablespoons all-purpose flour*
1 *stalk celery, chopped*
1 *carrot, pared and chopped*
1 *large potato, pared and cubed*
1 *tablespoon chopped fresh parsley*
½ *cup dry white wine*
⅔ *cup Fish Stock (see Index)*
1 *cup whipping cream*
Pinch of dried thyme
Pinch of ground allspice
1 *tablespoon lemon juice*
¼ *pound bay scallops (or sea scallops, cut into quarters)*
12 *clams, shucked, cut in half*
1 *pound flounder fillets, cut in pieces*
1 *egg yolk, lightly beaten with a few drops water*

I.   To make the pastry: Combine flour, salt, and sugar in a medium bowl. Cut in butter and shortening. Blend with a pastry blender until the texture of coarse crumbs. Stir in water to form a soft dough. Chill 1½ hours.

II.   Heat oven to 350°. To make the filling: Cook salt pork in a heavy saucepan over medium heat until golden. Remove with a slotted spoon. Drain on paper toweling. Reserve.

III.   Drain all but 2 tablespoons grease from pan. Add butter, onion, and garlic. Cook over low heat 4 minutes. Stir in flour; cook, stirring constantly, 2 minutes. Stir in reserved salt pork, celery, carrot, potato, and parsley. Add wine and Fish Stock. Heat to boiling; reduce heat. Simmer 5 minutes. Add cream; simmer until thickened, about 10 minutes.

IV.   Season vegetable mixture with thyme, allspice, and lemon juice. Stir in scallops, clams, and flounder. (See *Note* below concerning advance preparation.) Transfer to a 2-quart, deep-dish casserole or souffle dish.

V.   Roll out pastry so that it will hang over edge of casserole dish 1 inch all around. Press overhang against side of dish to seal and prevent shrinking. Cut a hole in center to allow steam to escape. Brush crust lightly with egg yolk and water. Bake until pastry is golden brown, 35 to 40 minutes. Let stand 5 minutes before serving.

Note: If preparing this dish in advance, let sauce cook completely before stirring in the seafood and covering with pastry. Otherwise fish will cook in warm sauce.

Serves 6.

POULTRY

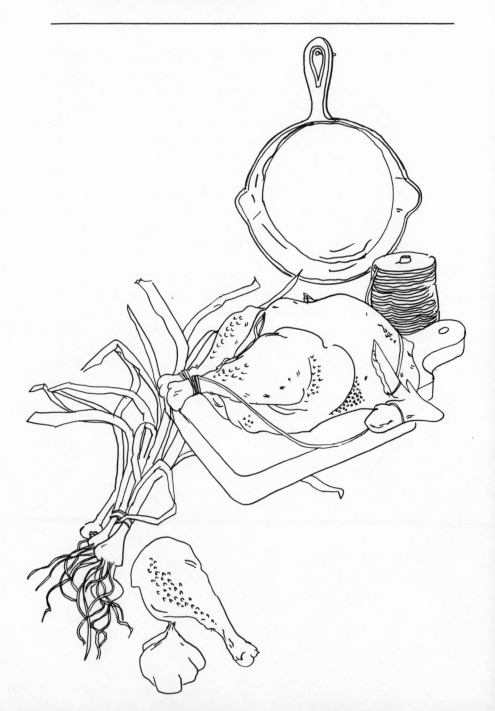

Chapter Five

Modern life may have a few compensations like food processors and microwaves, but there are drawbacks lurking under every pot cover.

Fifty years ago, for instance, no self-respecting cook would consider just dropping by a market and selecting a chicken for dinner from a pile of dead birds on ice. Instead, the lady of the house would knowledgeably visit her favored poultry butcher or chicken farm. After considerable inspection of the pullets' fine points (feet, crop, and tail feathers), she would select the correct breed she had in mind for a particular dish. Most often, the poor bird would be alive and kicking during its "physical," so the housewife would know with utter certainty about the freshness of her fricassee!

Today the idea of freshly killed poultry is anathema to most chicken-hearted shoppers, unless of course they happen to be religious Jews. More to the point, no one (not even a consumer with Home Ec credentials) can tell the difference between one tagged supermarket birdie and another.

In our grandmothers' day, a nominee for the chicken fryer or barbecue pit would not come within an inch of the flame unless it was a bona fide Rhode Island Red or Plymouth Rock. And a stewpot was an unthinkable repository for any hen other than a Buff Orpington.

Today if you tried quizzing a butcher about his pullets' ancestry, I think you might receive a few salty imprecations about your own!

Most everywhere in America we dine on "design-bred" chicken—fowl that has been mass-raised for multipurpose cookery sans individual character or savor. There is no sense in the world bemoaning the fact. And though I for one have had the good fortune to nibble on an honest-to-gosh *poularde de Bresse* in my time, all the poultry used in the recipes tested for this tome came from a supermarket meat counter just like yours.

As a prejudiced diner, however, I draw a hard and unswerving line at eating frozen chicken. Freezing frankly blunts any delicacy that Perdue and friends have left in the natural flavor and irremediably destroys all texture. So it is either *fresh* or a day of fasting at my table!

Roast chicken is a dish I equate with the Great Depression. Although, back in the days when President Hoover was promising a chicken in every pot, I was far too young to have appreciated the joys of *pot-au-feu.*

But I probably wouldn't have liked it much. As a small child, you see, I ate chicken only under duress. And frankly, I didn't care much for eggs either!

When I learned to cook (at age eleven or twelve), roast chicken entered my culinary repertoire with many caveats. My mother never quite trusted me to sew up a pullet after it had been stuffed, as I was at best a maladroit child. She was dead certain that even if I managed to truss up some poor bird without excessive bloodletting, I would probably leave the needle inside. Instead I was provided with toothpicks for skewers, instruments that usually broke in half before closure was effected. To pinion the legs, I settled on rubber bands. They snapped apart during the roasting period (and had to be fished out of the pan drippings) but were a preferred alternative to learning a proper slipknot! Small wonder the family ate their chicken braised most often.

The best roast chicken I have ever made is from a family recipe sent me years ago from an ardent fan who lives in Portland, Oregon. It comes with a historical note:

"Our family chicken recipe comes from my husband's great-grandmother. She lived to be 103 and brought this dish with her from Iowa as a present to her mail-order bridegroom."

PORTLAND, OREGON, BACON-STREAKED ROAST CHICKEN

1 *large onion, chopped*
½ *cup unsalted butter*
2 *medium potatoes, pared, cut into ¼-inch cubes*
2 *medium carrots, pared, cut into ¼-inch cubes*
1 *medium zucchini, cut into ¼-inch cubes*
¼ *cup chopped fresh parsley*
1 *tablespoon soy sauce*
½ *teaspoon salt*
¼ *teaspoon freshly ground pepper*
2 *whole chickens (about 2½ pounds each)*
1 *clove garlic, bruised*
4 *strips bacon*
1 *cup Chicken Stock (see Index)*
1 *tablespoon plus 1 teaspoon all-purpose flour*
1 *cup whipping cream*
2 *teaspoons strong coffee*
Salt and freshly ground pepper
Chopped fresh parsley

I. Heat oven to 375°. Cook the onion in ¼ cup butter in a large, heavy sauté pan over medium-low heat 5 minutes. Stir in potatoes, carrots, and zucchini; cook 2 minutes. Add ¼ cup parsley, the soy sauce, ½ teaspoon salt, and ¼ teaspoon pepper. Toss well; remove from heat.

II. Rub each chicken well, inside and out, with bruised garlic; discard garlic. Spoon half the stuffing into each chicken; truss. Place chickens in a roasting pan. Spread 1 tablespoon butter over each chicken. Place 2 strips bacon over each breast. Pour stock around chickens. Bake, basting every 20 minutes with pan juices, until chickens are tender, about 1½ hours. Remove trussing; place chickens on platter; keep warm.

III.   Remove excess fat from pan juices. Melt remaining 2
tablespoons butter in a medium saucepan over medium-
low heat; whisk in flour. Cook, stirring constantly, 2
minutes. Add pan juices and cream. Increase heat
slightly. Simmer until thickened. Stir in coffee. Season
to taste with salt and freshly ground pepper. Spoon ¼
cup sauce over chickens. Sprinkle chickens with parsley; pass remaining sauce.

Serves 4 to 6.

Having been raised in the suburban environs of New York
City, I knew no joys of regional cookery until I traveled to
Virginia as a freshman college student. But the conceit of
Southern food had long suffused my youthful imagination. Per-
haps "the mouth" for grits and gravy came from my assiduous
reading habits, as I dipped into Margaret Mitchell directly after
Beatrix Potter!

I well remember persuading my mother to attempt fried
chicken when I was just a kid. An experience not recalled with
any pleasure I might add, for though my poor parent diligently
floured and fried the chicken parts till golden in color (as Fanny
Farmer had so directed), her finished product was a disaster.
The platter looked (and smelled) authentic, but every piece was
bloody under the glistening upholstery. No one ate a wing!

The following Virginia formula (with cream gravy) is a
testament to more conspicuous consumption!

VIRGINIA FRIED CHICKEN WITH CREAM GRAVY

1 *chicken (about 4 pounds), cut into 10 pieces*
½ *cup plus 2 tablespoons all-purpose flour*
½ *teaspoon salt*
¼ *teaspoon freshly ground pepper*

Pinch of ground allspice
⅛ teaspoon freshly grated nutmeg
½ to ¾ cup unsalted butter
2 tablespoons vegetable oil
1 cup Chicken Stock (see Index)
1 cup whipping cream
Salt and freshly ground pepper
1 teaspoon bourbon
Steamed Rice (recipe follows)

I. Remove skin from chicken. Combine ½ cup flour, ½ teaspoon salt, ¼ teaspoon pepper, the allspice, and nutmeg in a large paper bag. Place chicken, a few pieces at a time, in bag. Shake to coat evenly with flour mixture.

II. Heat oven to 275°. Melt ½ cup butter with 1 tablespoon oil in a large, heavy skillet over medium-low heat. (Do not let butter burn.) Gently place chicken in skillet. Do not crowd pieces; use two skillets, if necessary. Sauté over medium-low heat until golden brown, about 12 minutes on each side. Add more butter and oil as needed. Remove chicken; drain on paper toweling. Place chicken in a shallow baking dish; transfer to oven. Bake chicken uncovered for at least 30 minutes and up to 1 hour.

III. Meanwhile, drain all but 2 tablespoons fat from skillet. Stir in 2 tablespoons flour over low heat; cook, stirring constantly, 2 minutes. Whisk in Chicken Stock, scraping bottom and sides of pan. Stir in cream; cook over low heat 20 minutes. Season to taste with salt and pepper. Just before serving, add bourbon. Spoon some of the sauce over chicken; pass remaining sauce. Serve with Steamed Rice.

Serves 4.

As a regional-bred fried chicken fancier, I would never serve any accompaniment to that dish other than steamed rice. I am forthrightly prejudiced on the subject of converted or instant rice—it's awful! Learn right here how to make rice in the Southern manner. One tip worth noting: Cooked rice triples in volume. Use ⅓ cup uncooked rice for each cupful desired.

STEAMED RICE

1⅓ *cups uncooked rice*
4 *quarts boiling, salted water*

I.   Add rice to 4 quarts boiling water in a 5-quart pot. Stir once with a wooden spoon so that rice does not stick to bottom of pan. Heat to boiling; reduce heat. Simmer until just tender, 12 to 15 minutes. Drain in a colander.

II.   Place colander with rice over 2 inches water. Heat water to boiling. Do not let water touch colander. Cover rice with one layer of paper toweling. Steam at least 15 minutes. Rice can be steamed for at least 45 minutes without damage.

Makes four 1-cup servings.

It's a long haul from Richmond, Virginia (and my first tasting of a properly sautéed chicken leg), to Kansas City, Missouri, where one of the most heralded chicken fryers of the nation practices her art. Producing, I might add, a radically divergent offering. Midwestern fried chicken is a crustier and gutsier delight—meant to be eaten exclusively with the fingers and dipped into gravy only when the tongue demands surcease. This recipe is the handiwork of "Chicken" Betty Lucas of The Newport Diner.

KANSAS CITY FRIED CHICKEN

1 *chicken (about 3½ pounds), cut into serving pieces*
1 *large egg*
⅔ *cup milk*
1½ *teaspoons salt*
1 *tablespoon freshly ground pepper*
1 *teaspoon chicken bouillon powder*
2 *cups plus 1½ tablespoons all-purpose flour*
1 *cup lard*
1 *cup vegetable shortening*
2 *cups milk or light cream*
Salt and freshly ground pepper

I.   Wipe the chicken with paper toweling to dry thoroughly.

II.   Combine the egg and ⅔ cup milk in a large bowl. Beat
       well. Dip the chicken pieces in milk mixture. Let excess
       drip off slightly. Place pieces on a large plate. Sprinkle
       generously on both sides with 1½ teaspoons salt, 1
       tablespoon pepper, and the bouillon powder.

III.   Place 2 cups flour in a large bowl. Roll chicken pieces,
       one at a time, in flour. Press and pound flour into
       chicken as much as possible.

IV.   Heat lard and shortening in a large, heavy skillet,
       preferably cast-iron. Add chicken pieces to skillet.
       Pieces can be close together, but should not touch. Fry
       chicken over medium-high heat until golden brown,
       about 7 minutes on each side. Reduce heat to medium-
       low. Cover the skillet about two-thirds of the way. Cook,
       turning the chicken several times, 20 minutes. (Chicken
       will be a deep copper color.) Reduce heat if pieces
       brown too quickly. Drain chicken on paper toweling.
       Keep warm.

V.   Drain all but 2 tablespoons grease from pan. Stir in 1½ tablespoons flour over low heat. Cook, stirring constantly, 2 minutes. Whisk in 2 cups milk. Boil until slightly thickened. Season to taste with salt and pepper. Pass gravy on the side.

Serves 2 to 4.

In the Florida Keys, chicken frying has been amended by several ethnic pot watchers. Expatriated Cuban cooks added a touch of native rum to a dish that black sharecroppers had traditionally seasoned with the juice of plentiful sour-sweet Key limes. The mixture (though unorthodox to any purist from other parts of Dixie) is justly celebrated in the coco-palm territory.

KEY WEST RUM AND LIME FRIED CHICKEN

1 *chicken (about 4 pounds), cut into serving pieces*
¼ *cup dark rum*
¼ *cup lime juice*
¼ *cup soy sauce*
½ *cup all-purpose flour*
½ *teaspoon salt*
¼ *teaspoon freshly ground pepper*
⅛ *teaspoon cayenne pepper*
⅛ *teaspoon paprika*
2 *cups vegetable oil*
Juice of 2 limes

I.   Place chicken pieces in a large bowl. Heat rum in a small saucepan to warm; ignite. Shake pan until flames subside. Add ¼ cup lime juice and the soy sauce. Pour over chicken. Marinate chicken, turning the pieces several times, 4 to 6 hours. Drain; pat dry with paper toweling.

II.   Combine flour, salt, pepper, cayenne pepper, and pa-
        prika in a large paper bag. Add chicken pieces. Shake
        to coat lightly with flour mixture.

III.   Heat oil in a 12-inch cast-iron skillet until very hot.
        Gently add chicken pieces. Fry chicken in oil, turning
        every 5 minutes, until crisp and cooked through, about
        25 minutes. Reduce heat if chicken browns too quickly.
        Drain on paper toweling. Sprinkle with the juice of 2
        limes; serve immediately.

                                                Serves 2 to 4.

The last nostrum for an "oven-fried" chicken comes from
Hannibal, Missouri—the same state responsible for "Chicken
Betty," but as far from Kansas City as a bird can fly.

This dish, born on the banks of the Mississippi, is reputed to
be as old as commercial coal stoves. What makes it notable is a
coating of high-fiber whole wheat flour and a relatively low
amount of butter. It's also decidedly *less work for mother!*

MISSOURI OVEN-FRIED CHICKEN

1 *chicken (about 4 pounds), cut into serving pieces*
2½ *cups milk (approximately)*
1 *tablespoon plus 1 teaspoon hot pepper sauce*
1 *tablespoon soy sauce*
1 *teaspoon salt*
6 *tablespoons stone-ground, whole wheat flour (available in health
    food stores)*
¼ *teaspoon freshly ground pepper*
¼ *teaspoon freshly grated nutmeg*
⅛ *teaspoon ground allspice*
¼ *cup unsalted butter*
½ *cup water*

I.   Place the chicken in a large bowl. Combine milk, hot pepper sauce, soy sauce, and ½ teaspoon salt. Pour over chicken. Add more milk if needed; chicken should be completely covered. Let stand at least 3 hours.

II.   Heat oven to 375°. Drain chicken, reserving milk mixture. Dry chicken on paper toweling. Combine flour, pepper, nutmeg, allspice, and ½ teaspoon salt in a large paper bag. Add chicken and shake to coat lightly. Reserve remaining flour mixture.

III. Melt butter with ¼ cup water. Place chicken pieces skin side down on a rack in a roasting pan. Bake, basting every 5 minutes with butter-water mixture, 30 minutes. Turn chicken over; continue to bake, basting every 5 minutes with pan juices, until chicken is golden and crisp, about 45 minutes. Transfer chicken to a serving platter; keep warm in a low oven.

IV.   Drain all but 2 tablespoons grease from the roasting pan. Place pan over medium-low heat; stir in 1 tablespoon reserved flour mixture, scraping bottom of pan. Cook, stirring constantly, 2 minutes. Add 1 cup reserved milk mixture and ¼ cup water. Cook until slightly thickened. Add more hot pepper sauce, if desired. Spoon some of the sauce over chicken; pass remaining sauce.

Serves 4.

The Shakers are a religious sect (a scant 250 years old) whose roots are pure Quaker. The earliest preachers were radical prophets obsessed with the notion of abstemious fasts, trances, and heavenly visions. The mighty "shakes" induced by these spiritual rigors led to their being dubbed "Shaking Quakers."

Early Shaker communities in the American Northeast believed in spare and simple pleasures. With simplicity came a rational measure of decorum. The makers of furniture and handicrafts that expressed absolute purity of line, Shakers took their philosophy of restraint into the kitchen as well.

"Shaker your plate!" was a typical table admonition to Shaker children from their parents who abhorred waste. The following straightforward recipe for chicken sautéed in cider comes from the apple-growing country of Hancock, Massachusetts. It characterizes this people's practice of cooking something simply delicious out of what was merely at hand.

SHAKER CHICKEN IN CIDER AND CREAM

2 *large red sweet apples, cored, cut into ½-inch-thick rings*
Juice of 1 lemon
1 *chicken (about 4 pounds), cut into serving pieces*
½ *cup unsalted butter*
1 *tablespoon vegetable oil*
½ *cup plus 3 tablespoons apple cider or fresh apple juice*
1 *cup granulated sugar*
1 *cup whipping cream*
2 *teaspoons grated lemon rind*
Salt and freshly ground pepper
Chopped fresh parsley
Steamed Rice (see Index)

I.   Heat oven to 350°. Place apple rings in a large bowl. Sprinkle with lemon juice; cover.

II.   Pat chicken dry with paper toweling. Heat ¼ cup butter and the oil in a large, heavy skillet over medium heat. Sauté chicken until golden brown, about 10 minutes on each side.

III.   Remove chicken to a plate. Drain all but 2 tablespoons
        grease from skillet. Stir in 3 tablespoons apple cider,
        scraping bottom of pan. Return chicken to skillet. Cook
        covered over low heat, turning chicken once, until
        tender, about 40 minutes.

IV.   Meanwhile, place sugar on a large plate. Press apple
        rings into sugar, coating well on both sides. Heat
        remaining ¼ cup butter in a heavy sauté pan over
        medium heat. Quickly sauté apple rings, a few at a
        time, until golden on both sides. Place on ovenproof
        plate in oven 20 minutes. (Recipe can be prepared
        several hours in advance to this point and kept at room
        temperature.)

V.   When chicken is tender, place in a shallow serving dish;
        surround with apple rings. Keep warm in a low oven.

VI.   Stir remaining ½ cup apple cider into skillet used for
        cooking chicken, scraping bottom and sides of pan. Add
        cream and lemon rind. Heat to boiling; reduce heat.
        Simmer until slightly thickened. Season to taste with
        salt and pepper. Pour sauce over chicken. Garnish with
        parsley. Serve with Steamed Rice.

Serves 4.

The following is a different kettle of fowl entirely—a transplanted Puerto Rican dish prepared in varying degrees of
hotness depending upon the variety of sausages available at your
local *bodega.*

My rendering is strictly 135th Street, New York City. I
acquired this treasured receipt from a Hispanic elevator man at
the Conde Nast building on Madison Avenue just prior to
automation. It is, parenthetically, the best party fare I've ever
consumed, too! If no chorizos are to be found in your locale,

however, this dish is equally palatable (if a jot less authentic) prepared with Italian sausages.

SPANISH HARLEM CHICKEN

¾ *pound eggplant, unpared, cut into ½-inch cubes*
Salt
1 *pound mixed hot and sweet chorizos (Spanish sausages)*
2 *tablespoons butter*
1 *chicken (about 4 pounds), cut into 10 serving pieces*
1 *large onion, chopped*
2 *large shallots, finely chopped*
2 *cloves garlic, minced*
1 *cup Italian green peppers, cut into strips*
1 *large fresh tomato, peeled, chopped*
1 *can (8 ounces) plum tomatoes*
1 *teaspoon granulated sugar*
1 *teaspoon chopped fresh basil or ½ teaspoon dried*
⅛ *teaspoon dried thyme*
¼ *teaspoon freshly ground pepper*
2 *cups Chicken Stock (see Index)*
1 *cup uncooked rice*
1 *cup raw corn kernels*

I.   Heat oven to 400°. Place eggplant cubes in a colander. Sprinkle well with salt. Let stand 30 minutes. Rinse with water; squeeze dry.

II.   Heat chorizos in a large, heavy pot or Dutch oven over medium-low heat. As sausages begin to render grease, increase heat slightly. Cook until golden brown on all sides, about 15 minutes; remove to a plate.

III.   Drain all but 1 tablespoon grease from pot. Add butter; Sauté chicken pieces over medium-high heat until well browned on both sides. Transfer chicken pieces to plate with sausages.

IV.   Add onion, shallots, and garlic to the pot. Cook, stirring constantly, 5 minutes. Stir in eggplant and green peppers; cook 3 minutes. Add fresh and canned tomatoes, sugar, basil, thyme, ½ teaspoon salt, and the pepper. (Recipe can be prepared several hours in advance to this point and kept at room temperature.)

V.   Stir in Chicken Stock, rice, and corn. Return chicken and sausages to pot, pressing down into rice mixture; cover. Heat to boiling; transfer pot to oven. Bake 35 minutes. Remove cover; bake 5 minutes longer.

Serves 4 to 6.

Another chicken bequest from my home state is a very old-fashioned dish that my grandmother cooked up to make good use of the stewing bird that seasoned her stock pot.

She prepared this chicken at least once a week (usually for Thursday night supper) and was the recipient of enriched leftover broth for quick soups and gravies on the six days that followed.

STEWED CHICKEN WITH GREEN SAUCE

2 *whole chickens (about 2½ pounds each)*
1 *clove garlic, bruised*
Salt
10 *peppercorns*
1 *carrot, chopped*
2 *leeks, trimmed*

1 *stalk celery, broken*
2 *sprigs parsley*
½ *cup lettuce (I use Boston)*
1 *slice lemon*
Water
2 *tablespoons butter*
2 *tablespoons all-purpose flour*
1 *tablespoon lemon juice*
Freshly ground pepper
3 *tablespoons whipping cream*
1 *egg yolk*
2 *tablespoons chopped chives*
⅓ *cup chopped, mixed fresh dill and parsley*
Steamed Rice (see Index)

I. Rub chickens well with garlic; discard garlic. Place
    chickens in a large, heavy pot. Add 2 teaspoons salt, the
    peppercorns, carrot, leeks, celery, sprigs of parsley,
    lettuce, lemon slice, and water to cover. Heat to boiling;
    reduce heat. Simmer just until tender, about 50 min-
    utes; remove scum with a spoon as it rises to the
    surface.

II. Heat broiling unit. Remove chickens from broth; strain
    broth and reserve. Cut chickens into serving pieces and
    place on a baking dish, skin side up. Broil until crisp;
    keep warm in a low oven.

III. Melt butter in a heavy saucepan over medium-low heat.
    Stir in flour; cook, stirring constantly, 2 minutes. Add 2
    cups reserved chicken broth. Simmer 5 minutes. Add
    lemon juice and salt and pepper to taste. Remove from
    heat.

IV. Beat cream with egg yolk in a small bowl. Stir in ¼ cup
    hot sauce. Stir this mixture back into sauce. Cook over

low heat 2 minutes. Do not boil. Stir in chives and mixed dill and parsley. Transfer chicken to a serving platter; pour sauce over. Serve with Steamed Rice.

Serves 6.

Speaking of chicken oddities, one more New York enterprise, but farther off my beaten path, is the following mirific notion: Buffalo's deep-fried chicken wings. I never heard of this local specialty until I sampled a platter recently during a stopover eating tour of the state. Buffalo Wings are excessively peppery outside with very tender flesh around the bones. They inevitably are dished up with a deep pile of celery sticks to stem the tang, along with a bowl of blue cheese dressing for skinny dips. The formula for this tasty treat is said to have originated at The Anchor Bar on Buffalo's Main Street. But my prescription was supplied by the most knowledgeable gastronome in town: Janice Okun, food editor of the *Buffalo Evening News*. So you had better believe it's *authentic!*

BUFFALO WINGS

Creamy Blue Cheese Dressing (recipe follows)
20 *to* 24 *small chicken wings*
Vegetable oil
¼ *cup butter*
6 *ounces Frank's Louisiana RedHot Sauce (see Note)*
4 *stalks celery, cut into strips about 3 inches long and ¼-inch thick*

I.   Make Creamy Blue Cheese Dressing.

II.   Cut tips off chicken wings; reserve for use in stocks. Cut remaining wings in half at the joint. Pat dry with paper toweling.

III.   Heat enough oil in a heavy pot to deep fry wings. (Oil should be very hot, but not smoking.) Add wings. Fry until golden brown and cooked through, about 12 minutes.

IV.   Meanwhile, heat butter and RedHot Sauce in a pot large enough to hold the wings. When wings are crisp, drain on paper toweling; stir wings into sauce, tossing well. Serve immediately with individual bowls of Creamy Blue Cheese Dressing and celery sticks.

Note: If you can't find Frank's sauce (made by Durkee), any spicy, hot barbecue-type sauce can be substituted.

Serves 4.

CREAMY BLUE CHEESE DRESSING

2 *tablespoons minced onion*
1 *clove garlic, mashed*
¼ *cup chopped fresh parsley*
1 *cup mayonnaise*
½ *cup sour cream*
1 *tablespoon lemon juice*
1 *tablespoon wine vinegar*
¼ *cup crumbled blue cheese*
Salt and freshly ground pepper to taste
Cayenne pepper to taste

I.   Combine all ingredients in a large bowl. Whisk until smooth. Chill well.

Makes about 2½ cups.

I am what epicures might call a quirky kitchen type. Native cuisine suits me best because it is so remarkably unconventional.

Certainly the recipes that capture my interest (and set the gastric juices flowing) involve the oddest of culinary couplings. Note, for instance, the following chicken barbecue, well-laced with Coca-Cola, from Georgia. The precept is handed down from Nathalie Dupree, glamorous director of Rich's Cooking School in Atlanta. Nathalie is a nonpareil teacher of elegant cookery, yet she avers this dish is "simply marvelous eatin'." Try her barbecue sauce on ribs, too. But never attempt to alter the essential ingredient. Tab, Pepsi, Royal Crown, or Dr. Pepper just won't make it here!

COCA-COLA BARBECUE SAUCED CHICKEN

Coca-Cola Barbecue Sauce (recipe follows)
2 small chickens (about 2½ pounds each), cut into pieces
1 clove garlic, bruised
Chopped fresh parsley

I.   Make Coca-Cola Barbecue Sauce.

II.   Heat oven to 350°. (See *Note*.) Rub each piece of chicken well with garlic; discard garlic. Spoon ½ cup barbecue sauce over the bottom of a shallow, heatproof baking dish. Place the chicken, skin side up, over the sauce. Spoon ½ cup more barbecue sauce over the top. Bake 30 minutes. Turn chicken over, basting with the sauce in the dish; bake 30 minutes longer.

III.   Heat broiling unit. Spoon half the remaining sauce over chicken. Broil until crisp, about 4 minutes. Turn chicken over; spoon on remaining sauce. Broil until crisp. Remove excess fat from sauce in baking dish. Garnish chicken with parsley.

Note: For outdoor cookery, cook chicken over low coals, basting frequently with barbecue sauce until all sauce has been used and chicken is tender.

Serves 6.

COCA-COLA BARBECUE SAUCE

2 *tablespoons butter*
1 *onion, finely chopped*
2 *cloves garlic, minced*
1 *bay leaf, crumbled*
2 *cups ketchup*
1 *small bottle (6 ounces) Coca-Cola*
1 *tablespoon Worcestershire sauce*
1 *teaspoon prepared mustard*
2 *teaspoons distilled wine vinegar*
Salt and freshly ground pepper to taste

I. Heat butter in a large saucepan over medium-low heat. Add onion and garlic. Cook 5 minutes; do not brown.

II. Add remaining ingredients. Simmer, stirring occasionally, 1 hour.

Makes about 1½ cups.

The South is rich in food oddities. From Greensboro, North Carolina, comes an exemplary sample—roast duckling basted with hot pepper jelly.

The last-named victual is dear to the hearts of all denizens who eat well below the Mason-Dixon line. A spicy hot emollient, served up with cold meats and all manner of roasted fowl, hot pepper jelly has also acquired a healthy reputation as an eclectic regional junk food. Aficionados spread the stuff on crackers

(Premium saltines are specified) that have been laved with a frosting of pure cream cheese!

Frankly, however, I would save my jar for a bout of more serious dining!

HOT PEPPER JELLY

1½ pounds juicy red apples
1½ cups water
2-inch strip lemon peel
7 cups granulated sugar, or to taste
¼ pound hot red peppers
¼ pound hot green peppers
1 large onion, cut into quarters
1 cup tarragon vinegar

I. Cut the apples into quarters, but do not remove skins or seeds; place in a large saucepan. Add the water and lemon peel; heat to boiling. Reduce heat; cook, covered, over medium-low heat 30 minutes. Remove from heat; let stand 30 minutes. Pour apple mixture into a jelly bag or a towel-lined colander over a pot. Let stand until mixture ceases to drip. Do not mash apples. (There should be about 2½ cups apple liquid.)

II. Heat apple liquid to boiling; add 2 cups sugar. Boil over medium heat until liquid sets when tested on a small, cold plate, about 35 minutes. Remove from heat.

III. Remove seeds from peppers; coarsely chop peppers. (Wash hands *thoroughly* afterwards.) Place peppers and onion in the container of a food processor. Process until fine. Transfer to a large saucepan. Add vinegar. Heat to boiling; boil 1 minute; add remaining sugar. Boil 4 minutes. Add apple liquid and boil over medium heat until liquid will set when tested on a small, cold plate, about 15 minutes. Pour into sterilized jars and seal. Shake jars as jelly cools to distribute peppers evenly. Serve with roasts or cold meats.

Makes 3½ pints.

The union of the preceding pepper jelly and a tender duckling is a food marriage made in heaven. The original Greensboro formula requests mallards, but I am sanguine on the subject, living in Long Island's duck precinct. Fresh duck may be hard to come by in the rest of the U.S., though. If you must buy yours *frozen*, thaw it in the original wrapping, in the fridge.

HOT PEPPER JELLY DUCKLING

2 *fresh ducks (about 5 pounds each)*
Salt
½ *teaspoon lemon juice*
2 *cloves garlic, bruised*
Freshly ground pepper
1 *onion, sliced*
½ *cup Hot Pepper Jelly (see preceding recipe)*
Watercress stems
Breaded Dumplings (recipe follows)
Hot Red Cabbage Slaw (see Index)

I.   Remove all fat and excess skin from neck and cavity area of ducks. Make sure the fat glands at the base of the tail have been removed. Remove any residue; rub each area with salt and lemon juice. Pierce the skin at ½-inch intervals along the thighs, back, and lower part of the breast. Place on a rack; let stand uncovered in a cool place overnight.

II.   Rub each duck inside and out with bruised garlic. Rub cavity with salt and freshly ground pepper. Place 1 bruised garlic clove in each cavity; place half the onion in each. Truss. Coat each duck with ¼ cup Hot Pepper Jelly. Let ducks stand 1 hour.

III.   Heat oven to 375°. Place ducks on a rack in a roasting pan. Ideally, ducks should be supported at least 2 inches above the bottom of pan (poultry racks are ideal for this). Roast 20 minutes. Turn ducks on one side; roast 30 minutes. Turn ducks on the other side; roast 30 minutes. Place ducks breast side up to finish roasting, about 25 minutes longer (about 1 hour and 45 minutes total). Remove grease from roasting pan with bulb baster as it accumulates. Duck should be a deep golden brown. If not brown enough, increase oven temperature during the last 20 minutes of roasting.

IV.   Cut duck into pieces. Arrange on a platter. Surround with watercress stems. Serve with Breaded Dumplings and Hot Red Cabbage Slaw.

Note: See All-American Cassoulet for use of leftovers.

Serves 6 to 8.

Breaded Dumplings are a purely Hungarian option for duck, which I discovered recently in a small restaurant in Cleveland, Ohio. Named "spats" on the bill of fare, these transplants from the Old Country are a kind of superlight *spatzle* (free-form fluffs of dough) that were poached first and then quickly sautéed in buttered bread crumbs. These dumplings are a wonderful adjunct to the Hot Pepper Jelly Duckling. I suggest you form yours as small as possible, however.

BREADED DUMPLINGS

2 *cups sifted all-purpose flour*
½ *teaspoon baking powder*
¼ *teaspoon salt*
2 *eggs, lightly beaten*
½ *cup milk*
⅛ *teaspoon freshly grated nutmeg*
3 *quarts water*
6 *tablespoons unsalted butter*
½ *cup bread crumbs*

I.   Combine flour, baking powder, and salt in a large bowl. Beat in eggs and milk. Beat until smooth. Add freshly grated nutmeg. (Dough will be quite sticky.)

II.   Heat the water to boiling. With a teaspoon, scoop up dough and drop into boiling water, using your finger to scrape dough off spoon. (Do not worry how the dumplings look. Some will have a spidery appearance.) Cook until done, about 1½ minutes. Drain on paper toweling. Transfer to a buttered plate. Cover until serving.

III.   Just before serving, melt the butter in a large sauté pan. Stir in bread crumbs. Cook over medium heat until golden. Reduce heat; stir in dumplings. Toss with bread crumbs until warmed through.

Serves 6.

A Thanksgiving turkey stuffed with a borrowed, New Orleans-style jambalaya is my own *boutarde* entirely. But it also happens to be the best dressing I have ever discovered for this bountiful bird. If you prepare the stuffing the night before

Thanksgiving (or any serious turkey-crowned occasion), do not stuff the cavity at that time—it can be unsafe. Either refrigerate the stuffing until the morning or tuck it into a convenient casserole and chill until it's time to pop it in the oven separately.

ROAST TURKEY WITH JAMBALAYA DRESSING

Jambalaya Dressing (recipe follows)
1 fresh turkey (about 20 pounds)
1 large clove garlic, bruised
Salt and freshly ground pepper
3 strips bacon
⅓ cup dry white wine
1 quart water
1 onion
1 stalk celery, broken
1 clove garlic
3 sprigs parsley
¼ teaspoon salt
4 peppercorns
1½ tablespoons unsalted butter
1½ tablespoons all-purpose flour
¼ cup whipping cream
Parsley sprigs

I.   Make Jambalaya Dressing.

II.   Heat oven to 325°. Remove giblets from turkey; reserve liver for another purpose; reserve remaining giblets for gravy. Wipe turkey with a damp cloth. Rub turkey well, inside and out, with bruised garlic, salt, and pepper. Stuff cavity with dressing; truss. Place turkey on rack in a roasting pan. Place bacon strips across breast. Cut a piece of cheesecloth to fit over turkey; soak cheesecloth in the wine; place over turkey. Pour any remaining wine over turkey. Roast 30 minutes.

III.   Meanwhile, combine giblets (not liver), water, onion, celery, garlic, 3 sprigs parsley, ¼ teaspoon salt, and the peppercorns in a large saucepan. Heat to boiling; reduce heat. Simmer until reduced to 2 cups. Strain giblet stock.

IV.   Baste turkey with giblet stock. Roast, basting with stock every 30 minutes, until legs move freely and juices run clear yellow when inner thigh is pierced with a fork, about 6 hours total. Increase oven temperature to 375°; remove cheesecloth and bacon during last 30 minutes of roasting to brown turkey. Transfer turkey to a carving board; let stand 15 minutes.

V.   Meanwhile, strain turkey drippings, removing excess fat. Melt butter in a medium saucepan over medium-low heat. Stir in flour. Cook, stirring constantly, 2 minutes. Whisk drippings and cream into saucepan; simmer 5 minutes. Taste and adjust seasonings. Garnish turkey with parsley sprigs. Serve with gravy and dressing.

Serves 8 to 10 (with leftovers).

A word here anent jambalaya. The following scaled-down version of the famed Creole dish makes a wonderful dinner entrée on its own. Prepare the jambalaya through the point where the ham, shrimps, and sausages are added, but do not add the cooked rice. Instead, stir in 1¼ cups uncooked rice and 2½ cups hot Chicken Stock (see Index also). Mix well. Cover and heat to boiling. Transfer to oven; bake in 350° oven 35 minutes. Remove cover; bake 5 to 6 minutes longer.

JAMBALAYA DRESSING

3¾ *cups Steamed Rice (see Index)*
2 *sweet Italian sausages*
1 *teaspoon olive oil*
1 *large onion, chopped*
2 *cloves garlic, minced*
2 *tablespoons unsalted butter*
½ *cup diced green bell pepper*
½ *cup diced red bell pepper*
2 *cups chopped, seeded, peeled tomatoes*
½ *teaspoon granulated sugar*
¼ *cup chicken broth*
1 *tablespoon chopped fresh or dried basil*
½ *teaspoon grated lemon rind*
¼ *teaspoon chili powder*
Pinch of dried thyme
1 *cup chopped, cooked ham*
½ *pound small shrimps, shelled, deveined*
Salt and freshly ground pepper

I. Prepare rice; reserve.

II. Sauté sausages in oil in a medium skillet over medium heat until well browned on all sides. Cool. Cut into ¼-inch slices; reserve.

III. Sauté onion and garlic in butter in a large skillet over medium heat until golden, about 5 minutes. Add green and red peppers; cook 3 minutes. Add tomatoes, sugar, broth, basil, lemon rind, chili powder, and thyme. Cook 5 minutes; transfer to a large bowl. Stir in ham, shrimps, reserved sausages, and rice. Season to taste with salt and pepper. Cool slightly before stuffing turkey.

Makes about 8 cups.

From Galveston comes an absolutely breathtaking variation on spicy Tex-Mex cookery. This devise for a smoky, tongue-sizzling broiler was given to me, off the cuff, by one of the best (and certainly most beautiful) cooks in the world: Houston's legendary cooking teacher and restaurateur, Mary Nell Reck.

GALVESTON STYLE TEX-MEX CHICKEN

1 *chicken (about 3½ to 4 pounds)*
1 *lemon, cut in half*
6 *cloves garlic, finely minced*
1 *tablespoon cayenne pepper*
2 *tablespoons paprika*
Salt

I.   With a sharp knife, remove backbone from chicken and save for use in stock. Split chicken in half. Rub each piece well on both sides with half a lemon. Rub each piece with garlic, then rub each piece with cayenne pepper and paprika. Place breast side up in a shallow baking dish. Let stand in a cool place (do not refrigerate), uncovered, for 24 hours.

II.   Heat oven to 350°. (See *Note.*) Place chicken breast side down on a rack in a roasting pan. Bake 30 minutes. Turn chicken over; sprinkle with salt. Bake until chicken is done, about 50 minutes.

III.   Heat broiling unit. Broil chicken on both sides until crispy and brown. Serve hot or at room temperature, carved into thin slices. This dish is also wonderful served cold with mayonnaise.

Note: To cook chicken on an outdoor grill, make sure the rack is high above the coals. Do not let the chicken catch fire. Cook, covered, turning several times, until the chicken is tender, about 1½ hours.

Serves 4.

If my introduction to Southern cuisine began when I went to college in Virginia, a decade elapsed before I tasted true Deep South cookery and recognized the difference!

In the mid-1950s, on wild impulse, I decided to fly to New Orleans for New Year's Eve. All flights from New York were booked, so with equal imprudence, I took a train to Washington and hopped the first Greyhound for Louisiana.

It was my initial sortie anywhere by bus and a totally dispiriting journey. The vehicle was crowded with servicemen returning home one day too late for the holidays, along with a motley crew of equally unhappy travelers. I particularly recall one old man who insisted that the driver stop at irregular intervals for the sake of his kidneys and a small, querulous child who cried for water the whole night long.

After twenty-four hours, I decamped at a bus stop in Alabama. Demanding my valise with no explanation, I promptly checked into the very best hotel in town.

I slept a day and a night, but managed to wake up in time for breakfast. The memory of that meal still whets my tongue. There were hot biscuits on the table, of course, and grits with syrup along with pale shavings of smoked ham and a mysterious chicken dish composed of crisp slices fried the color of molten gold before they were baked in a nest of velvet, peppery custard.

I never forgot that dish. Indeed, as you can see, I am still attempting to recapture that curious savor.

TUSCALOOSA CHICKEN CUSTARD

1 *chicken (about 3 pounds), cut into serving pieces*
1 *teaspoon salt*
½ *teaspoon freshly ground pepper*
¼ *cup chopped fresh mint leaves*
½ *cup plus 2 tablespoons butter*

1 *tablespoon vegetable oil*
Bouquet garni: 3 *sprigs parsley,* 1 *bay leaf, pinch of dried thyme,*
   1 *clove garlic*
¾ *cup Chicken Stock (see Index)*
4 *strips bacon*
2 *green onions, finely chopped*
½ *cup whipping cream*
½ *cup all-purpose flour*
⅛ *teaspoon ground allspice*
4 *eggs, lightly beaten*

I.   Place the chicken in a large bowl. Sprinkle with salt,
       pepper, and mint leaves. Rub each piece well with
       mixture. Let stand at least 30 minutes.

II.   Heat ½ cup butter and the oil in a large, heavy skillet
       (or 2, if needed) over medium heat. Add chicken pieces;
       sauté until golden brown on both sides.

III.   Reduce heat to medium-low. Place bouquet garni in
       center of pan; add Chicken Stock. Cover; cook until
       tender, about 35 minutes.

IV.   Meanwhile, sauté bacon until crisp. Crumble; reserve.
       Reserve bacon drippings.

V.   Heat oven to 375°. Rub a large, deep, heatproof baking
       dish with 2 tablespoons butter. With a slotted spoon,
       transfer chicken, skin side up, to dish. Sprinkle with
       chopped green onions. Place in oven.

VI.   Discard bouquet garni. Pour cooking juices from the
       skillet into a blender container. Add the bacon drip-
       pings, cream, flour, allspice, and eggs. Blend 1 minute.
       Scrape down sides; blend until smooth. Pour mixture
       over chicken. Sprinkle with crumbled bacon. Return to
       oven; bake until golden brown and puffed up, about 35
       minutes.

                                                  Serves 4.

MEAT

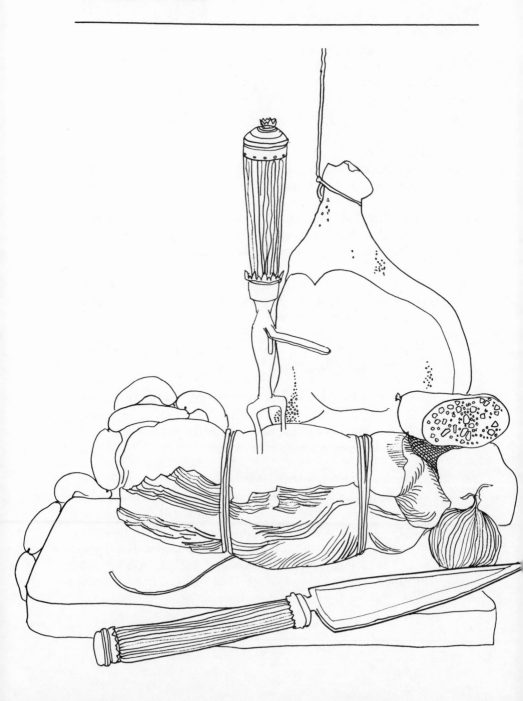

Chapter Six

I first sampled the wholesome meat cookery of the great American heartland when I was in my late twenties. At that time I was seriously courting a young lady whose father raised prize pigs in a little town an hour's ride from Columbus, Ohio.

She was not a typical farmer's daughter, and I was not a typical traveling suitor, but circumstances quite beyond our control placed us in these illogical roles.

A vital young woman with two small sons waiting out the snarls of a complicated divorce, my beloved was an unwanted visitor at her father's house. And I was the even more unwanted candidate (a swain, I might add, who was viewed with some unmasked suspicion by all of her family) who offered to take her away from it. Our alliance was not meant to be permanent; I know that now. But it was certainly rapid transit then! Every other weekend for almost half a year's time, I left New York to fly and entrain my way to central Ohio, plowing through snow and sleet and spring thaw to convince us both of my ardor.

Like a stoic, I plodded through enormous and enervating family dinners—quiz games played over bowls of steaming stew. The issue of my income and my prospects seemed far weightier than the substantial tureen of Swedish meatballs nesting on wreaths of home-rolled noodles before us all.

"Eat first; ask questions later," my lady's stepmother would laugh uneasily, as she ladled out the Saturday night fare. But the air was usually bluer than the rain of poppy seeds that fell on those very same noodles.

On odd occasions when we tried to sneak away on our own, there was nowhere to go. Greasy hamburger stands and chili parlors were all the culinary blandishments those rural parts offered. So we stayed and ate within our proscribed domestic circle most times. If you ask me what I remember best of those days of anxious loving, the answer comes fast—mud and shared misery. And sometimes, late-night meals taken after all the other family members had gone their separate ways to bed.

Perhaps we were watched; I don't think we cared. Together we would sit on the floor before an unlit fireplace like children, eating half-baked Ohio potatoes, split and sundered with fresh butter, and covered with a pure Midwest tranquilizer—creamed chipped beef. And we dreamed all the while of steak and the impossible future ahead.

A marriage license I never quite logged with Maggie. But her family's recipes made their way into my treasury of the grandest American cookery.

What I also recall of my bimonthly expeditions to Ohio (through the long-distance lens of time) is the absolutely dispiriting restaurant food I was served everywhere.

I usually dined "out" by myself on Sunday nights, trying to kill time before a midnight flight took me back to Manhattan. Since I ventured semiwestward some twenty-five or thirty occasions in that year, I had ample time to judge the local cuisine.

After several torpid samplings of French, Italian, Greek, and German fare, I assumed steak would be the next logical alternative. This was beef country after all! Subsequently, I selected a fancy chophouse and ordered the most expensive item on the menu: *New York Cut.* Implying, I assumed, a choice and rosy slice that would emulate my city's prime brawn.

What I was served up, however, turned out to be gray matter instead, masquerading as sirloin. Half-thawed, less than an inch in thickness, it was a cut that turned out to be a sworn enemy of both fork and knife! A steak with no flavor . . . no savor.

The next weekend, I ate Chinese.

Do not be misled by the following recipe's cognomen. This is the genuine article—a New York chef's finest testament to being at home on the range.

NEW YORKER'S STEAK

1 *boneless sirloin steak (3 pounds, about 3 inches thick)*
1 *clove garlic, bruised*
1 *tablespoon butter*
1 *tablespoon vegetable oil*
1 *shallot, minced*
1 *tablespoon Dijon mustard*
¼ *cup dry red wine*
½ *cup beef broth*
Chopped fresh parsley

I.   Heat oven to 400°. Rub steak on all sides with bruised garlic. Heat butter and oil in a large, heavy skillet over high heat. Brown meat well on all sides. Transfer steak to a heatproof platter.

II.   Drain all but 1 tablespoon grease from skillet. Sauté the shallot over low heat 5 minutes. Stir in mustard, wine, and broth. Heat to boiling; boil until liquid becomes syrupy. Pour over steak. Transfer platter to oven; bake steak about 15 minutes for medium-rare. Sprinkle with parsley. To serve, slice on the diagonal.

Serves 2 to 4.

A fairer estimate of the midwestern palate must be essayed on home territory. A remarkably wet Ohio weekend, as I recall, afforded me a recipe for meatballs that may appear slightly more Buckeye State than Scandinavian. But they'll pass muster at any *smörgåsbord!*

OHIO'S SWEDISH MEATBALLS

1 *pound ground beef*
¼ *pound ground veal*
½ *pound ground pork*
1 *cup fine dry bread crumbs*
1 *large onion, chopped*
½ *green pepper, chopped*
½ *cup milk*
2 *tablespoons chopped fresh dill*
2 *tablespoons chopped fresh parsley*
2 *shallots*
1 *clove garlic*
⅛ *teaspoon ground allspice*
2 *eggs*
1 *tablespoon caraway seeds*
1 *teaspoon salt*
¼ *teaspoon freshly grated nutmeg*
Freshly ground pepper
½ *cup butter*
2 *tablespoons vegetable oil*
1½ *cups whipping cream*
1 *cup sour cream*
Dill sprigs
Buttered noodles

I.   Combine ground meats and bread crumbs in a large
        bowl. Place onion, green pepper, milk, 2 tablespoons
        dill, the parsley, shallots, garlic, and allspice in a
        blender container or food processor. Blend until smooth.
        Add to meat mixture. Add eggs, caraway seeds, salt,
        nutmeg, and pepper to taste. Mix thoroughly; shape into
        small meatballs.

II.   Fry meatballs in butter and oil in a 10-inch skillet over medium heat, turning frequently, until brown, about 5 minutes. Place meatballs in a 2-quart saucepan. Mix whipping cream and sour cream in a small bowl; pour over meatballs. Simmer, uncovered, over low heat 1 hour. Garnish with dill sprigs. Serve with buttered noodles.

Serves 6 to 8.

In an honest environment one wants honest cookery. But for the life of this recipe collector, I don't know where or why the art of preparing plain food has gone. Good American cuisine, be it from the West, East, North, or South, is so varied and curiously tonic that to blunt it with sauce or sorcery is to overkill the golden goose.

My dismay at the state of the national appetite today stems from a lack of pride that most Americans take in their culinary heritage.

Perhaps it is not a permanent disaffection. A common maverick sensibility seems to swing us back from fad to fundamental in everything we do, art or politics. And I think it may be time for a "plain cooking" upswing. What follows is a hodgepodge of comestible Americana—pot roasts as varied as their inventors. The first is a virgin culinary effort of an oil man turned art collector who grows hydroponic herbs for a hobby. The second is some handiwork of Mildred Schulz of Golden, Colorado. Mrs. Schulz is one of a rare breed of instinctive cooks who simply put good things together and make a dish work!

OKLAHOMA CITY POT ROAST
WITH GREEN SAUCE

2 *tablespoons plus 1 teaspoon butter*
1 *small clove garlic, minced*
2 *medium onions, chopped*
2 *shallots, chopped*
1 *boneless chuck or rump roast (about 3½ to 4 pounds)*
1 *small clove garlic, bruised*
1 *tablespoon black peppercorns, crushed*
1 *teaspoon vegetable oil*
1 *cup beef broth*
1 *sprig fresh thyme or a pinch of dried*
2-*inch curl of lemon peel*
4 *to 6 medium potatoes, pared, cut into eighths, parboiled 15*
    minutes
6 *medium carrots, pared, cut into eighths, parboiled 5 minutes*
1 *small shallot, minced*
1½ *tablespoons freshly grated horseradish or 1 tablespoon*
    prepared horseradish
¾ *cup chopped fresh parsley*

I.   Melt 1 tablespoon butter in a large Dutch oven over
        medium heat. Sauté minced garlic, onions, and chopped
        shallots until golden, about 5 minutes; set aside.

II.   Rub meat well with bruised garlic. Press crushed
        peppercorns into meat. Heat 1 tablespoon butter and
        the oil in a heavy skillet over medium-high heat. Brown
        meat well on all sides. Transfer meat to the Dutch oven.
        Add beef broth, thyme, and lemon peel to skillet,
        scraping bottom and sides of pan. Pour over meat;

return Dutch oven to heat. Cook, covered, over medium-low heat 1½ hours.

III. Heat oven to 375°. Remove meat from Dutch oven. Strain liquid and reserve. Remove excess fat from meat liquid, reserving fat. Return meat and meat liquid to Dutch oven. Cook, covered, until meat is tender, about 45 to 60 minutes longer.

IV. Meanwhile, pour reserved fat into a shallow baking dish. Add potatoes, turning to coat well with fat. Place dish in oven. Bake potatoes, turning once, for 40 minutes. Add carrots; toss to coat. Bake 15 to 20 minutes longer.

V. Remove meat from Dutch oven. Place on a shallow serving platter; keep warm. Melt 1 teaspoon butter in a medium saucepan. Sauté minced shallot until soft, about 5 minutes. Add meat liquid, the horseradish, and parsley. Heat to boiling; boil 2 minutes. Pour over meat. Surround with potatoes and carrots.

Serves 4 to 6.

Do not be misled by the glittering moniker for Mrs. Schulz's pot roast. The name is meant to honor her home city (twenty-five minutes from Denver) rather than any high-toned slice of beef.

Her Golden Barbecued Pot Roast is, as one would suspect from a glance at the ingredient list, a rosy shade of barbecued bronze. All that glisters is your tongue—after the first heavenly bite!

GOLDEN BARBECUED POT ROAST

1 *small onion, chopped*
1 *boneless chuck roast (about 3½ to 4 pounds)*
1 *small clove garlic, bruised*
½ *cup beef broth (approximately)*
1 *can (8 ounces) tomato sauce*
2 *tablespoons brown sugar*
¼ *teaspoon paprika*
½ *teaspoon dry mustard*
¼ *cup lemon juice*
¼ *cup ketchup*
¼ *cup cider vinegar*
1 *tablespoon Worcestershire sauce*
Chopped fresh parsley

I.   Heat oven to 350°. Place chopped onion in bottom of a large Dutch oven. Rub meat well with bruised garlic; discard garlic. Add meat to Dutch oven. Cover; bake meat for 1½ hours. Add some beef broth if juices in bottom of pot begins to dry up.

II.   Combine tomato sauce, sugar, paprika, mustard, lemon juice, ketchup, vinegar, and Worcestershire sauce in a medium bowl. Pour over meat. Continue to cook, covered, until meat is tender, about 2 hours longer. Baste meat with sauce in pan every 20 minutes, adding more beef broth as needed.

III.   Remove meat from oven and place on a serving platter. Spoon 2 tablespoons sauce over the meat; sprinkle with parsley. Pass the remaining sauce.

Serves 4 to 6.

New Hampshire is a mixed bag of ethnocentricity. Almost entirely English, Scotch-Irish, and Welsh until the turn of the century, this spare, rocky land has given refuge of late to Albanians and Greeks who have taken the native fare they found in the White Mountains and altered it to suit their Balkan palates.

A particularly robust example of their culinary tampering is a pot of Anglo-Saxon corned beef, delicately sauced with yogurt and aromatic mustards.

WHITE MOUNTAIN SWEET AND SOUR CORNED BEEF WITH MUSTARD SAUCE

1 *corned beef (about 4 to 4½ pounds)*
Water
¼ *cup red wine vinegar*
1 *medium onion studded with 2 cloves*
1 *clove garlic, peeled*
3 *sprigs parsley*
1 *carrot, cut into quarters*
1 *stalk celery with leaves, cut into quarters*
10 *peppercorns*
2 *teaspoons crushed dried hot red peppers*
4-*inch curl of lemon peel*
⅛ *teaspoon dried thyme*
1½ *tablespoons butter*
1½ *tablespoons all-purpose flour*
1½ *tablespoons dry mustard*
1 *teaspoon Dijon mustard*
1 *tablespoon red wine vinegar*
½ *cup yogurt*
Salt and freshly ground pepper
Chopped fresh parsley

I.   Wipe meat with damp paper toweling. Place in a large pot. Add water to cover; add all ingredients through thyme. Heat to boiling; reduce heat. Simmer, partially covered, skimming surface as needed, until meat is tender, about 3 hours. Remove meat from pot; keep warm.

II. Heat liquid in pot to boiling; boil 5 minutes. Strain liquid; reserve.

III. Melt butter in a medium saucepan over low heat. Stir in flour and mustards; cook, stirring constantly, 3 minutes. Add 1½ cups reserved liquid, 1 tablespoon vinegar, and the yogurt. Cook until slightly thickened. Season to taste with salt and pepper. Spoon some of the sauce over the meat; sprinkle meat with parsley. Pass remaining sauce.

Serves 6 to 8.

Ten years after the Civil War, some Yankee peddler immigrated to Connecticut from Rhode Island and felt he had to celebrate the event in verse.

Home to silver teaspoons and new-fangled coffee machines,
The Nutmeg State is where I plan to die from over-eatin'
oysters, pumpkin, pickled tongue, and beans!

The following recipe is credited to the tiny city of Moosup (where a reader claims her great-grandmother invented it). This baked dish is no killer calorically. Rather, it is a fancyin'-up of plain Jane fare, but delectable for all the alleged source of culinary overkill (honey, mustard, and demon rum)! Serve it with brown rice or barley on the side, as an admirable antidote.

MOOSUP BOILED AND BAKED TONGUE

1 *corned beef tongue (about 3 to 3½ pounds)*
Water
1 *clove garlic*
1 *bay leaf*
1 *cinnamon stick*
¼ *cup red wine vinegar*
2 *tablespoons honey*
2 *tablespoons Dijon mustard*
1 *teaspoon dark rum*

I.   Place corned beef tongue in a large pot. Add water to cover, garlic, bay leaf, cinnamon stick, and vinegar. Heat to boiling; reduce heat. Simmer, partially covered, until tender, about 2 to 2½ hours. Let stand 5 minutes. Remove skin with a sharp knife.

II.   Heat oven to 400°. Place cooked tongue on a rack in a roasting pan. Combine honey, mustard, and rum. Coat meat with a fourth of the mixture. Bake tongue, basting every 5 minutes with remaining honey mixture, for 20 minutes.

Serves 6 to 8.

Our American palate is, by tradition, stouthearted. Europeans used to call us a "meat and potatoes nation." And our taste buds are still notoriously shy about any major culinary changes. It took two centuries and the indomitable Julia Child, regularly on the tube, before we attempted to master the art of French cooking, for heaven's sake. Now that we have finally cut the mustard and gotten *boeuf bourguignonne* under our collective belts, the national appetite is enflamed by rumor of more food shocks to come—namely, encroaching *nouvelle cuisine.*

However, do not throw away your old black skillet (or the chicken fryer) just yet. The media and a few Francophile gurus may predict a gustatory revolution is on the way. But I strongly suspect it will take more than a crew of darkly handsome chefs in white hats (bearing cookbooks as Bibles) to unhinge all of our long-established kitchen prerogatives! And neither Texas barbecues nor country fried ham is on the endangered species list, thank the Lord.

Speaking of which, my pet geographic garnering is a stewpot of zingy beef ribs, very Western-style, gilded with old-time cornmeal dumplings.

TEXAS SHORT RIBS: SABINE RIVER STYLE

FOR THE SHORT RIBS:
½ cup all-purpose flour
Salt and freshly ground pepper
½ teaspoon ground ginger
⅛ teaspoon ground allspice
3 to 3½ pounds beef short ribs
¼ cup plus 1 tablespoon butter
1 tablespoon vegetable oil
2 large onions, chopped
2 cloves garlic, minced
1 tablespoon finely chopped, fresh or canned jalapeño peppers
1 stalk celery, finely chopped
1 carrot, finely chopped
2 tablespoons brown sugar
½ teaspoon paprika
½ teaspoon dry mustard
2 tablespoons chili powder
¼ cup lemon juice
½ cup chili sauce
¼ cup red wine vinegar
1 can (17 ounces) plum tomatoes
2 tablespoons chopped fresh parsley

FOR THE DUMPLINGS:
1 *cup sifted all-purpose flour*
1 *cup yellow cornmeal*
2 *teaspoons baking powder*
1¼ *teaspoons salt*
1 *egg, lightly beaten*
¾ *cup milk*

I.   Heat oven to 350°. To make the short ribs: Combine flour, ½ teaspoon salt, ¼ teaspoon pepper, the ginger, and allspice in a large bowl. Roll ribs in flour mixture, pressing flour into meat with your fingers. Reserve 1 tablespoon flour mixture.

II.   Heat ¼ cup butter and the oil in a large Dutch oven over medium-high heat. Cook ribs, a few at a time, until well browned on all sides. Remove to a plate.

III.   Reduce heat; add 1 tablespoon butter to Dutch oven. Stir in onions, garlic, and jalapeño peppers. Cook over medium-low heat 5 minutes. Sprinkle with 1 tablespoon reserved flour mixture; cook 2 minutes longer.

IV.   Stir celery, carrot, brown sugar, paprika, mustard, and chili powder into Dutch oven. Mix well; add lemon juice, chili sauce, vinegar, tomatoes, ½ teaspoon salt, and ¼ teaspoon pepper. Heat to boiling; reduce heat. Simmer 5 minutes.

V.   Return meat to Dutch oven; transfer to oven. Bake, covered, turning meat every 30 minutes, 1½ hours. Uncover; bake 15 minutes longer. Remove excess fat from sauce.

VI.   Meanwhile, to make the dumplings: Combine flour, cornmeal, baking powder, and salt in a medium bowl. Beat in egg and milk to make a soft batter.

VII.   Remove Dutch oven from oven. Drop batter by table-
spoonfuls over and around meat. Cover; bake until
dumplings are firm, about 18 minutes. Sprinkle with
parsley before serving.

Serves 4 to 6.

O.K. What is burgoo and where did it come from?

The first query is best answered by detailing just what
burgoo *isn't*. It is not quite a stew. And definitely not a soup,
although to be truthful, some Kentucky diehards do slurp it up
from chowder bowls. A mixed meat dish, I would dub burgoo a
gallimaufry if ever I could learn to spell that word correctly!

There are burgoo masters in Louisville, as well as countless
numbers of burgoo contenders throughout the state of Kentucky,
who will argue for hours about the correct amount of salt and
pepper to use in this culinary masterpiece. One of the few points
of agreement among them is (1) that this local concoction must
be cooked and eaten out of doors and (2) that all burgoo must be
consumed *red hot!*

Contention between burgoo-ites concerns the disputed viands
that go into the pot itself. While specific origins are cloudy, it's
generally agreed that the dish started as a campfire meal, with
the kettle chockablock with fresh-caught rabbit, squirrel, and
fowl. The meats, bolstered by greens and tomatoes, were stirred
for hours, or until the pot watcher's fingers burned—from
fishing out delectable morsels to test for doneness.

My personal version of Kentucky Burgoo is somewhat more
civilized (composed solely of meats available at a butcher shop
rather than from a forest)—so leave your rifle over the mantel.
Bert Greene's unorthodox burgoo may also be eaten *indoors* with
utter equanimity.

Comforting and spicy at one and the same time, burgoo is a
dish that actually improves with time. On Derby Day in Kentucky, you may be sure that your steaming plateful was made
fully a week before. But like the bourbon in the dish, it is better
with age.

KENTUCKY BURGOO

½ *cup plus 1 tablespoon all-purpose flour*
Salt
½ *teaspoon allspice berries, crushed*
4 *boneless beef top chuck steaks (about 5 inches long each), all fat removed*
1 *chicken (about 3½ pounds), cut into 10 serving pieces*
½ *cup butter (approximately)*
3 *tablespoons vegetable oil*
3 *loin pork chops, cut into strips*
1 *large onion, chopped*
2 *shallots, minced*
2 *cloves garlic, finely minced*
1½ *cups chopped, seeded, peeled tomatoes*
½ *teaspoon chopped fresh basil, or* ¼ *teaspoon dried*
½ *teaspoon granulated sugar*
1 *cup Chicken Stock (see Index)*
½ *cup white wine*
1 *teaspoon crushed dried hot red peppers*
Freshly ground pepper
1½ *teaspoons bourbon*
2 *tablespoons chopped fresh parsley*

I. Heat oven to 350°. Combine ½ cup flour, 1 teaspoon salt, and the crushed allspice in a large bowl. Dredge steaks well with flour mixture, pressing flour into meat with your fingers; reserve. Coat chicken lightly with flour mixture.

II. Heat ¼ cup butter and 2 tablespoons oil in a large, heavy skillet over medium-high heat. Quickly sauté steaks until golden brown on both sides. Transfer to a large Dutch oven. Sauté chicken pieces in the skillet until golden brown on all sides, adding more butter and oil as needed; transfer to the Dutch oven. Sauté pork strips until brown; transfer to the Dutch oven. Stir chopped onion into meats.

III.   Drain all grease from skillet. Add 1 tablespoon butter and 1 tablespoon oil. Sauté shallots and garlic until golden, about 5 minutes. Stir in tomatoes; sprinkle with basil and sugar. Cook over low heat 20 minutes.

IV.   Pour tomato mixture over meats. Add Chicken Stock to skillet, scraping bottom and sides of pan; pour over meats. Add white wine and red peppers to Dutch oven; heat to boiling. Transfer to oven. Bake, uncovered, until meats are tender, about 1½ hours. (*Note:* If sauce around meats is too thin, mix 1 tablespoon softened butter with 1 tablespoon flour. Stir in around meats; cook until thickened.)

V.   Just before serving, season to taste with salt and pepper. Stir in bourbon; sprinkle with parsley.

Serves 4 to 6.

The West River Valley of southeastern Vermont grows some of the best eating apples in this country: the rosy McIntosh, Northern Spy, Newtown Pippin, and Winesap.

At one time there were probably more than 500 different varieties grown in Dummerston's orchards alone. Most have disappeared by now, but the snowbound denizens of the state would never have survived without its apples—not for nutritional value, but for the sweetening up of otherwise drab winter fare.

One of the most tonic New England couplings is roasted pork served with apple butter. The following precept (out of the West River Valley, coincidentally) unites the local fruit and meat in a most piquant alliance.

APPLE BUTTER ROASTED PORK

1 *roast pork loin (about 5½ pounds), chine bone cracked*
2 *cloves garlic, mashed*
1½ *tablespoons dry mustard*
1 *pint apple butter (recipe follows)*
1 *tablespoon caraway seeds*

I.   Rub the pork roast well with garlic and mustard. Spread 6 tablespoons apple butter over the top and sides of the roast. Sprinkle the top with caraway seeds. Let stand 1 hour.

II.   Heat oven to 300°. Cook pork slowly, basting frequently with pan juices and remaining apple butter, 1 hour for each pound, about 5½ hours total.

Serves 6.

Lazy chefs may buy their apple butter straight off a supermarket shelf and the dish will probably not suffer irremediable shock. However, the formula (for a low-sugar apple butter) is so easy to execute, one might consider putting up a batch for the heck of it!

LOW-SUGAR APPLE BUTTER

1 *pound green apples*
4 *cups apple cider (approximately)*
1 *cup granulated sugar*
1 *teaspoon ground cinnamon*
¼ *teaspoon ground ginger*
¼ *teaspoon freshly grated nutmeg*
Pinch of ground cloves

I.   Rinse apples; cut into quarters. Remove seeds, but do not pare. Place in a large pot and add enough apple cider to just cover. Heat apples and cider over medium heat; simmer until apples are reduced to a soft pulp, about 40 minutes. Cool.

II.   Place cooked apples with juices in a blender container or food processor. Blend until smooth. Press through a fine wire sieve to remove any residual skin or pulp.

III. Return mixture to pot. Slowly heat to boiling. Add sugar and spices. Reduce heat; simmer, stirring frequently, until mixture thickens and is reddish brown in color, about 45 minutes. Pour into sterilized jars and seal.

Note: This apple butter will not be as thick as commercial apple butter, since the sugar has been reduced one-third the amount usually required. The apple butter will thicken as it chills in a refrigerator.

Makes 2 pints.

Country ham is as *down home* as you can get in Dixie (anywhere from the Virginia Tidewater to the Rio Grande). The next bequest is yet another from Nathalie Dupree, the most impressive cook alive and well in Georgia today. Her advice is to fry a slice in Coca-Cola, black coffee, or red wine. Name your own poison!

COUNTRY FRIED HAM

2 *slices salted, sugar-cured, "country" ham, or 1 large ham steak (about ½-inch thick)*
3 *ounces Coca-Cola or 2 ounces water with 1 ounce black coffee or 2 ounces water with 1 ounce red wine*

I.　　　Heat a large skillet over medium heat. Add ham slices, with fatty edges laid against sides of skillet. Slowly fry until fatty edges are lightly browned. Turn ham over and continue to fry until browned. Keep warm on a platter in a low oven.

II.　　　Add Coca-Cola or other liquids to skillet. Heat to boiling; boil rapidly until juices thicken into a glaze, about 30 seconds. Pour over ham slices.

Serves 2.

It is a long drive from Atlanta to Dubuque, but true ham aficionados are advised to make the excursion posthaste. Iowa is the home of corn-fed pigs, and therein lies the wondrous taste difference according to food sleuths. And that's not hogwash!

My favored slice of ham has long been the Dubuque Fleur de Lis brand, so I speak with authority on the subject. The next culinary offering pairs this midwestern viand with a prodigious amount of beer—as a basting liquid. The result is a veritable taste-bender. The rosy ham is at its best (need I add) when the lager is Pickett's, the only beer brewed in the state of Iowa.

BEER-BAKED HAM

Beery Mustard Sauce (recipe follows)
1 smoked ham (about 10 to 12 pounds)
2 cans (12 ounces each) beer
Whole cloves
1 clove garlic
2 teaspoons Dijon mustard
1 cup light brown sugar

I.　　　Make Beery Mustard Sauce.

II.   Heat oven to 350°. Using a sharp knife, score top of ham in diamond patterns, cutting 1 inch deep. Place in a large pot. Pour the beer over the ham. Cover; bake 30 minutes.

III.   Remove ham from pot; place on a rack in a foil-lined roasting pan. Reserve beer in pot. Stud the top of the ham with whole cloves, placing a clove in the center of each diamond.

IV.   Mash the garlic with mustard in a small bowl. Add brown sugar and 3 tablespoons reserved beer. Mix well; spread over ham.

V.   Increase oven temperature to 400°. Bake ham 15 minutes. Pour 1 cup reserved beer over ham. Return to oven; bake, basting every 10 minutes with pan juices, 50 minutes longer. Reduce oven temperature to 350° if ham starts to burn. Cool on a rack. Serve slightly warm or at room temperature with Beery Mustard Sauce.

Serves 12 to 16.

Consider a mug of Pickett's beer (if you can import some) as the emollient in the following mustard sauce as well.

BEERY MUSTARD SAUCE

⅓ *cup English dry mustard*
⅓ *cup tarragon vinegar*
⅓ *cup beer*
3 *eggs*
6 *tablespoons brown sugar*
4 *tablespoons unsalted butter*

½ *teaspoon salt*
⅛ *teaspoon freshly ground pepper*
½ *teaspoon chopped fresh tarragon or a pinch of dried*

I. Place mustard, vinegar, and beer in a small bowl. Do not stir. Cover; let stand in a cool place 5 to 6 hours, or overnight.

II. Place mustard mixture in the top of a double boiler over hot water; whisk until smooth. Add eggs, one at a time, whisking vigorously after each addition. Gradually whisk in sugar until smooth. Beat in butter, salt, and pepper; cook until thick, about 5 minutes. Do not overcook or eggs will curdle. Stir in tarragon.

III. Spoon mustard sauce into a sterilized jar and seal. Refrigerate at least 24 hours before serving.

Makes about 1 pint.

The North Dakota bestowal to this volume represents a gastronomic mixed marriage. The dilled stew is clearly of Scandinavian heritage. But the style of cookery is curiously akin to the preparation of *blanquette de veau*, suggesting that one of the mates in the kitchen came from France.

Whatever the antecedance, this is one knockout dish! Compound the international anomaly by serving it over Pennsylvania Dutch dumplings or Irish boiled potatoes!

NORTH DAKOTA LAMB STEW

4 *pounds boneless lamb, cut into 1½-inch cubes*
2 *lamb bones (from your butcher)*
Water
2 *cups chicken broth*

3 *sprigs dill*
6 *sprigs parsley*
1 *large bay leaf*
12 *peppercorns*
2 *sprigs fresh thyme or ½ teaspoon dried*
1 *parsnip, cut into quarters*
1 *stalk celery, cut into quarters*
2 *carrots, cut into quarters*
1 *whole white onion, peeled*
Salt and freshly ground white pepper
3 *tablespoons butter*
1 *small yellow onion, finely chopped*
Pinch of ground allspice
3 *tablespoons all-purpose flour*
2 *teaspoons granulated sugar*
2 *tablespoons lemon juice*
Dash of hot pepper sauce
¼ *cup finely chopped fresh dill*
1 *cup sour cream*
Dill fronds

I.   Place meat and bones in a large pot; add cold water to cover. Heat to a rolling boil over high heat. Drain immediately; return meat and bones to pot. Rinse meat and bones in pot under cold running water until water runs clear. Drain.

II.   Place meat and bones in a large Dutch oven. Add chicken broth, 3 cups water, the 3 dill sprigs, parsley, bay leaf, peppercorns, thyme, parsnip, celery, carrots, white onion, and salt and white pepper to taste. Heat to boiling; reduce heat. Simmer, partially covered, until meat is tender, 50 to 60 minutes. Skim the surface as necessary.

III.   Drain meat, reserving liquid; discard bones and vegetables. Place meat in a large bowl; cover with aluminum foil to keep warm.

IV. Melt 3 tablespoons butter in a large, heavy saucepan. Add yellow onion; cook over low heat 5 minutes. Do not brown. Whisk in allspice and flour; cook, stirring constantly, 2 minutes. Add reduced liquid; whisk until smooth. Add sugar, lemon juice, hot pepper sauce, and finely chopped dill. Simmer until thickened, about 2 minutes. Place meat in the saucepan; cook until warmed through. (*Note:* Recipe can be prepared in advance to this point and refrigerated.)

V. Just before serving, stir sour cream into the saucepan. Heat over low heat for 2 minutes. Do not boil. Garnish with dill fronds.

Serves 6.

Delaware may have contributed the first log cabins to this country's architectural digest (the handiwork of Finnish settlers in 1638), but there are not many left on the territory today. An honest-to-goodness Finn is hard to find as well. Delaware's ethnic mix is reputedly 90 percent Yankee and 10 percent up for grabs. The prevailing foreign culture is reputedly East Indian these days!

One Eastern-inspired Wilmington recipe (for grilled lamb chops burnished with curry and garlic prior to the flame) may be just another culinary conundrum, but it's quite delicious! Try the dish with a dab of (hastily prepared) mint jelly, of equally dubious heritage.

CURRIED LAMB CHOPS WITH MOCK MINT JELLY

FOR THE MINT JELLY:
1 *jar (12 ounces) apple jelly*
¼ cup green crème de menthe

1 *tablespoon tarragon wine vinegar*
½ *cup chopped fresh mint*

FOR THE LAMB CHOPS:
4 *double lamb chops*
1 *clove garlic, bruised*
1 *teaspoon curry powder*
1 *tablespoon butter*
1 *tablespoon vegetable oil*
Salt and freshly ground pepper
2 *teaspoons chopped fresh mint*

I.   To make mock mint jelly: Place apple jelly in a large bowl. With a large wire whisk, beat in crème de menthe, vinegar, and ½ cup mint until smooth. Cover; chill well before serving.

II.   Heat oven to 400°. To prepare lamb chops: Rub lamb chops well with garlic; then rub each side with ⅛ teaspoon curry powder.

III.   Heat butter and oil in a large, heavy skillet over high heat. Quickly sauté chops until well browned on all sides. Transfer chops to a heatproof serving platter. Bake chops about 10 minutes for medium-rare. Season to taste with salt and pepper; garnish with chopped mint. Pass the mint jelly.

Serves 4.

Wyoming is a misanthrope's paradise—rocky, spare, practically treeless, and not too big on population either. The land, however, produces some of the best grass-fed lamb to be found in the U.S. today.

I have an old (1879) Wyoming formula for a roast that is marinated in buttermilk and a few other judicious seasonings for a long tenderizing period prior to the oven. This dish is obviously Cheyenne's magna contribution to American cuisine.

CHEYENNE BUTTERMILK-ROASTED LAMB

1 *leg of lamb (about 6 pounds)*
1 *clove garlic, cut into slivers*
2 *cloves garlic, mashed*
1 *tablespoon Dijon mustard*
½ *teaspoon soy sauce*
¼ *teaspoon freshly ground pepper*
3 *tablespoons olive oil*
¼ *cup buttermilk*
½ *cup dry white wine*
1½ *cups beef broth (approximately)*
2 *sprigs rosemary*
1 *tablespoon butter*
Salt and freshly ground pepper

I.   Pierce holes in the top of the lamb at 1½-inch intervals with an ice pick. Insert a sliver of garlic into each hole.

II.   Combine mashed garlic, mustard, soy sauce, and ¼ teaspoon pepper. Slowly beat in oil, a few drops at a time. Slowly add buttermilk. Pour this mixture over the lamb. Let stand at least 6 hours, basting lamb frequently with mixture that runs off.

III.   Heat oven to 400°. Place lamb on a rack in a roasting pan. Reserve excess buttermilk coating. Roast lamb at high heat, 15 minutes.

IV.   Combine excess buttermilk mixture, wine, and ½ cup beef broth. Pour around lamb into roasting pan. Add rosemary. Reduce oven temperature to 300°. Continue to roast lamb, 15 minutes for each pound, for medium-rare. Add remaining beef broth as the juices in pan begin to dry up.

V.   Remove excess fat from sauce; add butter. Season sauce to taste with salt and pepper. Serve sauce with lamb.
Serves 6 to 8.

LOAVES AND HOMELY CASSE-ROLES

Chapter Seven

Finding my home at the range was a matter of conscription rather than free will. A child of the Great Depression, I was channeled into light cookery early on by working parents who reasoned that my schoolwork could not possibly suffer more from my duties as a "mother's helper" *before* meals, than it did from my endless moviegoing *after* them.

As a result, I spent the better part of my formative years improbably wedged betwixt muses: Garbo, Dietrich, Fannie Farmer, and Irma Rombauer!

At first, I was merely a kitchen stand-in—picking up the groceries on my way home from class. I also did a little peeling and slicing on demand. That shortly led to a more important role: watcher of pots. At five every afternoon, while freer spirits played stickball or ring-a-levio, it was my assignment to turn up the gas jets under any food my mother had left partially cooked before she went to work. My attention span was slack, however. So periodically I burned something. It was this defection that actually prompted my debut as a chef.

Attempting to repair some utterly charred stew and dropping spoon after spoonful of peanut butter into the sorry pan (reputedly a cure-all for scorch in those prehistoric times) I remember thinking, "To heck with it. I couldn't possibly cook up anything worse!" I threw out the entire contents and started dinner from scratch!

In retrospect, the act seems signally audacious for a kid of eleven or twelve, but I was a born pragmatist (and an intrepid liar in the bargain). So, after ferreting out a recipe alike enough to the burnt offering plus a quick trip to the corner store for new ingredients, I produced my very first lamb stew.

I recollect it well because (on the counsel of Mrs. Simon Kander, culinary architect of *The Settlement Cook Book*), I added a handful of fresh peas to the casserole at the very end. Uncanned vegetables were an unlikely adjunct to any dish in our house, but I defended their alien presence with a myth. The greengrocer (Mr. Mulfetto), I announced, had obviously included a sack by error.

Apparently the ploy worked, for everyone admired peas in their stew—until the end of the month at least. Then, with terrible jeremiad, my scrupulous mother tallied up the monthly charges from our various grocers. Not only did the derelict peas appear on a statement, but a pound or so of stewing lamb came to light as well!

That is the reason I never saw Katharine Hepburn in *Sylvia Scarlett*, at least until the performance was revived on television in my advancing years. For I was barred from movie attendance seven terrible days for that misdeed.

It might have been worse. I fully anticipated a month's restriction, but parental consternation was mingled, even then, with grudging pride at my culinary accomplishment. And soon our family kitchen, equipped with Hoosier cabinet and dome-topped Frigidaire, became my uncontested bailiwick.

As a chef, I had certain near-fatal flaws. Namely, an incorrigible urge to excess. No recipe intrigued me in the pile of cookbooks I pored over for hours at a time unless it was of vaguely foreign derivation—best preceded by *le* or followed by *à la mode* in the index.

Sad to say, most of these highblown culinary efforts were downright indigestible. They were misfired bouts of cookery that attempted to emulate the rich and glamorous existence I hungered after in darkened movie theaters twice a week. My ultimate survival as a cook is only due to genetics. Luckily, I inherited a keen set of taste buds!

So, when a timbale (soufflé, mousse, or rissole) that I whipped up with the highest of hopes collapsed soggily or turned out to be less than tasty eating, I had the good judgment to turn to simpler, albeit homelier, fare.

My meat loaf, I am happy to report, has never faltered a jot in forty years!

Speaking of which, a bounteous assortment follows: seven of America's favored down-home bake-offs.

The first (circa 1935) came my way from a grandmotherly lady who lives in Omaha, Nebraska. She claims to have raised ten children on this delectable oaten devise, a dish that her family always referred to as "Mr. Roosevelt's Roast" until succeeding presidents made fiscal insecurity generic!

DEPRESSION MEAT LOAF

1¼ *pounds ground beef*
¼ *pound ground pork loin ends*
¼ *cup finely chopped onion*
1 *cup uncooked rolled oats*
1 *teaspoon salt*
¼ *teaspoon freshly ground pepper*
1 *teaspoon Dijon mustard*
¼ *cup ketchup*
1 *egg, lightly beaten*
1 *cup milk*

I.   Heat oven to 400°. Combine all ingredients in a large bowl. Mix thoroughly.

II.   Pack mixture into a lightly greased approximately 10- × 5- × 3-inch loaf pan. Bake 1¼ hours.

Serves 6 to 8.

New Jersey is where America's bumper crop of fennel grows. Coincidentally, the next meat loaf (utterly dependent upon the elusive flavor of that licorice-flavored stalk) hails from the Garden State—Trenton, to be exact.

In most cases, the recipes in this book can be made with some substitute for hard-to-find ingredients. Not Jersey Fennel

Loaf, however! But the delicacy of the dish is so rewarding, I bid you look hard and long at the greengrocer's before you pass it by.

JERSEY FENNEL LOAF

1½ *pounds ground beef*
½ *pound ground pork*
½ *teaspoon salt*
¼ *teaspoon freshly ground pepper*
2 *eggs, beaten*
1 *cup finely chopped onion*
1 *clove garlic, mashed*
½ *cup finely chopped raw fennel, fronds reserved*
1 *teaspoon fennel seeds, crushed*
¼ *teaspoon dried thyme*
½ *cup chopped fresh parsley*
Dash of hot pepper sauce
½ *cup chicken broth*
⅔ *cup fine bread crumbs*
3 *strips bacon*
1 *tablespoon butter*
2 *teaspoons all-purpose flour*
¼ *cup spicy tomato juice*
¼ *cup light cream*
2 *tablespoons chopped fennel fronds*

I.   Heat oven to 400°. Combine all ingredients through bread crumbs in a large bowl. Mix thoroughly.

II.   Trim one strip bacon to fit bottom of a lightly greased loaf pan. Place in center of pan lengthwise. Cover with half the meat mixture. Place another strip of trimmed bacon down center. Cover with remaining meat mixture. Place remaining strip bacon on the top. Bake the loaf 1¼ hours.

III.   Loosen the sides of the loaf when done. Carefully remove from pan with a spatula; keep warm. Remove excess fat from pan juices.

IV.   Melt butter in a saucepan over medium-low heat. Stir in flour; cook, stirring constantly, 2 minutes. Stir in degreased pan juices (you should have about ¼ cup), tomato juice, and cream. Heat to boiling; reduce heat. Simmer until thickened. Spoon a few tablespoons over the meat; garnish with fennel fronds. Pass remaining sauce.

Serves 6 to 8.

In case you are planning to skip the next meat loaf entirely, let me assure you that Chicken Dog is neither relation to canine nor crow. The recipe is over a century old and hails from the apple country of Arkansas (between Bentonville and Fayetteville). The disreputable moniker is just plain anonymous—but who cares when the eatin' is so "long-sweetnin'," as they say round those parts. Pass the cream gravy and hot biscuits, please!

CHICKEN DOG

1⅓ *cups milk, scalded*
7 *tablespoons butter*
2 *cups soft bread crumbs*
2 *cups chopped, cooked white chicken meat*
2 *eggs, lightly beaten*
1 *tablespoon chopped fresh parsley*
2 *teaspoons chopped fresh tarragon*
1 *tablespoon grated onion*
Salt and freshly ground pepper

2 *tablespoons all-purpose flour*
½ *cup milk*
½ *cup Chicken Stock (see Index)*
½ *cup sour cream*

I.   Heat oven to 375°. Pour scalded milk into a large bowl.
       Add 5 tablespoons butter; let melt. Add bread crumbs,
       chicken meat, eggs, parsley, tarragon, onion, ½ teaspoon
       salt, and ¼ teaspoon pepper. Mix thoroughly. Pat mix-
       ture into a buttered loaf pan. Place the loaf pan in a
       roasting pan; pour boiling water around the loaf pan to
       come halfway up the sides. Bake 1 hour.

II.   Carefully pour off juices; reserve. Unmold chicken loaf
       onto a platter. Keep warm. Remove excess fat from
       meat juices.

III.   Melt 2 tablespoons butter in a medium saucepan over
       medium-low heat. Stir in flour; cook, stirring con-
       stantly, 2 minutes. Add meat juices, ½ cup milk, and
       the Chicken Stock. Simmer until slightly thickened.
       Remove from heat; stir in sour cream, and salt and
       pepper to taste. Serve with the chicken loaf.

Serves 6 to 8.

There is a legend in Idaho about a pioneer woman named
Bronco Maggie who drove a freight wagon between Thompson
Falls, Montana, and Coeur d'Alene. Maggie was reputedly so
strong, she could "pick up a live deer by the antlers and throw it
down a root cellar." She was also supposed to be one heck of a
good cook!
   The following farago (well-laced with grated Russet Bur-
bank potatoes) is a more rugged loaf than any of the others
limned. But it is an old Idaho inspiration, perhaps from the oven
of Bronco Maggie herself.

TATER LOAF

1 *pound ground beef*
½ *pound ground veal*
¼ *pound ground pork*
¼ *pound cooked ham, chopped*
1 *teaspoon salt*
¼ *teaspoon freshly ground pepper*
2 *eggs, lightly beaten*
¼ *cup chopped green pepper*
¾ *cup chopped fresh parsley*
¼ *cup finely chopped fresh chives or green onion ends*
2 *tablespoons chopped fresh basil or 1 teaspoon dried*
1 *cup grated raw potatoes, squeezed dry*
1 *strip thick-cut bacon*
½ *cup beef broth*
1 *tablespoon butter*
1 *tablespoon all-purpose flour*
½ *cup whipping cream*
1 *egg yolk*

I.   Heat oven to 400°. Combine all ingredients through potatoes in a large bowl. Mix thoroughly. Form into a loaf in a shallow baking dish. Lay strip of bacon across the top lengthwise. Bake 1¼ hours.

II. Transfer meat to a platter. Keep warm. Remove scum from the baking dish. Remove excess fat from the juices. Pour beef broth into the dish, scraping bottom and sides of dish.

III. Melt butter in a medium saucepan over low heat. Stir in flour; cook, stirring constantly, 2 minutes. Add beef broth and juices from the dish and ¼ cup cream. Simmer until slightly thickened. Combine egg yolk with remaining cream. Stir into sauce; cook over low heat 2 minutes. Do not boil. Pass with the meat.

Serves 4 to 6.

I first tasted Clara Armstrong's zesty ham loaf more than twenty years ago. But truth to tell, I have never forgotten its special savor.

Her son Al (one of my oldest friends) had arranged a visit to his mother's home in Stafford Springs, Connecticut, for a weekend of highly cumulative consumption. What I recall best of the visit after all these years is Mrs. Armstrong's ceaseless good cooking and her utter lack of perturbation in the face of minor household disasters. My small Scotch terrier, Comfort, who had been housebroken at least a year prior to the visit, broke training on the living room broadloom (it was beige) within an hour of my arrival.

Mrs. Armstrong (a confirmed dog lover, it must be noted) refused to admit the enormity of the defection and would not allow the chastened pup to be tethered outside the kitchen door for the rest of his stay.

"Animals are animals, after all," was her only pithy reflection on the matter. "Now, let's have something to eat!"

The endless array of good things on her table (popovers, hot biscuits, buttery mashed potatoes, coleslaw, beet salad, raspberry jam, and sweet and sour peach pickle) has long since faded into the annals of great shared meals. But the flavor of her ham loaf seems lodged in my palate forever.

Mrs. Armstrong decamped her pretty, gingerbread Victorian house in Stafford Springs for the sunnier climes of Orlando, Florida, some while back. But the fact that she still makes this prodigious dish often is apparent from her (easy-as-pie) formula!

CLARA ARMSTRONG'S HAM LOAF

1 *cup fresh bread crumbs*
½ *cup light brown sugar*
2 *teaspoons Dijon mustard*
1½ *pounds uncooked smoked ham, ground*
1½ *pounds ground pork*

1 *cup milk*
2 *eggs, lightly beaten*
¼ *teaspoon salt*
¼ *teaspoon freshly ground pepper*

I.   Heat oven to 350°. Combine bread crumbs and brown sugar in a medium bowl. Toss with a fork until well mixed. Add mustard; mix well with your hands until mixture is crumbly. Measure ½ cup of the mixture. Reserve.

II.   Combine remaining crumb mixture with ham, pork, milk, eggs, salt, and pepper in a large bowl. Mix thoroughly.

III.   Shape meat mixture into a loaf in a shallow baking dish. Sprinkle reserved ½ cup crumb mixture over top and sides, pressing lightly into the meat. Bake 1 hour and 10 minutes. Serve at room temperature or well chilled.

Serves 8.

Here is another smoky New England loaf. This one (stolen from a pre-World War I cookbook, printed in Brattleboro, Vermont) is dubbed a "ham smash." The taste of apple cider in the basting liquid obviously makes it smashing!

CIDER-GLAZED HAM SMASH

FOR THE LOAF:
1½ *pounds uncooked smoked ham, ground*
½ *pound pork sausage meat*
1 *cup bread crumbs*

¼ *cup finely chopped onion*
1 *clove garlic, minced*
¼ *cup finely chopped green pepper*
¼ *cup chopped fresh parsley*
½ *cup apple cider*
2 *eggs, lightly beaten*
1 *teaspoon brown sugar*
½ *teaspoon dry mustard*
½ *teaspoon salt*
¼ *teaspoon freshly ground pepper*
¼ *teaspoon freshly grated nutmeg*
Pinch of dried thyme

FOR BASTING LIQUID:
1 *cup brown sugar*
2 *teaspoons tarragon vinegar*
2 *teaspoons Dijon mustard*
¼ *cup apple cider*

I.   To make the loaf: Heat oven to 350°. Combine all
          ingredients through thyme in a large bowl. Mix well;
          form into a loaf in a shallow baking dish. Bake 20
          minutes.

II.   To make the basting liquid: Meanwhile, combine all
          ingredients in a saucepan. Heat to boiling; boil 1 min-
          ute. Remove from heat.

III.   After 20 minutes, pour a third of the basting liquid
          over the loaf. Continue to bake, basting occasionally
          with remaining liquid until glazed, about 1¼ hours.
                                              Serves 4 to 6.

    Out of a fragmented Southern ledger comes the next
devise—named Pompey's Head after one of Rome's greatest
generals. (Rome, Georgia, did I hear you say?)

P's Head is a most arresting version of a meat loaf since it is no loaf at all, but rather, a huge pudding-like round. Formed as a ball, the meat is dusted with flour and melted butter as it bakes until the exterior is burnished the color of Southern terra firma. This dish, quite wonderful warm and freshly sliced, is just as savory sliced up the day after—if you are lucky enough to salvage any leftovers!

POMPEY'S HEAD

1 *pound ground beef*
1 *pound ground veal*
½ *pound pork sausage meat*
2 *onions, finely chopped*
1 *tablespoon Dijon mustard*
1 *minced fresh sage leaf or a pinch of dried*
Pinch of dried thyme
¼ *cup chopped fresh parsley*
¼ *teaspoon crushed dried hot red peppers*
2 *eggs, lightly beaten*
½ *cup beef broth*
Flour
6 *tablespoons melted butter*
1 *tablespoon butter*
¾ *cup beef broth*

I.   Heat oven to 500°. Combine all ingredients through ½ cup beef broth in a large bowl. Mix thoroughly.

II.   Shape the mixture into a ball; roll in flour. Place on a buttered, shallow baking dish. Make a 1-inch circular hole halfway through the center. Bake loaf 10 minutes.

III.   Reduce oven temperature to 350°. Drizzle loaf with melted butter, adding some to hole in center. Bake another 10 minutes. Remove from oven; sprinkle lightly with flour. Bake, basting every 15 minutes with butter and pan juices, 1 hour longer. Transfer to a serving platter; keep warm.

IV.   Remove scum from baking dish; remove excess fat from meat juices. Melt 1 tablespoon butter in a small saucepan over low heat. Stir in 1 tablespoon flour; cook, stirring constantly, 2 minutes. Add meat juices and ¾ cup beef broth. Simmer until slightly thickened. Serve with loaf.

Serves 6 to 8.

End of meat loaves—

Beginning of hash! The next honest American formula is from the receipt book of Angie Earl, a lady who ran the kitchen at Lion House in Salt Lake City, Utah, where all of Brigham Young's wives lived and died.

Ms. Earl's reputation as a hashslinger was obviously extraordinary, even in the light of contemporary tastes, for her prescription (only slightly amended here) holds up like a tabernacle!

ANGIE EARL'S ROAST BEEF HASH

5 *tablespoons butter*
1 *large clove garlic, minced*
2 *medium onions, chopped*
1 *green pepper, finely chopped*
½ *cup chopped celery*
4 *medium potatoes, cubed*
3½ *cups leftover roast beef*
1½ *teaspoons crushed dried hot red peppers*
1 *teaspoon chopped fresh basil or ½ teaspoon dried*
¾ *cup beef broth (approximately)*

¼ *teaspoon hot pepper sauce*
1 *teaspoon Worcestershire sauce*
½ *teaspoon salt*
¼ *teaspoon freshly ground pepper*
⅛ *teaspoon ground allspice*
1 *tablespoon wine vinegar*
Chopped fresh parsley

I.   Melt butter in a large, heavy skillet over medium-low heat. Add garlic and onions; cook 5 minutes. Add green pepper and celery; cook 5 minutes longer.

II.   Slowly stir potatoes and roast beef into skillet. Add red peppers, basil, beef broth, hot pepper sauce, Worcestershire sauce, salt, ground pepper, and allspice. Mix well. Cook over medium-low heat, tossing occasionally, for 30 minutes. Add more beef broth if mixture becomes too dry.

III.   Heat oven to 325°. Transfer skillet to oven. Bake 30 minutes. Sprinkle with vinegar. Heat broiling unit. Broil hash for a minute or so until the top is very crusty. Garnish with parsley.

Serves 6.

For a hash of another color, ponder on the next golden Wisconsin bequest. A hot potato salad completely dependent on thick wedges of spicy, pink summer sausage.

I never make this dish without a healthy supply of ethnic German wurst on hand in the fridge or freezer. The best summer sausage I have ever eaten in this country is produced by a butcher named Hoff in the tiny farming village of Brownsville, Wisconsin. Mr. Hoff's flavorsome sausage has taken first prizes at the Wisconsin State Fair competition since 1977 and garnered a grand championship in the national competition as well. I discovered his ineffable wurst on a visit to Wisconsin friends some years back and became a deep-dyed fan at first bite. Happily, I have become the beneficiary of several "sticks" at Christmastime ever since. The dish is quite delicious with any Thüringer-type sausage, but, in my opinion, only Hoff's confers it with divinity.

HOT SPUD SALAD WITH SUMMER SAUSAGE

3 *strips bacon, cut into 1-inch-long pieces*
1 *tablespoon butter*
1 *large clove garlic, minced*
4 *green onions, chopped*
2 *large potatoes, sliced ¼ inch thick*
Pinch of dried thyme
⅛ *teaspoon crushed dried hot red peppers*
½ *pound summer sausage, cut into chunks (I prefer Hoffs; see*
    Note)
2 *tablespoons red wine vinegar*
Salt and freshly ground pepper
2 *tablespoons chopped fresh parsley*

I.   Render bacon in a large skillet over medium-low heat. Do not brown. Add butter and garlic; cook 4 minutes.

II.   Stir in green onions, potatoes, thyme, and red peppers. Mix well; add sausage. Cook, stirring occasionally, until potatoes are tender, about 20 minutes. Sprinkle with vinegar; cook 5 minutes longer. Season to taste with salt and pepper. Garnish with chopped parsley.

Note: For mail order, write: Hoff's United Food, Main Street, Brownsville, WI 53006.

Serves 2 to 4.

The next contribution (from at least half a continent east of Brownsville, Wisconsin) is the handiwork of Helen Wilber, food editor of the Providence, Rhode Island, *Journal-Bulletin*. Like me, Helen is a devoted aficionado of leftovers. Her prescription for a bonus Yorkshire-type pudding that uses up practically anything stashed away in the refrigerator (except fruit and salad) is based on an old and thrifty New England proposition. Helen's version (to make a bad pun) *providentially* gives it pizzazz!

HELEN WILBER'S BONUS YORKIE PUDDING

3 *tablespoons butter*
2 *eggs*
1 *cup milk*
1 *cup all-purpose flour*
Salt
1 *small onion, sliced*
1½ *to 2 cups leftover meat (beef, chicken, lamb, etc.)*
1 *cup gravy*
1 *cup leftover, or mixed, frozen vegetables*
Freshly ground pepper

I.　　Heat oven to 425°. Place 2 tablespoons butter in a deep, 2-quart soufflé dish. Place in oven until butter is sizzling hot.

II.　　Place eggs, milk, flour, and ½ teaspoon salt into a blender container. Blend 1 minute. Scrape down sides; blend until smooth.

III.　　Pour half the batter into the heated soufflé dish. Bake 12 minutes.

IV. Meanwhile, sauté the onion in 1 tablespoon butter in a large sauté pan until golden. Stir in meat; cook 3 minutes. Add gravy, vegetables, and salt and pepper to taste. Cook until warmed through.

V. Pour meat mixture over baked pudding in soufflé dish. Spoon remaining half of the batter over the top. Bake 12 minutes longer.

Serves 4.

I suspect that dyed-in-the-cotton Southerners will balk at my inclusion of Grits Soufflé, calling it simply another plain Jane casserole. But that regional specialty (particularly in this Tennessee rendering paired with ham and cheese) is so downright economical and upstandingly wholesome, I felt it deserved a random salute here.

For the uninitiated, grits are the hulled kernels of white corn that have been dried and ground to a fare-thee-well! Very nutritious in the bargain, too!

GRITS SOUFFLÉ

2½ tablespoons butter
4 tablespoons freshly grated Parmesan cheese
1 tablespoon minced shallots
⅓ cup minced cooked ham
2 teaspoons Madeira
1 cup water
1 cup milk
½ teaspoon salt
½ cup white hominy grits (I use Quaker enriched)
4 egg yolks
¼ teaspoon freshly grated nutmeg
Dash of hot pepper sauce

½ *cup grated Swiss or Jarlsberg cheese*
¼ *cup whipping cream*
Salt and freshly ground pepper
5 *egg whites*

I.   Heat oven to 400°. Rub a 1-quart soufflé dish with ½ tablespoon butter and sprinkle with 1 tablespoon Parmesan cheese. Set aside in a cool place.

II.   Melt 1 tablespoon butter in a small sauté pan; add shallots; cook over medium heat until golden. Add ham and Madeira; cook, stirring constantly, until all liquid is absorbed, about 5 minutes. Set aside.

III.   Combine the water, milk, and salt in a medium saucepan; heat to boiling. Stir in grits; return to boiling. Reduce heat and cook, stirring constantly, until thick and tender, 5 to 8 minutes. Add 1 tablespoon butter. Reduce heat to low. Beat in egg yolks, one at a time, beating well after each addition.

IV.   Transfer grits-yolk mixture to a large bowl; stir in the ham mixture, nutmeg, hot pepper sauce, Swiss cheese, 2 tablespoons Parmesan cheese, the whipping cream, and salt and pepper to taste. Beat the egg whites in a large bowl until stiff but not dry; stir a third of the beaten whites into the grits mixture. Fold in the rest. Pour into the prepared soufflé dish; sprinkle the top with remaining 1 tablespoon Parmesan cheese. Bake 30 to 35 minutes. (Slightly less cooking time will produce a moister center.) Serve immediately.

Serves 4 to 6.

From upper Michigan comes a pasty (pronounced past-ēē), a hearty meat 'n' vegetable turnover with decided roots in Cornwall, England. However, the donor of this recipe, Sandra Silfven, aforementioned food editor of the *Detroit News*, avers that the prescription "goes back to my husband's Scandinavian relatives in the copper country at the turn of the century."

An ethnic throwback or not, The Silfven Pasty is an addictive habit at my house—for brunch, lunch, and sometimes even dinner!

THE SILFVEN PASTY

FOR THE PASTRY:
1 *cup plus* 2 *tablespoons all-purpose flour*
1 *teaspoon salt*
4½ *tablespoons butter*
4 *to* 5 *tablespoons cold water*

FOR THE FILLING:
2 *tablespoons olive oil*
2 *cups cubed boneless steak (about 1 pound)*
1 *medium onion, chopped*
1 *cup chopped carrots*
1 *cup chopped rutabaga (yellow turnip)*
1 *teaspoon beef bouillon powder*
½ *teaspoon salt*
¼ *teaspoon freshly ground pepper*
2 *tablespoons melted butter*

I.   To make the pastry: Combine flour and 1 teaspoon salt in a medium bowl. Cut in butter by bits. Blend with a pastry blender until the texture of coarse crumbs. Add enough of the water to make a soft dough. Chill 1 hour.

II.   Heat oven to 450°. To make the filling: Heat olive oil in a large, heavy skillet over high heat. Quickly sauté meat, a few pieces at a time, until well browned.

Transfer meat to a large bowl. Add onion, carrots, rutabaga, bouillon powder, salt, and pepper. Mix well.

III. Divide dough in half. Roll out each half into an 11-inch circle. Line a 9-inch pie plate with one circle, leaving ½ inch hanging over the edge. On one side of pastry, place half the filling. Fold the other half of pastry over the filling; crimp edges to seal. Cut a slit in the top of the pastry to allow steam to escape. Repeat procedure for remaining pastry and filling.

IV. Bake pasties 15 minutes. Reduce oven temperature to 350°; bake 45 minutes longer. If pasties become too dark, cover loosely with aluminum foil.

V. Remove pasties from oven. Pour 1 tablespoon melted butter into each vent hole. Cover with a tea towel; let steam 15 minutes before serving.

Serves 4.

More ethnocentricities.

As you may have surmised, my good friend Mary Surina of San Pedro, California, is one of my favorite American cooks, particularly by virtue of her Yugoslavian stirring-arm. Mary describes herself as "just a little old lady with a big heart who loves people." What she neglects to say is that she loves to cook, too!

Try the Surina method for San Pedro "soul food"—tuna and spaghetti. It's a surprise.

SPAGHETTI TONNATO

¼ *cup olive oil*
1 *large onion, chopped*
2 *cloves garlic, minced*

1 *cup chopped, seeded, peeled fresh tomatoes*
1 *can (8 ounces) plum tomatoes*
Pinch of granulated sugar
1½ *teaspoons chopped fresh basil or* ¾ *teaspoon dried*
¼ *teaspoon ground allspice*
½ *teaspoon salt*
¼ *teaspoon freshly ground pepper*
2 *cans (6½ ounces each) tuna, drained*
1 *small clove garlic*
½ *teaspoon anchovy paste*
8 *ounces spaghetti*
1 *tablespoon butter*
3 *tablespoons minced fresh parsley*
Freshly grated Parmesan cheese

I.   Heat oil in a large saucepan over medium-low heat. Cook onion and garlic until soft, about 5 minutes. Add fresh and canned tomatoes, sugar, basil, allspice, salt, and pepper. Simmer 10 minutes. Stir in tuna; simmer 20 minutes longer.

II.   Mash 1 small clove garlic with anchovy paste and 1 teaspoon tomato-tuna mixture. Stir into the saucepan. Simmer 5 minutes.

III. Meanwhile, place the spaghetti in boiling, salted water in a large saucepan. Cook until tender, about 5 minutes. Drain. Wipe out pot; return spaghetti to pot over low heat. Toss spaghetti with 1 tablespoon butter until very hot.

IV.   Sprinkle tomato-tuna mixture with minced parsley. Serve with spaghetti. Pass the freshly grated Parmesan cheese.

Serves 4.

I admire all the logic behind fast food, but I simply hate the way it tastes, unless it is pizza, of course. Pizza is a private passion stretching back to the time when the lovely, crusty stuff was only eaten in oven-warmed cantinas (by large Italian parties) and never, never sold frozen or reheated by the slice.

My favored pizza parlors in America (a purely prejudiced judgment, I confess) are Uno's and Due's in Chicago, Illinois. These establishments bake a marvelous, gooey pie; and while the management is zealous about guarding family secrets, I have tried to duplicate their efforts for you (at home) in a regulation apartment stove. Uno's makes a deep-dish pizza (like *calzone*) in rounds. I have come up with a similar formulary, which makes two pies. But one may be frozen before baking.

CHICAGO DEEP-DISH PIZZA

FOR THE CRUST:
1½ *cups milk*
6 *tablespoons butter*
2¼ *teaspoons granulated yeast*
¼ *cup lukewarm water*
2 *tablespoons granulated sugar*
1 *teaspoon salt*
⅓ *cup yellow cornmeal*
3 *eggs, beaten*
5 *cups all-purpose flour (approximately)*

FOR THE TOMATO SAUCE:
2 *tablespoons butter*
2 *cloves garlic, minced*
1 *onion, finely chopped*
2 *cans (17 ounces each) plum tomatoes*
1 *can (8 ounces) plum tomatoes*
½ *cup tomato sauce*
2 *teaspoons granulated sugar*

2 *teaspoons chopped fresh basil or ½ teaspoon dried*
¼ *cup chopped Italian parsley*
1 *teaspoon dried oregano*
2 *teaspoons salt*
½ *teaspoon freshly ground pepper*
¼ *teaspoon freshly grated nutmeg*
⅛ *teaspoon ground allspice*

FOR THE FINAL ASSEMBLY:
Vegetable oil
1½ *pounds sweet Italian sausage*
¾ *pound mozzarella cheese, cut into thin slices*
¾ *pound mozzarella cheese, coarsely grated*
⅓ *cup freshly grated Parmesan cheese*

I.   To make the crust: Scald the milk; add the butter by bits. When butter melts, let mixture cool to lukewarm.

II. Combine the yeast, lukewarm water, and sugar in a small bowl. Let stand 10 minutes.

III. Pour the lukewarm milk into a large bowl. Stir in the yeast mixture, salt, cornmeal, eggs, and 3 cups flour. Stir until smooth; add enough of the flour to make a sticky dough, about 1½ cups. Scrape onto a floured board and knead 15 minutes, adding ½ cup more flour if needed. Place in a lightly greased bowl; cover with plastic wrap and then with a heavy towel. Let rise in a warm place until doubled in bulk, about 1½ hours.

IV. Punch down dough. Re-cover; let rise until doubled in bulk, about 1½ hours.

V.   Meanwhile, to make the tomato sauce: Melt the butter in a heavy saucepan over low heat. Add garlic and onion; cook until tender, about 5 minutes. Add remaining ingredients for the sauce. Heat to boiling; reduce heat. Simmer over medium-low heat until very thick, about 1½ hours.

VI.   Heat oven to 400°. Lightly grease two 9-inch round pans that are 2 inches deep. Divide the dough in half; roll each half into 10½-inch circles. Line each pan with dough and press over bottom and slightly more than halfway up the sides of the pans.

VII.   Rub a heavy skillet with oil; sauté the sausage in the skillet until brown on all sides. Cover; cook, shaking the pan frequently, for 5 minutes. Drain on paper toweling; slice ½-inch thick.

VIII.   Place the sliced mozzarella over the bottom of each crust. Spread half the tomato sauce over cheese in each pan. Then place half the sausage over each. Next, sprinkle half the grated mozzarella and Parmesan cheese over each pie. Bake until crisp and golden, about 25 minutes. Let stand 5 minutes before slicing.

Serves 8.

Different from any other cuisine in the U.S., the spicy fare of the Southwest acquired a Spanish accent from the intrepid Franciscan monks who settled Arizona, New Mexico, and Nevada in the sixteenth century. The basic ingredients, however, are 100 percent native—cultivated by the Indians who predated those latter-day conquistadors in the territory.

For ethnic starters, sample my pet New Mexican kitchen prerogative.

TAMALE PIE

¾ cup yellow cornmeal
1 cup cold water
2 cups boiling water

2 *tablespoons unsalted butter*
¼ *pound sausage meat*
¾ *cup finely chopped onion*
1 *large clove garlic, minced*
2 *tablespoons chili powder*
¼ *teaspoon ground cumin*
¾ *pound ground beef*
¼ *teaspoon hot pepper sauce*
1 *stalk celery, chopped*
1 *small Italian green pepper, finely chopped*
1½ *cups chopped, seeded, peeled fresh tomatoes*
2 *ears corn*
1 *teaspoon salt*
¼ *cup sliced, pitted black olives*
½ *cup grated Monterey Jack cheese*
¾ *cup grated mild Cheddar cheese*

I.   Gradually stir the cornmeal into the cold water. Stir this mixture into the boiling water in a heavy saucepan. Heat to boiling, stirring constantly; reduce heat to medium low. Add butter. Cover; cook, stirring occasionally, 35 minutes.

II. Meanwhile, cook the sausage meat in a large heavy skillet, breaking it up with a fork, over medium heat until it begins to lose its pink color. Add the onion and garlic; cook 5 minutes. Stir in the chili powder and cumin. Add the ground beef; continue to cook, breaking up meat with a fork, until beef loses its color, about 5 minutes.

III. Stir hot pepper sauce, celery, and green pepper into the skillet. Cook 5 minutes. Add tomatoes; cook, stirring occasionally, 5 minutes.

IV.   Using a sharp knife, cut halfway down through the corn kernels on each cob. Using the back of the knife, scrape cobs to remove remaining kernel bits and milky residue. Add to tomato-meat mixture. Cook 10 minutes. Season with salt.

V.   Heat oven to 350°. Lightly butter a 10-inch round baking dish, at least 2 inches deep. Spread two-thirds of the cornmeal mixture over sides and bottom. Spoon meat filling evenly in dish; arrange the olive slices over the top. Sprinkle with grated Monterey Jack cheese. Cover with Cheddar cheese.

VI.   Spoon the remaining cornmeal mixture evenly over the top of the pie to form a crust. (If cornmeal has become too thick to spread, thin with a few drops of boiling water.) Bake until golden brown, about 45 minutes. Let stand 10 minutes before serving or serve at room temperature.

Serves 4 to 6 as a main course.

A far cry from traditional Tex-Mex cookery, southwestern American dishes are heartier (and more outdoorsy) in character and dependent on three local staples: chili peppers, tomatoes, and corn. Indeed, the last victual is so much a part of the *gringo* diet that most New Mexican and Arizonan small towns perpetually smell of corn silk—the way Spanish villages are redolent of olive oil.

Have a trio of treasured chili inspirations, noted on native soil, and remanded to New York for taste tempering. The first was acquired in Nevada—along with a divorce (not mine!).

RENO CHILI

1 *pound dried pinto beans, soaked overnight in cold water*
6 *tablespoons butter*
1 *tablespoon vegetable oil*
1½ *pounds beef steak, cut into strips 2 inches long, ½-inch wide*
1½ *pounds lean beef, ground*
3 *onions, chopped*
2 *cloves garlic, minced*
4 *tablespoons chili powder, or to taste*
2 *large tomatoes, chopped*
1 *can (10 ounces) mixed tomatoes and green chiles*
1 *teaspoon brown sugar*
1 *bay leaf, crumbled*
Pinch of dried thyme
1 *teaspoon cayenne pepper*
½ *teaspoon ground allspice*
½ *teaspoon crushed dried hot red peppers*
1 *teaspoon soy sauce*
Dash of hot pepper sauce
¾ *cup beef broth (approximately)*
½ *cup beer*
1 *teaspoon salt*
½ *teaspoon freshly ground pepper*

I.   Drain soaked beans. Place in a large pot of water. Heat to boiling; reduce heat. Simmer, stirring occasionally, until tender, about 1 hour. Drain beans.

II.   Heat oven to 300°. Heat 3 tablespoons butter and the oil in a large, heavy skillet over medium heat. Pat beef strips dry with paper toweling. Sauté, a few pieces at a time, until well browned on both sides. Transfer to a large Dutch oven.

III.   Add ground beef to skillet. Cook over medium-high heat, breaking up lumps with a wooden spoon, until lightly browned. Transfer, using a slotted spoon, to the Dutch oven.

IV. Drain all grease from skillet. Add 3 tablespoons butter. Sauté onions, scraping bottom and sides of pan, over medium-low heat 3 minutes. Add garlic, cook 3 minutes longer. Transfer to the Dutch oven.

V. Stir chili powder into meat mixture. Add fresh tomatoes and mixed tomatoes and green chiles. Sprinkle with brown sugar. Stir in remaining ingredients except beans. Heat to boiling; transfer to oven. Bake, covered, until meat is tender, about 2 hours.

VI. Stir beans into Dutch oven. Bake, uncovered, 30 minutes longer, adding more beef broth if beans become too dry.

Serves 6 to 8.

Cowpuncher Beans come as a grant from an Arizona fan who earnestly felt the recipe belonged in this honest food collection. She was right as the rain!

Granted the dish *is* somewhat on the hot side, but cold beer makes a perfect antidote, I've discovered!

COWPUNCHER BEANS

¾ pound dried pinto beans
4 quarts water
2 strips bacon
¼ pound salt pork, diced
1 pound lean pork, cut into strips 2 inches long, ½-inch thick
1 pound round steak, cut into strips 2 inches long, ½-inch thick
2 onions, chopped
3 cloves garlic, minced

½ *teaspoon dried oregano*
⅛ *teaspoon ground cumin*
3 *tablespoons chili powder*
1 *teaspoon salt*
¼ *teaspoon freshly ground pepper*
3 *cups canned plum tomatoes*
1 *medium jalapeño, or hot green pepper, seeded, minced*
1 *teaspoon Worcestershire sauce*
¼ *teaspoon hot pepper sauce*

I. Place the beans in a large, heavy saucepan. Add 8 cups water. Slowly, heat to boiling; boil 2 minutes. Remove from heat. Let stand 1 hour. Drain. Wipe out pot and return beans. Cover with 8 cups water. Heat to boiling over medium heat; reduce heat. Simmer until barely tender, about 30 minutes. Drain; reserve.

II. Sauté the bacon strips in a large Dutch oven until crisp. Remove bacon. Reserve.

III. Add the salt pork to the Dutch oven; sauté until golden brown. Remove with a slotted spoon. Reserve.

IV. Add half the pork strips to the Dutch oven; brown well on both sides. Remove with a slotted spoon. Sauté remaining pork; remove. Repeat process, in two batches, with beef strips. Reserve.

V. Add onions and garlic to Dutch oven. Sauté over medium heat until golden, about 5 minutes. Return pork and beef strips to the Dutch oven; stir in oregano, cumin, chili powder, salt, and pepper. Mix well. Add reserved salt pork, tomatoes, and jalapeño. Cook, covered, over low heat until meat is almost tender, about 1 hour. Stir in reserved beans, Worcestershire, and hot pepper sauce. Cook, covered, 30 minutes. Taste; adjust seasonings. Crumble bacon over top before serving.

Serves 6.

You may be certain that "the eyes of Texas are upon you" whenever you write a word about Lone Star fare or print a recipe for any dish with geographic ties from Amarillo to Corpus Christi. I conned the following chili devise from a cookbook-collecting cowhand who resides in Lubbock, with a hand-over-the-heart promise that his identity would never be revealed!

RED-NECK CHILI

1 *pound dried pigeon peas (grandules), soaked overnight in cold water*
5 *tablespoons olive oil*
1 *pound chorizos (Spanish sausages), cut into ½-inch thick slices*
3 *pounds stewing beef, cut into 1-inch cubes*
2 *medium onions, chopped*
3 *cloves garlic, minced*
2 *Italian green peppers, chopped*
3 *tablespoons chopped fresh or canned jalapeño peppers*
2 *tablespoons masa harina (corn flour, available at Spanish grocers)*
3 *tablespoons chili powder*
1 *teaspoon ground cumin*
1 *teaspoon crushed dried hot red peppers*
1½ *cups chopped, seeded, peeled fresh tomatoes*
1 *can (17 ounces) plum tomatoes*
1 *teaspoon salt*
¼ *teaspoon freshly ground pepper*
1½ *cups beef broth (approximately)*

I.   Drain soaked beans. Place in a large pot of water. Heat to boiling; reduce heat. Simmer, stirring occasionally, until tender, about 1 hour. Drain.

II.   Heat oven to 350°. Heat 2 tablespoons oil in a large Dutch oven. Saute chorizos until crisp and golden on both sides, about 10 minutes. Remove with a slotted spoon to a plate.

III.   Wipe out Dutch oven. Add 3 tablespoons oil. Pat beef cubes dry with paper toweling. Saute beef over medium heat, a few pieces at a time, until well browned on all sides. Transfer to plate with chorizos.

IV.   Add onions, garlic, green peppers, and jalapenos to Dutch oven. Cook over medium-low heat 5 minutes.

V.   Return meats to Dutch oven. Stir in masa harina, chili powder, cumin, and red peppers. Mix well; add tomatoes, salt, pepper, and beef broth. Heat to boiling; cover. Transfer to oven; bake until meat is tender, 2 to 2½ hours.

VI.   Stir beans into meat mixture. Bake, uncovered, 30 minutes. (If beans seem too dry, add more broth.)

Serves 8.

The last bean mandate is from the Northeast, just to make a topical change of venue. The following pottage was first tasted in Portland, Maine, offered up as "My Boston Grandmother's Frenchified Baked Beans."

A little sleuthing after dinner produced a grandparent who was obviously a *Toulousaine* before she became a proper Bostonian. But that is the very nature of this crazy mixed up cuisine of ours, after all!

ALL-AMERICAN CASSOULET

1 *pound dried marrow or pea beans, soaked overnight in cold water*
¼ *cup diced salt pork*
½ *pound sausage meat, shaped into 8 small patties*

1¼ *pounds lamb shoulder chops with bones, excess fat removed, cut*
    into 1-inch pieces
1 *clove garlic, minced*
5 *tablespoons butter*
1 *cup coarsely chopped onions*
1 *cup coarsely chopped leeks*
½ *cup coarsely chopped carrots*
1 *can (17 ounces) plum tomatoes*
1½ *cups beef broth*
½ *cup white wine*
½ *teaspoon fresh thyme or a pinch of dried*
1 *bay leaf, crumbled*
Salt and freshly ground pepper
2 *cups leftover duck, cut into chunks*
1 *cup bread crumbs*
Chopped fresh parsley

I.   Drain beans. Place in a large pot; cover with water. Heat to boiling; reduce heat. Simmer, stirring occasionally, 30 minutes. Drain.

II.   Meanwhile, sauté salt pork in a large, heavy skillet over medium heat until golden. Remove with a slotted spoon; drain on paper toweling; reserve.

III.   Drain off all grease from skillet. Sauté sausage patties until golden brown on both sides. Remove with a slotted spoon. Drain on paper toweling; reserve.

IV.   Drain all but 1 tablespoon grease from skillet. Add half the lamb pieces; sprinkle with half the garlic. Sauté over medium heat until well browned on all sides. Remove with a slotted spoon. Repeat step with remaining lamb and garlic. Reserve.

V.   Drain all grease from skillet. Add 1 tablespoon butter; sauté onions over medium-low heat 5 minutes. Add leeks, carrots, tomatoes, broth, wine, thyme, and bay leaf. Mix well, scraping bottom and sides of skillet. Combine with beans and reserved salt pork. Season to taste with salt and pepper.

VI. Heat oven to 350°. Rub a large Dutch oven with 1 tablespoon butter. Spoon a third of the bean mixture over the bottom. Add half the duck meat, half the reserved sausage, and half the reserved lamb. Spoon a third of the bean mixture over the top. Add remaining meats; top with remaining bean mixture. Bake, uncovered, 35 minutes.

VII. Meanwhile, melt 3 tablespoons butter in a large skillet over medium heat. Stir in bread crumbs. Cook, stirring constantly, until golden.

VIII. After 35 minutes, spoon bread crumbs over bean mixture. Increase oven temperature to 400°. Bake 20 minutes. Break crumb topping into cassoulet with a spoon. Bake 10 minutes longer. (If bean mixture becomes too dry, add some beef broth.) Sprinkle with parsley.

Serves 6 to 8.

More New England mixed ancestry. A Connecticut version of *ratatouille* dubbed "Eight Layer Dinner." The following dish is devised of any and every thing in the garden and larder. Easy on the budget, it is even easier on the utilities as all ingredients go into the pot together.

EIGHT LAYER DINNER

3 *tablespoons unsalted butter*
1½ *pounds baking potatoes, pared, cut into ⅛-inch thick slices*
4 *ounces salt pork, cut into ¼-inch thick strips*
1 *large clove garlic, minced*

3 *stalks celery, diced*
1 *large red bell pepper, finely chopped*
1 to 1½ *pounds beef shoulder steak, cut into pieces ¼-inch thick, 4*
    inches square
Salt and freshly ground pepper
1 *large onion, sliced*
1 *large green bell pepper, finely chopped*
1 *can (17 ounces) plum tomatoes*
¼ *cup chopped fresh parsely*

I.   Heat oven to 325°. Rub the bottom of a 3-quart Dutch
      oven with 1 tablespoon butter. Layer the sliced potatoes
      over the bottom.

II.   Render the salt pork in a large heavy skillet over
      medium heat until crispy. Remove with a slotted spoon;
      spread evenly over potatoes in Dutch oven.

III. Pour off all but 2 teaspoons grease from skillet. Sauté
      garlic over medium-low heat 3 minutes. Spoon over
      potatoes. Add the celery and then the red pepper.

IV.   Heat remaining butter with oil in skillet over medium-
      high heat. Sauté meat, a few pieces at a time, until well
      browned on both sides. As the meat is done, place over
      red pepper in Dutch oven.

V.   Sprinkle meat lightly with salt and pepper. Place sliced
      onion over meat, then the green pepper, and, finally, the
      tomatoes. Sprinkle tomatoes with salt and pepper.

VI.   Bake covered in oven until meat is tender, 1½ to 2
      hours. If mixture seems too wet, bake uncovered 15
      minutes. Sprinkle with parsley before serving.

                                          Serves 4 to 6.

HOT AND COLD VEGETABLES

Chapter Eight

My mother was a lady of some very odd conceits. For one thing, she implicitly believed in convenience foods. In fact, she lives in memory as the only woman I ever met who managed to serve canned, creamed onions, frozen cauliflower, canned carrots and peas, and two kinds of instant potatoes at the same Thanksgiving dinner. These were accompaniments, I might add, to a turkey so lacking in flavor that bottled Heinz ketchup surreptitiously addressed the bird at her table!

To be complimentary, my mother's cooking was expedient at its best. Of course, she worked for years and years, so her culinary energies were limited. But even in later life after she had retired from industry to devote herself to a second marriage and the late bloom of homemaking, she obdurately refused to buy or chop up fresh vegetables. Why? "Too much trouble," proclaimed my intolerant parent.

Another of my mother's crotchets was that she sincerely believed she had altered the course of American slang. How? By inventing new expressions. "I find myself making up new catch phrases all the time," she once declared with total lack of modesty. "Not even thinking, the words come out of my mouth. And before you can say Jack Robinson, other people are saying the same damned thing! I want to tell you, these expressions have become very, very *popular* in our language! If I had a copyright on any of them . . . we'd all be millionaires today!"

What were some of the magical phrases to which my mother laid authorial claim? Well, they were certainly aphorisms very much in common usage. "For crying out loud!" was one of her earliest brainstorms. She insisted it had first been uttered in the middle of a deadheat World Series baseball game when an umpire miscalled a ball for a strike. "I guess people in the bleachers heard me say it," she later recalled, "and it kinda stuck!"

Another phrase my mother asserted she had coined was an utterance of approval she used quite often.

"That guy . . . sure knows his onions," the lady would announce with grave authority whenever she discovered some particularly knowledgeable practitioner in her orbit. Be it Einstein or merely Oscar of the Waldorf, the compliment was unvarying, *"He sure knows his onions!"*

If I inherit any maternal gifts, none are tinged with my parent's enormous self-confidence. Yet, she would be the first to admit, I certainly know my onions in the kitchen!

Indeed my affection for the common garden ally *(Allium cepa)* is so great that I rarely cook up a vegetable dish that is not somehow tinged (even in the smallest way) with the aromatic savor of onion or its garden cousins, shallot, leek, scallion, or garlic.

Ancient Turks believed that onion's creation was originally a devilish exercise. They claimed that when Lucifer was expelled from heaven he landed on Earth and the first onion bulb grew simultaneously. Be that as it may, the onion is an angelic bequest for gastronomy, no matter how it got here.

For starters, observe this aromatic plant in its purest form—a lovely old-fashioned vegetable flummery, snatched from *The Women's Temperance League Receipt Book,* printed in Helena, Montana, but laced with wine by this tippling chef.

The dish's flavor depends on the confederacy of honest-to-gosh real onions, shallots, and garlic for its mettle. So do not be tempted to emulate my mother at the stove, please!

ONION BREAD PUDDING

6 *thin slices French- or Italian-type bread, toasted, buttered*
4 *tablespoons butter*
4 *large onions, coarsely chopped*

3 *large shallots, chopped*
1 *clove garlic, chopped*
1 *chopped sprig fresh thyme or* ⅛ *teaspoon dried*
¼ *teaspoon freshly grated nutmeg*
⅛ *teaspoon ground cloves*
⅛ *teaspoon ground allspice*
¼ *cup grated Gruyère cheese*
Salt and freshly ground pepper
¼ *cup whipping cream*
¼ *cup dry white wine*
2 *tablespoons freshly grated Parmesan cheese*
Chopped fresh parsley

I. Heat oven to 350°. Arrange buttered toast on the bottom of a shallow, buttered baking dish.

II. Heat 2 tablespoons butter in a large, heavy skillet. Add onions, shallots, garlic, and thyme. Cook over low heat, stirring occasionally, 20 minutes. Increase heat; cook until all liquid has evaporated and onions are lightly browned.

III. Transfer onion mixture to a food processor container (or run through a food mill). Blend until smooth. Add nutmeg, cloves, allspice, 3 tablespoons Gruyère cheese, and salt and pepper to taste. Spoon over toast.

IV. Combine whipping cream and white wine in a small bowl; pour over onion mixture. Sprinkle with remaining 1 tablespoon Gruyère cheese and the Parmesan cheese. Dot with remaining 2 tablespoons butter. Bake until lightly browned and bubbly, about 30 minutes. Sprinkle with parsley before serving.

Serves 6.

Arizona's grapefruit groves and onion fields bloom cheek by jowl. The notion of combining the communal harvest in a salad bowl dates back to the early 1930s. I discovered the next recipe in a huge pile of dusty newspaper and magazine clippings that I inherited from a New York evacuee making tracks to Scottsdale, funnily enough. She hadn't looked at her collection in thirty years, and most of the yellowed scraps shattered on contact. This prescription survived the rigors of time and is worthy of some revival at your next dinner table or outdoor picnic.

ARIZONA GRAPEFRUIT SLAW

2 *large grapefruit*
1 *medium red onion, thinly sliced, circles separated*
Peel of 1 orange, thinly slivered
1 *clove garlic, finely minced*
½ *teaspoon sea salt*
1 *teaspoon Dijon mustard*
Juice of 1 lemon
½ *cup olive oil*
Juice of 1 orange (about ¼ cup)
Freshly ground pepper
1 *bunch watercress leaves*

I.   Peel the grapefruit. Using a very sharp knife, remove all pith. Slice across grapefruit, cutting into rounds about ¼ inch thick. Cut each segment apart. (There should be about 3 cups fruit.) Place in a serving dish. Place circles of onions over the top of the grapefruit. Sprinkle with slivered orange peel.

II.   Mash garlic and salt with the back of a spoon in a medium bowl. Stir in mustard and lemon juice. Very slowly whisk in oil. Mixture will be quite thick. Thin with orange juice. Pour over salad. Sprinkle with freshly ground pepper. Cover; chill thoroughly.

III.   Just before serving, garnish with watercress leaves. Toss salad at the table.

Serves 4.

I had sung the praises of the next recipe donor (Mrs. Irma Wehausen of Golden, Colorado) in several cooking tomes before I actually met the lady. That omission was happily corrected by a visit to the Centennial State for Thanksgiving in 1980. Mrs. Wehausen is a lady of formal manner, but formidable culinary accomplishment, a gift she deprecates as simply "home-style cooking." Her contribution to this green-thumbed chapter is a Coloradan put-up of (far-from-ordinary) pickled beets, a treasure any pantry cupboard across the nation would gladly prize.

This rosy condiment takes a mere week of "sittin'" before it may be consumed, but the end result makes grand eating, I assure you. Particularly in concert with the Chicken Püt Pie limned earlier.

IRMA WEHAUSEN'S PICKLED BEETS

10 *medium fresh beets*
Water
2 *cups granulated sugar*
2 *cups distilled white vinegar*
2 *teaspoons whole mixed pickling spices*
1 *medium onion, thinly sliced*

I.   Wash beets; trim, leaving ½ inch of beet top intact. (Reserve beet tops for Mildred Schulz's Beet Top Soup; see Index.) Place beets in a large pot; add water to cover. Heat to boiling; reduce heat. Simmer until beets are tender, but still firm, about 15 minutes. Drain. Cover with cold water. Let cool. Peel beets; cut into ⅛-inch-thick slices. (You should have about 6 cups.)

II.   Combine 2 cups water, the sugar, vinegar, and pickling spices in a large saucepan. Heat to boiling; add sliced beets. Reduce heat; simmer 10 minutes.

III.   Transfer beets to a large bowl with a slotted spoon. Add sliced onion; mix well.

IV.   Return syrup in saucepan to boiling; simmer until reduced slightly, about 4 minutes.

V.   Place beet-onion mixture into sterilized jars. Pour enough hot syrup into each jar to cover beets. Seal. Let stand unrefrigerated 1 week. Chill well before serving.

Makes about 4 pints.

The following recipe (for Grandmother Clarke's Fried Carrots) comes from a true friend in Santee, California, who was a pen pal of mine for over a year before we actually met.

I am, you see, an assiduous letter writer and an equally devoted recipient of mail. As a small child, I used to affix my name to every advertising coupon and circular that appeared in my mother's consignment of monthly magazines just to encourage an active correspondence. And the postman on our Humphrey Street route not only rang twice, he got to know my name very, very well—from the intense volume of my answers.

In later life, fan letters happily take up the slack.

My acquaintance with Jody Gillis dates back to the publication of my last cookbook, *Kitchen Bouquets.* A perfect stranger, she wrote me such a loving note about my book, it elicited a good cry and an instant reply. Thus began what some, including the lady's tolerant husband, considered to be Olympian cross-country communication.

Jody Gillis is the director of a very special cooking school at a choice gourmet cookware shop in La Mesa, called Something More. More to the point, she is also a lady of decidedly pragmatic bent. After six or seven months of hot and heavy *billets-doux*, she suddenly phoned me in New York one day.

"Bert," she declared a bit breathlessly. "I am going into the hospital for an operation. I've never had surgery before in my whole life and I am *petrified*. I decided there were only two ways to face the inevitable: see a shrink or call you!"

Fortunately for both of us, Jody is abloom with good health and back to writing long, long letters from California on the most bizarre collection of assorted stationery in the western world. A sheet of notepaper, emblazoned with circus wagons in luminescent shades of pink and green, bears the following inscription:

Bert,

This was my maternal grandmother's recipe. She used to put me on her big kitchen work table when I was tiny and let me help cook. Grandmother Clarke grew up on a Southern plantation and was one of the best cooks in the world. Unfortunately, few of her recipes were saved when she died because she never measured or wrote anything down.

. . . She fried almost anything she could think of in cornmeal. This dish was her own invention one night when she had some cooked carrots left over. I had to do the recipe from memory . . . but I doubt you'll ever find anything like it in any cookbook but yours—if you use it! It's really good and unusual and *so* nostalgic for me!

Love,

Jody

GRANDMOTHER CLARKE'S FRIED CARROTS

12 to 16 small carrots, pared
Salt
2 eggs, beaten
Yellow cornmeal
Hot bacon drippings

I.   Cook the carrots in boiling salted water in a medium saucepan until barely tender, about 10 minutes. Do not overcook; carrots should be slightly crisp. Drain and let cool. Cut each carrot lengthwise into 3 pieces.

II.   Sprinkle carrots lightly with salt. Dip into beaten eggs; roll in cornmeal. Fry in about 1-inch bacon drippings in a large skillet over medium heat until golden. Drain on paper toweling. Keep warm until ready to serve.

Serves 4 to 6.

Jody Gillis is a deep-eyed okra lover. When I went to California on a teaching spree last year, she insisted I catechize San Diegans about the joys of true Southern cookery. My students matriculated in a crash course of undercooking okra (among other things) that I had acquired in New Iberia, Louisiana, the year before.

The greens themselves (out of season on the West Coast in November) were hand delivered by me, via TWA jet from Balducci's in New York, making it a truly intercontinental seminar.

BLANCHED OKRA IN THE CAJUN STYLE WITH MUSTARD SAUCE

1½ pounds fresh okra, trimmed
2 egg yolks

1 *tablespoon Dijon mustard*
Juice of ½ lemon
Dash of hot pepper sauce
½ cup frozen unsalted butter
Salt and ground white pepper

I.   Cook okra in boiling salted water in a medium sauce-pan for 4 to 5 minutes. (Okra should be slightly crunchy, or it will turn into a pasty mass.) Drain; keep warm.

II.   Combine the egg yolks, mustard, lemon juice, and hot pepper sauce in the top of a double boiler. Place over simmering water and stir until slightly thickened. Cut in the frozen butter by bits until smooth and thick. If the sauce begins to thicken too quickly, remove from heat while adding the butter. (If the sauce should curdle, beat in a few drops of boiling water until smooth.) Add salt and white pepper to taste. Pour sauce over okra; serve immediately.

Serves 4.

Hoppin' John is a traditional good luck dish served in the South at New Year's Eve dinner. My version, slightly altered as to the nature of the legume (frozen instead of dried), hails from Paris, Missouri, home of my earliest mentor on the joys of the American table, Mary Margaret McBride.

HOPPIN' JOHNNY

1 *package (10 ounces) frozen black-eyed peas*
2 *strips bacon*
1 *small onion, chopped*
1 *clove garlic, minced*
1 *cup cooked rice (see Steamed Rice in Index)*

2 *tablespoons red wine vinegar*
Salt and freshly ground pepper
¼ *cup finely chopped fresh chives or green onion ends*
2 *tablespoons chopped fresh parsley*

I.   Drop frozen peas into boiling salted water in a medium saucepan. Simmer until tender, about 20 minutes. Drain, reserving ¼ cup cooking liquid.

II.   Sauté bacon strips in a large, heavy skillet over medium heat until crisp. Drain on paper toweling. Reserve.

III.   Stir onion into bacon drippings in skillet. Cook 3 minutes. Add garlic; cook 2 minutes longer. Stir in drained peas and the rice. Cook, stirring constantly, until warmed through. Add vinegar and enough reserved cooking liquid from peas to moisten mixture, 2 to 3 tablespoons. Cook 5 minutes.

IV.   Season to taste with salt and pepper. Crumble reserved bacon over the top. Sprinkle with chives and parsley.

Serves 4 to 6.

Addiction is said to be a great leveler.

I, for instance, have no tolerance for alcohol. Too much Scotch or vodka makes me sick, instead of merely mellow. And hard drugs are as alien as space travelers. Never having mastered the proper inhalation of a cigarette (no less a joint) has also kept me less than transported by nicotine.

In the late sixties, I was once gifted with a packet of *enriched* chocolate chip cookies. However, the only residual high of that experience was an elevated appetite. After I gained ten pounds virtually overnight, I gave up tripping forever.

My sole vice is no less caloric—just a more familiar procliv-ity. The fix? Mashed potatoes!

I have doted on this sensual side dish since childhood, but I readily confess I never properly learned to prepare a potful until I was past forty years of age.

As a novitiate in my mother's kitchen, I followed the exam-ple of all expedient potato mashers and churned the cooked tubers with a wire thong. This was an implement that kneaded the potatoes to a pulp certainly, but left a few unsquashable lumps amid the velvet no matter how much warm milk or butter was added.

Since then, I have discovered the one sure method for preparing a flawless drift of mashed potatoes requires an even more old-fashioned tool—a hand ricer. Food processors simply will not do the trick, as the action of the blade draws out excess starch.

The most felicitous raw ingredient for a pot of *supermashed* is the baking potato. Be sure to presoak pared potatoes for at least fifteen minutes (in icy cold water) before setting them on the stove. The cold bath removes a healthy measure of starch prior to cookery. I usually quarter my potatoes as well, to shorten the boiling time. Actual stove times vary, but twenty minutes should suffice. The only seasoning in the water should be a measure of salt, the amount dependent upon one's dietary concern.

A good cook will drain and rice cooked potatoes as soon as they are fork tender. I always add a smallish lump of sweet butter to the pan before the ricing procedure begins to keep the strands from sticking. Further enrichment is up to you. Greene's rule of thumb: one-half stick butter to about three cups of cooked potatoes; cream added at your own discretion (over low, low heat) until the mixture in your saucepan resembles a February blizzard!

Perhaps I love the mashed potato so well because it makes such an exemplary leftover. Consider a panful of Pennsylvania Dutch Potato Dumplings from Lancaster as a prandial phoenix for the next night's dinner party!

PENNSYLVANIA DUTCH POTATO DUMPLINGS

3 *cups cold mashed cooked potatoes*
1 *cup all-purpose flour (approximately)*
2 *egg yolks*
½ *cup grated Swiss or Parmesan cheese*
½ *teaspoon freshly grated nutmeg*
¼ *cup butter, melted*
Salt and freshly ground pepper

I.   Heat oven to 300°. Place potatoes on a floured surface or in a large bowl. Work in 1 cup flour, the egg yolks, cheese, and nutmeg by hand, adding more flour, if necessary, to make a soft dough. Roll into ropes about 1 inch in diameter. Slice into 1-inch lengths. Press ends of dumplings with the tines of a fork.

II. Drop dumplings, 8 to 10 at a time, into a large kettle of boiling salted water; cook dumplings until they float to the top, about 2 minutes. Remove with a slotted spoon; drain on paper toweling. Keep warm in oven. (If making in advance, reheat for 20 minutes in a low oven.)

III. Just before serving, pour melted butter over dumplings; sprinkle with salt and pepper. (If serving with a bland dish, sprinkle grated Parmesan over the top as well.)

Serves 6.

I never knew, until I started seeking out ethnic recipes for this collection, that as many Basques live in Idaho today as do in Andorra, principal city of the Pyrenees. Sheep raisers mostly, these émigrés dwell remarkably close to Sun Valley, dining magnificently on mother-tongued versions of local produce. Witness for starters:

BASQUE BAKED POTATOES

4 *large Idaho baking potatoes*
6 *tablespoons butter, softened*
1 *clove garlic, minced*
½ *green pepper, finely chopped*
2 *tomatoes, peeled, seeded, chopped*
Pinch of granulated sugar
2 *slices prosciutto, chopped*
2 *teaspoons chopped fresh parsley*
½ *cup whipping cream*
Salt and freshly ground pepper

I.   Heat oven to 375°. Bake potatoes until tender, about 1 hour.

II.   Meanwhile, melt 2 tablespoons butter in a medium-size, heavy skillet over medium-low heat. Stir in garlic; cook 3 minutes. Stir in green pepper and tomatoes; sprinkle with sugar. Cook until tomatoes are tender, about 20 minutes. Increase heat slightly. Add prosciutto; toss until all liquid has evaporated. Stir in parsley. Reserve.

III.   Slice the tops off the potatoes. (Reserve for use at another time.) Scoop out insides of potatoes into a medium bowl, leaving a ¼-inch-thick layer of potato in each shell as a base. Add 4 tablespoons butter and the cream to potatoes in the bowl. Mix well, but do not mash. Potatoes should be coarse in texture. Season with salt and pepper to taste.

IV.   Spoon potato mixture into shells without mashing. Mound tomato mixture over the tops. Bake 20 minutes before serving.

Serves 4.

A blushing potato dish that is a favorite of mine (particularly when it is paired with a crimson slice of beef) comes from a Charlestonian friend who explains that her father's mother loved the color pink extravagantly—in her garden, in her drawing room, even on her buffet table. So she added a mite of tomato to a classic family dish. *Et voilà!* Potatoes through rose-tinted glasses!

ROSY SCALLOPED POTATOES

1½ *pounds potatoes*
1 *cup milk*
1½ *cups whipping cream*
1 *large clove garlic, mashed*
1 *teaspoon tomato paste*
1 *teaspoon Dijon mustard*
1 *teaspoon salt*
¼ *teaspoon ground white pepper*
1 *tablespoon butter*

I. Heat oven to 400°. Pare potatoes; slice ⅛ inch thick. Place in a large saucepan. Combine milk, cream, garlic, tomato paste, mustard, salt, and white pepper in a small bowl. Pour over potatoes. Heat potato mixture to boiling, stirring constantly.

II. Rub a gratin dish or shallow baking dish with 1 tablespoon butter. Spoon in the potato mixture. Bake potato mixture 1 hour. Reduce oven temperature slightly if potatoes brown too much. Potatoes are excellent hot, room temperature, or cold.

Serves 4.

More Southern offerings: A Georgian farmhouse supper of greens, unpeeled taters and fatback, cooked together to a fare-

thee-well! This dish makes a wondrous adjunct to a summer
outdoor grill, or barbecue at any season!

GEORGIA GREEN BEANS AND NEW POTATOES

1¼ *pounds mature green beans, trimmed, broken into 1-inch pieces*
2 *ounces fatback, rinsed, cut into strips*
½ *teaspoon salt*
½ *cup strong Chicken Stock (see Index)*
6 *to 8 small new potatoes, unpared*

I.   Combine green beans, fatback, salt, and Chicken Stock
            in a large saucepan. Heat to boiling; reduce heat.
            Simmer, covered, 30 minutes.

II.   Add potatoes; cover. Cook, stirring occasionally, for 30
            minutes. (All liquid should be absorbed by this time.) If
            too wet, increase heat and cook, uncovered, until fairly
            dry.

Serves 4.

According to a fairly reliable ex-Nebraskan of my acquaintance, Omaha boardinghouses once carried discreet placards in
their lace-curtained windows announcing, "venison, fowl, bird,
or fish cooked in any manner you like." A parenthetic mandate
to potential residents was added as well: "You may smoke in the
parlor, put heels on the fireplace fender, or spread a buffalo robe
on the green grass. But please do not pick the dandelions!"

With good reason, because the good Nebraskan housewife
turned the greens into a breakfast pie.

The following homely recipe comes to my breakfast table with
bacon and eggs, but it also makes a dandy lunch or supper,
paired to a platter of cold ham or tongue.

DANDELION GREEN BAKE

2½ *pounds dandelion greens or 2 pounds dandelion greens mixed*
with ½ pound arugula
3 *tablespoons unsalted butter*
2 *tablespoons all-purpose flour*
¾ *cup milk, scalded*
⅓ *cup grated Swiss or Jarlsberg cheese*
⅛ *teaspoon freshly grated nutmeg*
1 *teaspoon red wine vinegar*
Salt and freshly ground pepper
¼ *cup fine bread crumbs*

I.   Heat oven to 425°. Rinse greens under cold running water. Remove tough center ribs. Coarsely chop.

II.   Heat a large pot of salted water to a rolling boil. Add chopped greens. Return to a rolling boil; drain immediately under cold running water. Drain thoroughly. Squeeze out all liquid with your hands.

III.   Melt 2 tablespoons butter in a medium saucepan over low heat; whisk in flour. Cook, stirring constantly, 2 minutes. Whisk in milk; beat until smooth. Stir in grated cheese, nutmeg, and vinegar. Add salt and pepper to taste. Stir in chopped greens. Spoon mixture into a lightly greased 8-inch glass pie plate.

IV.   Melt remaining 1 tablespoon butter in a small sauté pan over medium heat. Stir in bread crumbs. Cook until lightly browned. Spoon over dandelion mixture; bake until bubbly, about 20 minutes.

Serves 4.

Former Hungarians make up a healthy chunk of urban Ohio's population. From their Old Country gardens, they have fortuitously brought an unpronounceable and practically unspellable vegetable dish (*Füszeres Vöröskáposzta Köménymaggal*) that is a culinary marriage-made-in-heaven with duck, goose, or crisp roasted pork.

HOT RED CABBAGE SLAW

1 *onion, finely chopped*
1 *green pepper, finely chopped*
3 *tablespoons vegetable oil*
1 *medium red cabbage (about 1½ pounds), shredded*
1 *teaspoon caraway seeds*
2 *bay leaves*
1 *teaspoon granulated sugar*
1 *tablespoon wine vinegar*
Salt and freshly ground pepper

I. Sauté onion and green pepper in oil in a large pot or Dutch oven until wilted, about 6 minutes. Add cabbage, caraway seeds, bay leaves, sugar, and vinegar. Toss well; cover and cook over low heat 1 hour. (If cabbage becomes too dry, add a few tablespoons of water.) Discard bay leaves. Season to taste with salt and pepper.

Serves 6.

A cabbage of a different color and nationality (Irish heritage here) comes from South Philadelphia, Pennsylvania.

This dish, curiously enough, is almost as marriageable with duck, goose, and roast pork as the preceding devise. But Phillykraut won't hurt a platter of pork tenderloin or a mess of franks, either.

What makes this sauerkraut so special? A spot of gin. (Seventh ingredient from the top!)

SOUTH PHILADELPHIA SAUERKRAUT

2 *pounds sauerkraut*
2 *tablespoons butter*
1½ *cups chopped, seeded, peeled tomatoes*
¼ *teaspoon granulated sugar*
¼ *cup Chicken Stock (see Index)*
1 *cup white wine*
1 *tablespoon gin*
1 *tablespoon caraway seeds*
⅛ *teaspoon ground allspice*
Salt and freshly ground pepper
¼ *cup chopped fresh parsley*

I.   Rinse sauerkraut under cold running water. Drain.

II.   Melt butter in a medium saucepan over medium heat. Add tomatoes, sugar, and Chicken Stock. Simmer 10 minutes. Stir in drained sauerkraut, wine, and gin. Increase heat slightly; cook 5 minutes.

III.   Reduce heat; add caraway seeds and allspice. Cook, partially covered, over low heat 45 minutes. If mixture seems too dry, add more butter. Season to taste with salt and pepper. Sprinkle with parsley.

Serves 4 to 6.

The last cabbage dish in my vegetable album contains not a speck in its formula. Dubbed *maquechoux* (masked cabbage) by the Cajuns of Louisiana, it is made of corn, tomatoes, peppers, and onions instead. And a wonderful case of false identity for your dinner table.

LOUISIANA MAQUECHOUX

6 *ears fresh corn*
2 *slices bacon*
1 *large onion, chopped*
1 *large green pepper, seeded, chopped*
2 *ripe tomatoes, seeded, chopped*
1 *teaspoon granulated sugar*
¼ *cup milk*
¼ *cup whipping cream*
¾ *teaspoon salt*
¼ *teaspoon freshly ground black pepper*
1 *tablespoon butter*

I.   Cut corn kernels from 2 ears of corn; place in a medium bowl. Using a sharp knife, cut the corn from the remaining cobs in the following manner: slice halfway into the kernels the full length of the cob. With the back of the knife, rub up and down each cob to remove all pulp and juice. Add to the whole kernels in the bowl. The mixture will resemble scrambled eggs.

II.   Sauté the bacon in a large, heavy skillet until crisp. Remove bacon; drain on paper toweling. Sauté onion and green pepper in bacon drippings until soft, about 4 minutes. Add tomatoes and sugar; cook, uncovered, 3 minutes. Reduce heat to medium. Add corn, milk, cream, salt, and pepper. Cook, stirring constantly, until corn is tender and mixture is creamy, 8 to 10 minutes. If mixture is too wet, increase heat for a few minutes. Stir in the butter; crumble cooked bacon over the top.

Serves 6.

From Detroit, a Greek-American version of raw spinach and rice baked together like a classic Mediterranean *risotto*. How this dish acquired its pejorative name I cannot tell you—but it is well worth remembering!

GREENHORN RICE

3 *tablespoons unsalted butter*
1 *tablespoon olive oil*
1 *medium onion, finely chopped*
3 *shallots, finely chopped*
1 *clove garlic, minced*
1 *cup raw rice*
1 *cup hot chicken stock*
½ *teaspoon salt*
¼ *teaspoon freshly ground pepper*
¼ *teaspoon freshly grated nutmeg*
3 *sprigs chopped fresh thyme, or* ¼ *teaspoon dried*
1 *pound fresh spinach, trimmed, washed, finely chopped*
½ *cup whipping cream*

I.   Heat oven to 375°. Heat the butter with oil in a Dutch oven over medium-low heat. Stir in onion; cook 2 minutes. Add the shallots, garlic, and rice. Cook, stirring constantly, until rice turns milky in color, about 4 minutes. Add the chicken stock, salt, pepper, nutmeg, thyme, and chopped spinach. Stir over medium-high heat until well mixed and until liquid comes to the boil.

II.   Place Dutch oven covered in oven until rice mixture dries out, about 15 minutes.

III. Remove pot from oven. Turn off oven heat. Stir cream into rice. Return covered to oven for 5 minutes.

Serves 4 to 6.

A special bonus from a South Dakota kitchen follows. "At its best when the peas are picked no longer than one-half hour before the dish is to be made," is the way I got this receipt (from a *Beaver Valley Church Bulletin*). Scandinavians like their peas practically uncooked as well. With luck, I get to the greengrocer on the same day the dish is to be prepared. But South Dakota Svenska Ärter never fails to delight my table companions!

SOUTH DAKOTA SVENSKA ÄRTER

2 *cups shelled fresh peas (about 2 pounds)*
3 *tablespoons butter*
¼ *cup water*
½ *teaspoon salt*
¼ *teaspoon ground white pepper*
¼ *cup whipping cream*
1 *egg yolk*
2 *tablespoons chopped fresh mint*
1 *teaspoon confectioners' sugar*
Pinch of cayenne pepper

I.   Combine the peas, butter, water, salt, and white pepper in a medium saucepan. Heat to boiling over high heat; reduce heat. Simmer 3 minutes.

II.   Combine the cream and egg yolk. Remove peas from heat; stir cream-yolk mixture into the peas. Return to low heat; stir until slightly thickened. Do not boil. Add mint, sugar, and cayenne pepper to taste. Serve immediately.

Serves 4.

Another South Dakota donation. This one acquired from a makeup artist in Hollywood, California, who traded recipes all the while she slathered pancake on my face for an appearance on "The Merv Griffin Show." The lady was born in Garretson,

South Dakota (of Norwegian stock), and the following cold salad is her family formula verbatim. She called it a salad. I prefer it as a cold first course. The only trick to making it is the saving up of sufficient pickle juice. But that's really no hardship. Particularly if you have a hamburger afficionado on the premises.

COLD DILLED CARROTS

4 *large carrots, cut into strips 2 inches long, ¼-inch thick*
1½ *cups dill pickle juice*
1 *cup sour cream*
1½ *tablespoons finely chopped chives*
¼ *cup chopped fresh dill*
Salt and freshly ground pepper

I.   Simmer carrots in pickle juice in a small saucepan over medium heat until tender, about 15 minutes. Let cool in juice. Chill carrots overnight in juice.

II.   Beat the sour cream in a large bowl until smooth. Add chives and 3 tablespoons dill. Drain carrots; toss into sour cream mixture. Season to taste with salt and pepper. Transfer to a serving dish. Sprinkle with remaining 1 tablespoon dill. Chill until ready to serve.

Serves 4.

Anent pickle juice: The best recipe for homemade dills that I have ever sampled comes from Morrison, Colorado. The donor is a young, energetic (and talented) mother of three named Linda Herbert. Linda gifted me with several jars of these crunchy green condiments over the years. But now that her wonderful (and easy) recipe is public domain, I suspect I will have to make my own. These pickles mature in six weeks and keep indefinitely. The brine also works wonders with the aforementioned carrots.

LINDA HERBERT'S OLD-FASHIONED DILLS

10 *cups water*
2 *cups cider vinegar*
1 *cup kosher or pickling salt*
40 *to* 50 *small cucumbers (gherkins), rinsed*
Fresh dill tops gone to seed or fresh dill sprigs with dried dill
seeds

I. Combine water, vinegar, and salt in a medium saucepan. Heat to boiling, stirring to dissolve salt; remove from heat. Cool 10 minutes.

II. Pack cucumbers into sterilized 1-pint jars. Add 3 dill tops with seeds to each jar; or add 3 fresh dill sprigs with 1½ tablespoons dried dill seeds to each jar. Pour vinegar mixture into each jar to cover. Seal. Place in hot water bath 10 minutes. Cool upside down.

III. Let pickles stand at least 8 weeks before using. Serve well chilled.

Makes about 12 pints.

A wilted green salad is an entirely Southern conceit—meant to be frothed up the moment before it is actually served. The greens may be washed and refrigerated well in advance, however, and all the dressing ingredients assembled. The whisking time? Three minutes flat!

What goes well with a wilted green salad, you ask? In a word, *chili.*

WILTED GREEN SALAD

2 *heads Boston, Bibb, or romaine lettuce (or a combination)*
4 *eggs*
¼ *cup water*
¼ *cup red wine vinegar*
Salt and freshly ground pepper
¼ *cup bacon drippings*
Dash of lemon juice

I. Separate lettuce leaves. Wash well; dry in a salad basket or with paper toweling. Place in a large bowl.

II. Beat the eggs until frothy. Beat in water, vinegar, and salt and pepper to taste.

III. Heat the bacon drippings in a small saucepan over low heat. Remove from heat; stir in egg mixture. Return to low heat and cook, stirring constantly, until sauce thickens. Add lemon juice. Do not let boil. Pour sauce over lettuce leaves in bowl. Toss well; serve immediately.

Serves 4 to 6.

There are certain lapses of culinary sensibility in the U.S. that even a deep-eyed chauvinist (like me) cannot extol with good grace. One such idiosyncracy is the Midwest and Western penchant for cold, glutinous courses (like Seven-Up Salad, Rainbow Mold, or Cherry-Cola Surprise). But then I am equally ill at ease with the French notion of splicing icy sherbets into the dead center of a full-course dinner.

Aspics and their like seem to be perfect luncheon or supper food (usually in conjunct with some cold meat, fish, or cheese) but spare me them as side dishes! One of the best of these quivering salads I have ever unmolded (and as awe-inspiring as the sunrise over Rangoon) came my way from a zealous reader in Texarkana. How she came to Burmese eggs, however, I cannot tell you. But some cook's secrets are best left unquestioned.

BURMESE EGGS ARKANSAS STYLE

3 *cups Chicken Stock (see Index)*
¼ *cup red wine vinegar*
Juice of ½ lemon
2 *tablespoons unflavored gelatin*
1 *teaspoon salt*
¾ *cup thinly sliced radishes*
1 *package (10 ounces) frozen mixed vegetables, thawed under hot running water, drained*
3 *green onions, tops and bottoms, cut into ¼-inch slices*
¼ *cup finely chopped green pepper*
1 *cup mayonnaise*
1½ *teaspoons curry powder*
Pinch of cayenne pepper
5 *cold, hard-cooked eggs, cut in half*

I.   Combine Chicken Stock, vinegar, and lemon juice in a medium saucepan. Sprinkle gelatin over the top; soften. Stir over low heat until gelatin dissolves. Add salt. Cool.

II.   Lightly oil a shallow, 6-cup ring mold. Press radish slices on sides and bottom. Chill at least 30 minutes.

III. Combine mixed vegetables, green onions, and green pepper in a large bowl. Beat mayonnaise, curry powder, and cayenne pepper in small bowl until smooth. Stir into vegetable mixture; mix well.

IV.   Stir gelatin mixture over ice until syrupy. Carefully

spoon about ⅓ cup gelatin over radishes in mold. Place mold in freezer until almost set, but still syrupy.

V.   Combine remaining gelatin mixture with vegetable mixture; mix well. Spoon half the mixture into the mold. Place in freezer 5 minutes. Arrange egg halves, cut side down, around the mold in a spoke pattern. Cover with remaining vegetable mixture. Cover; refrigerate 6 hours or overnight. To unmold, dip in hot water for a few seconds. Cover with a serving plate; turn over.

Serves 6 to 8.

My late mother had yet *another* expression. She used it frequently in her later life, although I do not recall her ever claiming to have originated it.

"It's a great life, kid," she would pronounce wryly, "if you don't weaken!"

Depleted on the subject of vegetables both hot and cold, I present my last notion. This thoroughly illegitimate stir-fry is arbitrarily served half hot and half cold. I uncovered it in Sacramento not too long ago and liked it so much that it has joined the Greene repertory of fast-faster-fastest foods!

SACRAMENTO CHINATOWN HOT SALAD

1 *cup coarsely chopped lettuce*
1 *cup coarsely chopped watercress*
3 *tablespoons vegetable oil*
1 *red bell pepper, seeded, cut into thin strips*
6 *small green onions (3 inches long each), cut down the centers*
1 *small zucchini, cut into this strips, 2 inches long, ¼-inch wide*
1 *teaspoon crushed dried hot red peppers*
8 *ounces sirloin steak, cut into thin strips*
6 *ounces fresh green beans, cut in the French style, cooked 1 minute in boiling salted water, drained*

¼ *cup chopped green onion ends*
1 *tablespoon Dijon mustard*
1 *tablespoon soy sauce*
2 *tablespoons red wine vinegar*
Salt and freshly ground pepper

I.   Combine lettuce and watercress in a large serving bowl. Set aside.

II.   Heat 2 tablespoons oil in a wok or heavy sauté pan over medium heat. Add red bell pepper; cook, stirring constantly, 5 minutes. Add green onions; cook 1 minute. Remove both to a medium bowl with a slotted spoon.

III.   Add zucchini to the pan; cook, stirring constantly, 2 minutes. Transfer to the bowl with pepper and green onions.

IV.   Add 1 tablespoon oil and dried red peppers to the pan. Increase heat slightly; quickly sauté meat on both sides. Add cooked red pepper, green onions, zucchini, green beans, and chopped green onion ends. Toss well.

V.   Combine mustard, soy sauce, and vinegar in a small bowl. Pour over vegetable-meat mixture in the pan. Toss well. Season to taste with salt and pepper. Pour mixture over lettuce and watercress. Toss well; serve immediately.

Serves 2 as a main course;
more as a luncheon dish.

PIES AND SWEETS

Chapter Nine

Somewhat sweeter-toothed than most, I must confess to feeling positively cheated at any meal that ends with mere cheese and fruit! That classical finish may have satisfied the likes of Brillat-Savarin and a few other gastronomes who came down the pike after him, but Greene's mouth definitely requires more dulcet treatment.

Small wonder that my father once dubbed me "the dentist's best friend." For I was a tad with such a proclivity for dessert that twice-yearly checkups for cavities became mandatory well into middle age!

My love for the ultimate sweet, I will state here and now, is mated with unabashed chauvinism. I think America's largess of dairies, orchards, and sugar refineries has produced some of the most memorable desserts man has ever dipped a spoon into! That opinion, however, is tempered by a prewar recollection of old-timey goodness—cream so dense and ivory-thick (sans ultra-pasteurization) that one could spread it with a knife on a sponge cake as frosting; and vine-ripened berries that came into season (as God planned it) but once a year.

The last-named victual was once so eagerly awaited that kids like myself dreamed of nothing but pink ice cream (in Technicolor) for ten eager months of the year.

Strawberries. If one was raised in the East or Midwest (or practically anywhere aside from the Sun Belt), these treats never appeared on the family table until mid-June, and then in such rosy, juice-stained profusion that they were imbibed nightly. That is, until some member of the household (like me) broke out with a rash of hives!

Fruit festivals were annual summer events in these United States in the early half of the twentieth century. And men of good appetite (like my own father) would think nothing of

cranking up their Reos or Hupmobiles and traveling thirty or
forty miles to some hamlet where a church supper or a pink
Sunday had gained far-reaching reputation because of the qual-
ity of the fruit and the quantity of the whipped cream.

Quirky Captain James Handly of Quincy, Illinois, was a
gentleman of bright ideas who marked the last Sunday in
September on the calendar as National Apple Day, back in 1905.
It was the captain's sweet notion that mankind should pay
tribute to the many virtues of this rubicund orb by a day of
heavy-duty consumption. And apple pie-eating contests were
merely one of the obligations.

As an early entrant to one of these pie-eating competitions, I
must confess that the love of apples alone does not ensure
championship. Even in the 1930s, entrepreneurism hopelessly
rigged these events for anyone with half a palate. Not only were
the apples canned, they were flavored with some synthetic
cinnamon mucilage and encased in purest pasteboard. I dropped
out of the race after two bites!

My mother, whose prowess as a cook has hardly been
extolled in these pages, was yet a wondrous baker and an
amazingly light-fingered pastry maker when I was young. Later
in life, she claimed the gift had vanished (from disuse, I suppose),
but the sweet memory of her buttery, frangible piecrusts will
remain with me forever.

A seminal devise for apple pie came about during my long
tenure as co-owner of The Store in Amagansett, where our
towering pastries ran sky-high in size (and price!). Years later,
after The Store had been sold, I visited a good friend in West
Townshend, Vermont, over Labor Day. Taking an obligatory
hike through the woods on a cool September afternoon, we came
upon a long abandoned apple orchard in what once had been a
rolling, mountainside farm. The apple trees were now hemmed
in by thick, towering pines. The trunks were gnarled, the
branches unpruned and obviously unsprayed for generations.
The fruit, however, was delectable. Rosy pink *under* the skin,
these were prime McIntosh apples. They grew high and one had
to climb to pick them. But they were well worth the effort,

tasting slightly sourish and icy to the bite. Fruit so perfect for pie, in fact, that we collected half a bushel in makeshift containers of sweaters, jackets, and assorted scarves. That yield produced the best all-American apple pie I have ever tasted!

The pie's geographic heritage? The crust was a Midwestern bequest made of unbleached flour, butter, and shortening flavored with Californian orange juice and bright slivers of peel. The lattice topping was a purely Southern conceit seasoned with a mid-Atlantic bouquet of honey, vanilla, and cinnamon. Two kinds of sugar (brown and white) sweetened those tart New England apples. The final touch, an upholstery of crumbs intersecting the fretwork crust, was obviously borrowed from the Pennsylvania Dutch. And that, I guess, almost covers the nation!

In my prejudiced opinion, there is no better dessert to be found in the world. I eat it—never with cheese—but topped with gobs of whipped, unsweetened cream, or, as my late father always called for his apple pie, "Allah Moe!"

ALL-AMERICAN APPLE PIE

Orange Crust Pastry (recipe follows)
7 to 8 medium tart apples
⅓ cup plus 1½ tablespoons all-purpose flour
¾ cup granulated sugar
¾ teaspoon ground cinnamon
⅛ teaspoon freshly grated nutmeg
½ teaspoon grated orange peel
½ teaspoon vanilla
½ cup honey
⅓ cup dark brown sugar
Pinch of ground ginger
3½ tablespoons unsalted butter
1 egg, beaten

I.   Make Orange Crust Pastry.

II.   Pare and core apples; cut into ½-inch slices. Place in a
        large bowl; toss with 1½ tablespoons flour. Add granu-
        lated sugar, ½ teaspoon cinnamon, the nutmeg, orange
        peel, and vanilla. Mix well. Stir in honey; let stand 1
        hour.

III.   Heat oven to 450°. Combine remaining ⅓ cup flour,
        remaining ¼ teaspoon cinnamon, the brown sugar, and
        ginger in a small bowl. Work in 2 tablespoons butter
        with your fingers until mixture is mealy.

IV.   Roll out half the dough; line a 9-inch pie plate. Trim.

V.   Drain apple slices, reserving liquid. Set ¼ cup crumb
        mixture aside. Layer apples with remaining crumbs in
        pastry shell. Use crumbs like mortar to build fruit up.
        Dot apples with remaining 1½ tablespoons butter.
        Sprinkle with 5 tablespoons reserved apple liquid.

VI.   Roll out remaining dough. Cut with a sharp knife into
        ½-inch wide strips. Weave strips into a lattice pattern
        over apples. Flute edges. Sprinkle remaining crumbs in
        holes of lattice. Brush pastry edge and strips with
        beaten egg.

VII.   Bake pie on an aluminum foil-lined baking sheet 5
        minutes. Reduce oven temperature to 350°; bake 50 to
        55 minutes longer.

Serves 8.

Bert Greene's kitchenry is obviously a patchwork of the
world's best recipes. My favored orange-spiked pie pastry was
originally the handiwork of Rose Naftalin, whose cookbook,

Grandma Rose's Book of SINFULLY DELICIOUS Cakes, Cook-
ies, Pies, Cheese Cakes, Cake Rolls and Pastries is a worthy
addition to any good cook's library.

ORANGE CRUST PASTRY

2½ cups all-purpose flour
½ teaspoon salt
½ cup cold unsalted butter
½ cup cold vegetable shortening
1 teaspoon grated orange peel
4 tablespoons cold orange juice

I. Sift flour with salt into a large bowl. Cut in butter and
    shortening; add orange peel. Blend with a pastry
    blender until the texture of coarse crumbs.

II. Using a fork or knife, cut orange juice into flour
    mixture to form a soft dough. (Do not overwork.)
    Refrigerate 1 hour before using.

Makes enough for two 9- or
10-inch single crusts, or one
9- or 10-inch double-crust pie.

The following receipt for Twelve-Apple Pie for Twelve
People comes from another devoted letter-writing friend who
lives in Soap Lake, Washington. My correspondent, who is
responsible for some wondrous recipes like this tonic apricot-
tinged apple formula, asks for utter anonymity in this tome, "So
my neighbors won't think that I am getting uppity in my old
age!" Her recipe is one she inherited from her mother-in-law, "a
very dear lady who came from a large family in Ephrata." My

friend also abjures the unwary cook "to only bake this super pie when some big eaters are in residence!" But that's *your* moral dilemma.

TWELVE-APPLE PIE FOR TWELVE PEOPLE

Darlene Schulz's Pie Pastry (recipe follows)
1 *package (6 ounces) dried apricots*
1 *cup orange juice*
¾ *cup granulated sugar*
1 *curl orange peel (about 4 inches)*
12 *tart green apples*
2½ *tablespoons all-purpose flour*
1¼ *cups light brown sugar*
1 *teaspoon vanilla*
1 *teaspoon grated lemon rind*
3 *tablespoons unsalted butter*
1 *egg, beaten*

I.   Make Darlene Schulz's Pie Pastry.

II.   Combine apricots, orange juice, granulated sugar, and orange curl in a medium saucepan. Heat to boiling, stirring constantly; reduce heat. Simmer over medium-low heat until apricots are tender, about 20 minutes. Cool. Finely sliver the orange peel.

III.   Heat oven to 425°. Roll out half the dough and line a ceramic or glass 10-inch pie plate. Trim.

IV.   Pare and core apples; cut into ½-inch slices. Place in a large bowl; toss with the flour. Add brown sugar and vanilla. Stir in cooled apricot mixture and slivered orange peel. Mix well.

V.   Layer a third of the apple mixture in the pastry shell. (Do not let slices sit until syrupy.) Sprinkle with ½ teaspoon lemon rind. Dot with 1 tablespoon butter. Layer another third of the apple mixture into shell. Sprinkle with remaining ½ teaspoon lemon rind. Dot with 1 tablespoon butter. Add remaining apple mixture, piling apples high in center. Dot with remaining 1 tablespoon butter. Roll out remaining dough. Place over apples. Seal and flute edges. With a sharp knife, cut 4 slits in top of pie to allow steam to escape. Brush pastry with beaten egg.

VI.   Bake pie on an aluminum foil-lined baking sheet 15 minutes. Reduce oven temperature to 350°; bake 45 minutes longer.

Serves 12.

One of the best (and briefest) pastry formulas in my bake-off repertoire is the donation of my good friend Darlene Schulz. One of the best cooks in Brownsville, Wisconsin, and the surrounding environs, Darlene brought this vinegar-tinctured recipe for piecrust from South Dakota when she married and emigrated some while back. The culinary exercise has given architecture to some mighty impressive desserts ever since!

DARLENE SCHULZ'S PIE PASTRY

2 cups plus 2 teaspoons all-purpose flour
2 teaspoons granulated sugar
1 teaspoon salt
¾ cup lard
1 egg, beaten
1½ teaspoons wine vinegar
2 tablespoons cold water

I.   Sift 2 cups flour with sugar and salt into a large bowl. Cut in lard. Blend with a pastry blender until the texture of coarse crumbs.

II.   Combine egg, vinegar, and water in a small bowl. Using a fork or knife, cut into flour mixture to form a soft dough. (Do not overwork.) Sprinkle with remaining 2 teaspoons flour. Chill 1 hour before using.

Makes enough for two 9- or
10-inch single crusts, or one
9- or 10-inch double-crust pie.

From the Kent County Apple Festival in Michigan comes a mirific notion for a grated apple-custard pie (dubbed "Shredded Treat") that more than lives up to its name. This dish is positively addictive whether one is apple lover or no!

"SHREDDED TREAT" APPLE PIE

Darlene Schulz's Pie Pastry (see preceding recipe)
1 tablespoon grated orange peel
2 teaspoons grated lemon rind
¼ cup orange juice
1 tablespoon lemon juice
4 cups grated, pared raw apples (about 2¼ pounds)
1½ cups granulated sugar
1½ tablespoons all-purpose flour
2 eggs, beaten
2 tablespoons whipping cream
Whipped cream or vanilla ice cream

I.   Make Darlene Schulz's Pie Pastry.

II.   Heat oven to 450°. Combine orange peel, lemon rind, orange juice, and lemon juice in a large bowl. Grate apples and add to mixture as you grate them. Stir in sugar, flour, and eggs. Mix well.

III.   Roll out half the dough and line a 9-inch pie plate. Trim. Spoon grated apple mixture into shell.

IV.   Roll out remaining dough. Cut with a sharp knife into ½-inch-wide strips. Weave strips into a lattice pattern over apple mixture. Flute edges. Brush pastry with 2 tablespoons whipping cream.

V.   Bake on an aluminum foil-lined baking sheet 10 minutes. Reduce oven temperature to 350°; bake 30 minutes longer. Serve warm with whipped cream or vanilla ice cream.

Serves 8.

During the past year and a half, I have been lucky enough to teach cooking in more than seventy American cities. One benefit of all that cross-country stove-hopping is a valise full of unusual native receipts that return home with the chef.

In my book, the only unsuccessful class I ever taught was the one where no one proffered a maxim for Grandma's fudge or Aunt Em's buttermilk waffles. (Name and place on request!)

From Hoosier country (Indiana), I received the following note, not too long ago.

Dear Mr. Greene,

Last fall I attended your cooking class at The Pan Handler in Indianapolis. I enjoyed it very much. We discussed recipes and I told you about a favorite of mine . . . a pie that was passed down to me from the "Amish people."

This being such an unusual pie, I thought you would be interested . . .

Most sincerely,

Mrs. Dorothy (Dottie) Johnson

More than interested, I was enthralled. The bequest was for my favorite kind of dessert; a culinary oddity composed of a delicate island of cake afloat on a sea of lemon sauce. The "Montgomery" who gave it name I will probably never know, but the aforementioned Dottie Johnson gets a salvo of grateful thanks right here and now!

MONTGOMERY PIE

Short Crust Pastry (recipe follows)
2 eggs
¼ cup lemon juice
2 teaspoons grated lemon rind
½ cup granulated sugar
1½ cups plus 2 tablespoons all-purpose flour
1 cup water
4 tablespoons butter, softened
⅔ cup granulated sugar
1 tablespoon baking powder
1 cup milk

I. Make Short Crust Pastry.

II. Heat oven to 350°. Roll out pastry and line a 9-inch pie plate. Trim and flute edges.

III. Beat 1 egg with lemon juice, lemon rind, ½ cup sugar, 2 tablespoons flour, and 1 cup water in a medium bowl. Pour into shell.

IV. Beat butter with 1 egg in a large bowl. Slowly beat in ⅔ cup sugar and the baking powder. Add milk in three parts, alternating with three parts of the remaining 1½ cups flour. Beat until smooth. Spoon mixture over filling in shell. Bake until a toothpick inserted in center comes out clean, 35 to 40 minutes. Cook on a wire rack. To serve, cut into wedges. Spoon the sauce over the top.

Serves 6 to 8.

SHORT CRUST PASTRY

1 *cup all-purpose flour*
¼ *teaspoon salt*
4 *tablespoons cold unsalted butter*
1½ *tablespoons cold vegetable shortening*
2½ *to 3 tablespoons cold water*

I. Sift flour with salt into a large bowl. Cut in butter and shortening. Blend with a pastry blender until the texture of coarse crumbs. Add just enough water to form a soft dough. Chill 1 hour before using.

Makes enough for one 8- to 9-inch single-crust pie.

I never heard of Funeral Pie until I went to an Irish-Catholic wake in south Philadelphia a year or so ago. Strictly speaking, it was a dessert eaten out of context but quite delicious nonetheless. The origin of this dish is the Pennsylvania Dutch country southwest of Philadelphia. There among the Mennonites it has been a tradition for years to send some baked gift to the family of the deceased. Nuts and raisins are the chief ingredients of this offering, and on a less moribund note I would beg you to consider the homely legacy for your next Thanksgiving dinner. It makes a nice change from mince and pumpkin. And think of therapeutic table conversation once you reveal the dessert's true cognomen!

FUNERAL PIE

Darlene Schulz's Pie Pastry (see Index)
2 *cups raisins*
1 *cup orange juice*
1 *cup water*
1 *teaspoon grated orange peel*
¾ *cup plus 1 tablespoon granulated sugar*
2 *tablespoons cornstarch*
¾ *teaspoon ground allspice*
⅛ *teaspoon freshly grated nutmeg*
1 *tablespoon lemon juice*
½ *cup chopped walnuts*
1 *egg, beaten*
Whipped cream or vanilla ice cream

I.   Make Darlene Schulz's Pie Pastry.

II.   Heat oven to 425°. Roll out half the dough and line a 9-inch pie plate. Trim.

III.   Combine the raisins, orange juice, water, and orange peel in a medium saucepan. Heat to boiling; reduce heat. Simmer over medium heat 5 minutes.

IV.   Combine ¾ cup sugar, the cornstarch, allspice, and nutmeg in a small bowl. Stir this mixture slowly into raisin mixture. Cook, stirring constantly, until thickened, about 2 minutes. Stir in lemon juice and walnuts. Pour into pie shell.

V.   Roll out remaining dough. Cover raisin mixture. Trim and flute edges. Cut slits in top of pie to allow steam to escape. Brush with beaten egg; sprinkle with remaining 1 tablespoon sugar.

VI.   Bake pie until golden, 20 to 25 minutes. Serve warm
        with whipped cream or vanilla ice cream.

Serves 8.

In New Iberia, Louisiana, there is a wonderfully artful
dessert that can only be secured by calling Mrs. Usea Bourque
and placing an order several weeks in advance. For Mrs.
Bourque makes her double-crust cream pies at home, as a favor
to local aficionados only. These pies are widely heralded on Mrs.
Bourque's home territory, but I heard a mouth-watering report
of them about 150 miles away in New Orleans. The recipe for
this soothing custard tart was passed down in Mrs. Bourque's
family (from mother to daughter) for over a century. She gave it
to me two years ago—and now it's yours as well!

TARTE AU BOUILLE GINGEMBRE

Tart Pastry (recipe follows)
2 egg yolks
⅓ cup granulated sugar
3 tablespoons cornstarch
1 teaspoon ground ginger
2 tablespoons cold milk
2 cups hot milk
2 tablespoons cold unsalted butter
1 teaspoon vanilla

I.   Make Tart Pastry.

II.   Beat egg yolks and sugar with a wire whisk in the top
        of a double boiler until light. Mix cornstarch, ginger,
        and cold milk in a small bowl; stir into egg yolk

mixture. Whisk in hot milk. Cook over boiling water, stirring constantly, until consistency of a thick white sauce, about 30 minutes. Beat in butter by bits. Beat in vanilla. Refrigerate covered with waxed paper until cold, about 15 minutes.

III.   Heat oven to 400°. Roll three-fourths of the dough into a large circle. Line a 9-inch pie plate. (Pastry is fragile, so patience is a must here.) The pastry should hang over the edge slightly, about ½ inch. Spoon custard into pastry shell.

IV.   Roll out remaining dough between 2 sheets of lightly floured waxed paper to a 10-inch circle. (Pastry will be paper-thin.) Remove top piece of waxed paper. Invert pastry onto custard, gently removing remaining paper.

V.   Carefully tuck top crust under custard at edge with a spoon. Fold overhanging edge of bottom crust up over the top crust. Press edges lightly with a fork. Bake until golden, 25 to 30 minutes. Cool completely on a wire rack.

Serves 8.

TART PASTRY

3 *tablespoons softened vegetable shortening*
⅓ *cup granulated sugar*
1 *egg*
2 *tablespoons milk*
2 *teaspoons vanilla*
1 *teaspoon baking powder*
1 *to* 1½ *cups all-purpose flour*

I. Cream shortening and sugar in a large bowl. Add egg; beat until smooth. Beat in milk and vanilla. Stir in baking powder and enough flour to make a stiff dough. Refrigerate 4 hours or overnight before using.

Makes enough for two 9-inch single-crust tarts or one 9-inch double-crust tart.

Peach and Almond Grunt (originally tasted in Nashua, New Hampshire) is a first cousin to New England's other traditional fruit oddities like cobblers, slumps, and dowdies. The *grunt* is a sort of deep-dish pie blanketed with crumbs instead of crust.

I suggest you make it any time from late July to early October, when the peaches turn gold-crimson in color and the juice runs free as the Pemigewasset River.

PEACH AND ALMOND GRUNT

2½ pounds fresh peaches
2 cups granulated sugar
¼ cup bourbon
1 tablespoon orange juice
1 teaspoon grated orange peel
⅛ teaspoon almond extract
4½ tablespoons unsalted butter
¾ cup toasted blanched almonds, ground
½ cup all-purpose flour
Pinch of salt
¼ teaspoon ground cinnamon
1 teaspoon vanilla
2 tablespoons whipping cream
Amaretto-flavored whipped cream or vanilla ice cream

I.   Place peaches in boiling water 1 minute to loosen skins; drain. Peel; remove peach pits; cut each peach into 8 slices.

II.   Place sliced peaches with 1½ cups sugar, the bourbon, orange juice, orange peel, and almond extract in a large saucepan. Heat to boiling; reduce heat. Simmer 10 minutes. Drain peach slices in a colander over another saucepan, reserving liquid. Reserve slices. Heat peach liquid to boiling; boil until thick and syrupy, about 14 minutes. (Do not burn.)

III.   Grease a shallow, 2½-quart baking dish with ½ table-spoon butter. Arrange well-drained peach slices over the bottom. Pour only enough reduced liquid over the top to barely cover the fruit. Cool.

IV.   Heat oven to 400°. Combine ground almonds, remaining ½ cup sugar, the flour, salt, and cinnamon in a large bowl. Cut in remaining 4 tablespoons butter. Blend with a pastry blender until the texture of coarse crumbs. Add vanilla and 2 tablespoons whipping cream. Mix well. Sprinkle mixture over the top of the peaches.

V.   Bake grunt 20 minutes. Let stand 10 minutes before serving with Amaretto-flavored whipped cream or vanilla ice cream.

Serves 6 to 8.

The next formula for an Impossible Pie was uncovered in *The Naper Sampler*, a cookbook published by The Naperville School of Illinois. A plastic-bound copy of this local food collection was sent to me by Jeanette Deschamps, a resident of Naperville, who knew I was hot on the trail of regional cuisine.

To be sure, *The Naper Sampler* is no instant gold mine to gourmands. But weed through the canons for "Wacky Cake," "Play Dough," "Mock Veal Cutlets," and Guacamok Dip," and you will find the following wonderful offering.

A dessert that is concocted entirely in a blender container (in less than five minutes) and baked for a mere hour, Impossible Pie surely represents fast food's finest hour.

IMPOSSIBLE PIE

3 *eggs*
¼ *cup unsalted butter, cut into bits*
½ *cup all-purpose flour*
1 *cup granulated sugar*
2 *cups milk*
¼ *teaspoon salt*
½ *teaspoon baking powder*
1 *teaspoon vanilla*
2 *tablespoons orange liqueur*
1 *cup grated fresh coconut*

I. Heat oven to 350°. Place all ingredients in the order given in a blender container. Blend at low speed 30 seconds. Blend at high speed 2 minutes.

II. Pour mixture into a lightly greased, 10-inch ceramic quiche pan or glass pie plate. Bake 1 hour. Cool completely on a wire rack.

Serves 8 to 10.

Key Lime Mousse is a strictly Florida dividend, an airy, sour-sweet rendering of that state's green citrus harvest. I must confess that I have never been able to acquire any Key limes to make an authentic mousse on local turf, so do not feel similarly deprived. Merely make do with conventional limes—the mousse will be monumental anyhow!

KEY LIME MOUSSE

4 *Key limes, or 3 regular-sized limes*
4 *eggs, separated*
1½ *cups granulated sugar*
1 *tablespoon unflavored gelatin*
¼ *cup cold water*
1 *teaspoon cornstarch*
¼ *cup Grand Marnier liqueur*
1½ *cups whipping cream*
3 *tablespoons confectioners' sugar*
¾ *cup whipping cream*

I.   Roll the limes back and forth on a flat surface for a few minutes to release juices. Grate the rind from the limes; reserve. Squeeze the juice; reserve.

II.   Beat the egg yolks with granulated sugar until mixture is lemon colored and forms a ribbon when spooned back on itself.

III.   Soften the gelatin in ¼ cup cold water. Place over hot water and stir until gelatin is dissolved.

IV.   Combine the cornstarch and a third of the lime juice in a large bowl; whisk until smooth. Add remaining juice, reserved rind, and gelatin. Stir well; add to the beaten egg yolk mixture. Transfer to the top of a double boiler and cook, stirring constantly, over hot water until it begins to thicken. Add 2 tablespoons Grand Marnier; cook 1 minute. Chill until set.

V.   Whip 1½ cups cream with confectioners' sugar and remaining 2 tablespoons Grand Marnier until stiff. Beat the egg whites until stiff. Fold the cream and then the egg whites into the lime mixture. (If the mixture has become lumpy, beat until smooth with a few drops of boiling water before adding whipped cream and egg whites.) Spoon into a soufflé dish or serving bowl. Whip ¾ cup cream until stiff; pipe a decorative lattice design over the top. Chill for 4 hours before serving.

Serves 8 to 10.

My first and only trip to Puerto Rico was blemished by an extraordinary quest for chocolate flan. I had had this dessert on my initial dinner outing in Old San Juan, and I became so infatuated with the elusive flavor of the velvety bronze custard that I went through every possible means to secure the recipe. This included a visit to the minister of the Interior, who sagely persuaded me that culinary matters are internal rather than inter-territorial.

Eventually (by bribing a waiter) I managed to acquire enough information about the ingredients to reconstruct a pale imitation of this elegant dessert in my own kitchen. But truth to tell, the seasoning wanted spirit somehow. After many tests (and failures), Phillip Schulz, my cooking associate, and I went over every possible flavoring agent that might be responsible for the lack of piquancy. We started with A (anise), B (banana), C (coffee), and on until we reached R (rum). Instantly, we knew the subtle element our flan lacked. Rum—only a tablespoon—was added, but at last the flan flew!

PUERTO RICO CHOCOLATE FLAN

1 *cup granulated sugar*
2 *cups milk*
½ *cup whipping cream*
½ *teaspoon vanilla*

2 *ounces sweet cooking chocolate, broken into pieces*
2 *tablespoons creme de cacao liqueur*
1 *tablespoon golden rum (I prefer Puerto Rican Bacardi)*
3 *eggs*
3 *egg yolks*
½ *cup whipping cream, whipped (optional)*

I.   Heat oven to 350°. Warm a 1-quart soufflé dish in oven 5 to 6 minutes.

II.   Meanwhile, heat ½ cup granulated sugar in a small saucepan over high heat until sugar starts to melt; cook, stirring constantly with a wooden spoon, until sugar liquifies. Reduce heat; cook, stirring constantly, until caramel turns deep golden. Remove from heat.

III.   Pour caramel into the warmed soufflé dish, turning dish to coat bottom and sides. Invert dish on a piece of aluminum foil (to prevent drippings from hardening on any work surface); let stand to cool. (Do not worry if caramel does not look smooth.)

IV.   Heat milk, cream, and vanilla in a medium saucepan over low heat. Add broken chocolate; heat until mixture is smooth and all chocolate thoroughly dissolves. Add crème de cacao and rum; remove from heat.

V.   Beat eggs and egg yolks in a large bowl. Beat in ½ cup sugar until light and lemon colored. Gradually pour the warm chocolate-milk mixture into the egg mixture, stirring constantly.

VI.   Pour custard into caramel-coated soufflé dish. Place dish in a roasting pan on middle rack in oven. Pour boiling water into roasting pan to half the depth of the soufflé dish. Bake until a knife inserted in center comes out fairly clean, about 1 hour. (Do not let water in roasting pan boil; if it begins to boil, add cold water.) Cool flan on a wire rack; refrigerate at least 6 hours or overnight.

VII.　To unmold flan: heat 1 inch of water in a skillet to boiling; turn off heat. Dip a sharp knife in water; run it around the sides of the flan. Dip bottom of soufflé dish in skillet for a few seconds. Place a serving dish over the soufflé dish and invert; remove soufflé dish. Decorate flan with swirls of whipped cream if desired.

Note:　Flan may be prepared through step 3 and left standing 4 to 5 hours before you proceed with next steps.

Serves 8.

Ohio, it has been said, is an olfactory wonderland. Cincinnati smells of juniper berries from its gin distilleries; Cleveland smells of salt brine and, when the lake breezes blow in spring, of shrimp and shellfish, too. Akron smells of rubber. Best of all the scents to me is the Sunday perfume of buttermilk waffles in Lebanon. The most famous restaurant in town is The Golden Lamb. I ate there almost thirty years ago, but I can only hope the policy of freshly made hot cakes, slathered with buttermilk fudge and homemade ice cream for Sunday dinner, still obtains. If not, have this beautific substitution!

BUTTERMILK WAFFLES
WITH BUTTERMILK FUDGE SAUCE

FOR THE BUTTERMILK FUDGE SAUCE:
2 *ounces unsweetened chocolate*
2 *ounces semisweet chocolate*
2 *tablespoons unsalted butter*

2 *tablespoons light corn syrup*
½ *cup granulated sugar*
¾ *cup whipping cream*
2 *tablespoons buttermilk*

FOR THE BUTTERMILK WAFFLES:
3 *eggs, separated*
⅓ *cup unsalted butter, melted*
2 *cups buttermilk (approximately)*
1¾ *cups sifted all-purpose flour*
1 *teaspoon baking soda*
2 *tablespoons granulated sugar*
Confectioners' sugar
Vanilla ice cream

I.   To make the buttermilk fudge sauce: Combine chocolates with butter in the top of a double boiler over simmering water. Stir until smooth. Add corn syrup, sugar, whipping cream, and buttermilk. Cook, stirring constantly, 10 minutes. Cool. Refrigerate in a jar until ready to use.

II.   To make the waffles: Beat the egg yolks in a large bowl until light. Beat in melted butter and 2 cups buttermilk.

III.   Sift the flour with baking soda and granulated sugar in a small bowl. Add to yolk-buttermilk mixture. Beat until smooth. (Add more buttermilk if batter seems too thick.) Beat egg whites until stiff; fold into batter.

IV.   Spoon batter into a preheated waffle iron. Bake until steam has stopped coming from edges of iron, about 5 minutes. (Waffles should be crisp and golden.) Remove waffles. Keep warm on a rack in a low oven until all waffles are prepared.

V.	Reheat buttermilk fudge sauce in the top of a double boiler until smooth and warmed through. Sprinkle the waffles with confectioners' sugar. Place a scoop of vanilla ice cream on each serving. Spoon fudge sauce over the top (plus a dab of whipped cream, if you dare!).

Serves 6 to 8.

From Ashland, Kentucky, comes the humblest regional American dessert I know: pan-fried pears. Of course, tradition decrees it is best to use the blue graniteware frying pan your grandmother used. ". . . And fresh honey from a feudin' hive up Big Sandy Creek won't hurt the dish a mite, neither!" That is the definitive word from the recipe's donor, Jean Ingalls, who passed her family treasure along to me last spring. No wonder some Blue Grass preacher once declared that "Heaven is obviously a Kentucky sorta place!"

PAN-FRIED PEARS WITH CLABBERED CREAM

2 *tablespoons honey*
½ *cup water*
4 *fresh ripe pears, pared, cored, cut in half*
Fresh raspberries or strawberries
¼ *cup Clabbered Cream (see Index)*

I.	Combine honey and water in a large sauté pan. Heat to simmering over medium-low heat, stirring to dissolve the honey. Add pears, cut side down. Cover; simmer 8 minutes. Turn pears over. Cover; simmer until tender, about 8 minutes.

II.	Transfer pears to a serving dish with slotted spoon. Boil liquid in sauté pan until syrupy. Pour over pears. Serve warm or at room temperature, decorated with fresh raspberries or strawberries. Serve with about 1 tablespoon Clabbered Cream for each person.

Serves 4.

The most lofty tart in my sweet repertoire is a tranquil lemon compound—French in derivation perhaps but 100 percent American in its unorthodox formula. This prodigious golden achievement is the handicraft of a young chef at La Métairie restaurant in Greenwich Village, Jane Keller. Jane is pretty, talented, and generous in the bargain. Sharing her recipe with me, she cautioned that the tart should be baked ". . . only until the center is solidish to the touch of a finger."

The female touch, evidently—my tart cracked in the center twice during the testing. But otherwise it was perfection!

LEMON TART

½ recipe Orange Crust Pastry (see Index)
6 eggs
⅔ cup granulated sugar
Juice of 4 lemons
1½ cups whipping cream
6 tablespoons butter, melted

I.　　　Make a half recipe of Orange Crust Pastry.

II.　　　Heat oven to 400°. Roll out pastry on a lightly floured board. Line a 10-inch, loose-bottom tart pan. Line pastry with aluminum foil; weight with beans. Bake 10 minutes. Remove foil and beans; bake 5 minutes. Cool. Reduce oven temperature to 325°.

III.   Beat the eggs and sugar in a large bowl until light and
        lemon colored. Add lemon juice, cream, and melted
        butter. Pour into shell. Bake until firm, about 45 min-
        utes.

Serves 6 to 8.

Ice cream and ices were the pleasures of my childhood. I
know that seems tame stuff compared with the highs of today's
roller-disco generation. But, truth to tell, I dearly adored the
mundane when I was young.

I spent my summers hoarding up nickels for visits from
either the Eskimo Pie man or the hokey-pokey wagon. Both were
a breed of primitive vendor who seemed to vanish from the
suburban sprawl long before the outbreak of World War II, and
I cannot accurately remember much of their offerings—except
for the mode of conveyance. The Eskimo Pie man always carried
his wares (chocolate-covered slabs of vanilla ice cream) in a
portable ice chest that was strapped to his broad back. The chest
had to be removed and set on the ground before he could reach
into its vapory depths to make a new transaction. The hokey-
pokey wagon, on the other hand, was a two-wheeled enterprise
that was generally trundled into a neighborhood after sundown,
when the bosky light sheltered its wares from any overhygenic
scrutiny.

Hokey-pokeys sold neither ice cream nor ices, but rather a
mysterious concoction all their own which was held in parental
disfavor because of its dubious origin. From under a gaudily
striped umbrella, the purveyor dispensed small, pleated cups of
shaved ice, liberally sludged with a choice of flavorings, to a
crowd of mesmerized young buyers lined up for the privilege.

It cost two cents a throw for the option of a neon-orange,
neon-lemon, or neon-lime syrup that turned each snowdrift
container brilliantly aglow, and stained hands, shirt, and hand-
kerchiefs the same lethal shade for weeks afterward. For an

additional penny, the hokey-pokey man added a spritz of a particularly phosphorescent, magenta-hued liquid. Neither cherry, strawberry, nor currant, the flavor tasted exactly the way it was named by the kids on my block in Jackson Heights, "Dirty Red."

Almost forty years have passed since my first infatuation with frozen sweets. But the old appetite is still whetted by the mettle of sugar, ice, and fruit in some wondrous (if gumstinging) conjunction. For starters, have the following native bouquet!

My Thanksgiving table has been made bright for years with the addition of a New England table relish (concocted of fresh, uncooked cranberries, pineapple, and oranges). Recently, I froze the stuff instead. Not exactly a classic sorbet, but like enough to be its twin, this old-fashioned sweet is dubbed a *shrub!*

CRANBERRY SHRUB

1 *package (1 pound) cranberries*
2 *cups coarsely chopped, fresh pineapple*
1 *cup superfine sugar*
½ *cup chopped seeded orange pulp*
1 *tablespoon finely slivered orange peel*
1 *tablespoon orange liqueur*
Curls of orange peel
Sweetened whipped cream (optional)

I.   Combine cranberries, pineapple, sugar, orange pulp, and orange peel. Process in a food processor (or in batches in blender) with rapid on-off turns until coarsely chopped. Transfer to a large, metal bowl. Stir in orange liqueur.

II.   Either pour mixture into the canister of an ice cream freezer and proceed according to manufacturer's directions, or cover the metal bowl and place in freezer until frozen 2 inches in from the sides, about 2 hours. Scrape down frozen part; beat with an electric mixer until uniform in texture; return to freezer. Repeat process twice, allowing mixture to freeze solid after the final beating. To serve, garnish with curls of orange peel. Or top with sweetened whipped cream.

Makes about 5 cups.

The next two sherbets have varying geographic origins. The Red Currant Thaw is a North Dakota beneficence and the Blueberry Freeze was discovered in Vermont. However, they are both old formulas, easier to make than ice cream because they take less freezing time—which means less work for mother (or brother, as the case may be!). They are also darned good to eat. The red currant mix will alter any ideas you had of that sourish fruit after a first taste, I promise. The Blueberry Freeze is somewhat of a more mystical merger: sour cream turns the Green Mountain State fruit a blushing purple color and adds a tart flavor that invigorates the spoon. You'll love it, too!

RED CURRANT THAW

1 *pint fresh red currants, stems removed*
1 *cup granulated sugar*
1 *cup water*
3 *tablespoons orange juice*
2 *tablespoons kirschwasser (cherry brandy)*

I. Combine currants, sugar, and water in a medium saucepan. Heat to boiling; reduce heat. Simmer 5 minutes. Cool.

II. Process in a food processor (or in batches in a blender) until smooth. Press through a fine sieve over a large, metal bowl to extract seeds. Stir in orange juice and kirschwasser.

III.   Either pour mixture into the canister of an ice cream freezer and proceed according to manufacturer's directions, or cover metal bowl and place in freezer until frozen 2 inches in from the sides, about 2 hours. Scrape down frozen part; beat with an electric mixer until uniform in texture; return to freezer. Repeat process twice, allowing mixture to freeze solid after the final beating.

Makes about 1 quart.

BLUEBERRY FREEZE

1 *bright-skinned orange*
8 *sugar cubes*
3 *tablespoons orange juice*
1 *pint blueberries, hulled*
¾ *cup granulated sugar*
¾ *cup water*
1 *tablespoon lemon juice*
½ *teaspoon ground cinnamon*
½ *cup sour cream*

I.   Rub the surface of the orange with sugar cubes to extract the oil of the fruit. Place cubes, 3 tablespoons orange juice, the blueberries, sugar, water, lemon juice, and cinnamon in a medium saucepan. Heat to boiling; reduce heat. Simmer 10 minutes. Cool.

II.   Process in a food processor (or in batches in blender) until smooth. Transfer to a large, metal bowl. Beat in sour cream.

III.　　　Either pour mixture into the canister of an ice cream freezer and proceed according to manufacturer's directions, or cover metal bowl and place in freezer until frozen 2 inches in from the sides, about 2 hours. Scrape down frozen part; beat with an electric mixer until uniform in texture; return to freezer. Repeat process twice, allowing mixture to freeze solid after the final beating.

Makes about 1½ quarts.

South Carolina has a long history of dessert-loving citizens. I have in my possession a yellowed Charleston dinner menu (circa 1898) that describes a meal which ends with eight pies, two floating islands, syllabub, a bowl of mousse, and benne wafers—with a ginger ice to clear the palate afterward.

Calorically, I eschew all the foregoing sweets (except for that sharp-tongued ice!). The devise for it is printed below. But be forewarned, it is truly a *zinger!* At my table I often anesthetize the bite with drifts of whipped cream.

GINGER-LEMON ICE

12 *large lemons*
4 *cups water*
3 *cups granulated sugar*
1 *tablespoon grated lemon peel*
1½ *tablespoons grated fresh ginger root*

I.　　　Cut lemons in half. Scoop out pulp; discard seeds. Place pulp in a blender container; puree until smooth.

II.　　　Heat water and sugar in a large saucepan to boiling.

Boil 5 minutes. Remove from heat. Stir in lemon puree, lemon peel, and ginger. Cool.

III.   Either pour mixture into the canister of an ice cream freezer and proceed according to manufacturer's directions, or pour into a large metal bowl, cover, and place in freezer until frozen 2 inches in from the sides, about 2 hours. Scrape down frozen part; beat with an electric mixer until uniform in texture. Return to freezer. Repeat process twice, allowing mixture to freeze solid after the final beating.

Makes about 1½ quarts.

The dream berries of my youth come home to roost in two favored varieties of sweet maturity. The first is a street ice (a fabrication of fruit, sugar, cream, and water), only vaguely connected to the slurps dished up by my chimerical friend, the hokey-pokey man.

This rosy treat was concocted by Salvatore DiLorenzo of Mulberry Street, in New York's Little Italy. He served it and espresso alone for years and years at his small establishment near Spring Street. For the same spate of time, I attempted to duplicate the magic of his ice at home, with a signal lack of success. Shortly before he retired and shuttered his small business forever, Mr. DiLorenzo confided the secret of the wondrous strawberry sherbet. "Raspberries," he said succinctly. "I add raspberries! Makes it sweeter!"

NEW YORK-STYLE STRAWBERRY ICE

1 *quart fresh strawberries, hulled*
1 *package (10 ounces) frozen raspberries, thawed, juice reserved*
1 *cup granulated sugar*
¾ *cup cold water (approximately)*
½ *cup whipping cream*

I.   Combine strawberries, raspberries, sugar, and 1½ cups liquid (about ¾ cup raspberry juice, plus water). Process in a food processor (or in batches in blender) until smooth. Transfer to a large, metal bowl.

II.   Beat the cream until soft peaks form. Fold into strawberry mixture.

III.   Either pour mixture into the canister of an ice cream freezer and proceed according to manufacturer's directions, or cover metal bowl and place in freezer until frozen 2 inches in from the sides, about 2 hours. Scrape down frozen part; beat with an electric mixer until uniform in texture; return to freezer. Repeat process twice, allowing mixture to freeze solid after the final beating.

Makes about 1¼ quarts.

Ice cream in Kansas is reputedly richer than the kind they make in Philadelphia (which contains the highest degree of butterfat in the country). Why? Because their whipping cream is still resolutely non-ultrapasteurized. From Topeka, coincidentally, comes my favorite strawberry ice cream—all gussied up with cognac and kirschwasser, just like some eastern recipe. Only it's better, because the berries bloom later on the Great Plains.

STRAWBERRY ICE CREAM

1 *quart fresh strawberries, hulled*
⅓ *cup granulated sugar*
2 *teaspoons kirschwasser (cherry brandy)*
1¼ *cups granulated sugar*
3 *egg yolks*
2 *tablespoons cornstarch*
2 *cups whipping cream*

¼ *cup milk*
1 *vanilla bean (1½ inches long)*
2 *teaspoons unsalted butter*
2 *teaspoons cognac*
2 *tablespoons orange liqueur*

I.   Cut strawberries in half; reserve 1 cup. Combine re-
        maining strawberries, ⅓ cup sugar, and the kirsch-
        wasser. Process in a food processor (or in batches in
        blender) until smooth. Let stand 1 hour.

II.   Beat 1¼ cups sugar and the egg yolks in top of a 2-
        quart double boiler until thick and lemon colored. Beat
        in cornstarch until smooth. Beat in ¼ cup whipping
        cream and the milk; add vanilla bean. Heat mixture
        over simmering water, stirring frequently, until thick
        enough to coat a spoon. Remove from heat. Remove
        vanilla bean. Split bean, scraping seeds into mixture;
        discard bean. Stir in butter and cognac. Cool.

III.   Mince reserved strawberries. Combine with vanilla
        custard in a large bowl. Add pureed strawberries,
        remaining 1¾ cups cream, and the orange liqueur. Pour
        into the canister of an ice cream freezer and proceed
        according to manufacturer's directions.

                                        Makes about 1½ quarts.

The greengage plums of Williamsburg, Virginia, bloomed
long before I went to college there in the 1940s. It is rumored
that Thomas Jefferson originally invented an ice cream from
this native fruit. Whatever, it is quite a traditional Virginian's
summer treat on The Duke of Gloucester Street. My version is at
variance with the mint edition of this recipe, since it may be

made with any color plums in season. If you are determined to be a traditionalist or have a greengage tree on the premises, however, be my guest!

WILLIAMSBURG PLUM ICE CREAM

3 *egg yolks*
1¼ *cups granulated sugar*
1 *cup warm light cream*
1½ *pounds fresh, tart plums (see Note)*
2 *tablespoons orange liqueur*
1 *cup whipping cream*
¼ *cup lemon juice*

I. Beat the egg yolks and the sugar in the top of a double boiler until light and lemon colored. Stir in light cream. Cook over simmering water, stirring frequently, until thick enough to coat a spoon. Cool.

II. Drop the plums in boiling water for about 2 minutes to loosen the skins. Peel; remove pits.

III. Process peeled plums in a food processor (or in batches in blender) until smooth. Transfer to a large bowl. Add cooled custard, the orange liqueur, whipping cream, and lemon juice. Mix well. Pour into the canister of an ice cream freezer and proceed according to manufacturer's directions.

Note: The original Williamsburg receipt for plum ice cream used greengage plums. If you have that variety, use about 1½ cups fresh plums. Also, ¼ teaspoon green food coloring is usually added to give the desired shade of greengage. That's up to you.

Makes 1½ quarts.

CAKES AND
COOKIES

Chapter Ten

Culinary debts are rarely paid in full.

I, for instance, have never properly acknowledged the overwhelming influence of the late Dione Lucas (my first and only cooking teacher) on my kitchen sensibilities.

Dione was a handsome Englishwoman, presumably of high birth, who, through some Gilbert and Sullivan-like inadvertence had been apprenticed to a French chef at an early age. Her lineage, like her cryptic domestic status, was a well-guarded secret. But early on, I adjudged Dione to be of blood royal (a duchess, to say the very least) by the degree of hauteur she exhibited while performing the most demeaning scullery tasks.

Dione (it was pronounced Dee-*oh*-knee) was at the helm of a small, storefront cooking school named Le Cordon Bleu when I first came into her orbit. The time was barely after the end of World War II and the Manhattan culinary academy doubled as an omelet shop at midday in order to support its chic East Side address. Like a few other curious wage earners in the territory, I appeared at the lunch counter one day. And, knowing little of French cookery, ordered an *omelette brouillé* blindly.

Until that first bite, I had considered omelets to be a purely American kitchen exercise. But never again. For there was nothing to compare with the like of Mrs. Lucas's airy fabrication. The color? Pure gold. The texture? A compound of ozone and fire encircling a heart of runny velvet. Definitely kin to no other egg I had ever tasted.

I consumed two portions at that first visit—to Mrs. Lucas's deep pleasure, as I recall. For she herself was the short order cook!

Garbed in an apron over a long, flowing gown, her arms clattering with gold baubles, and her hair (the color of cinnamon bark) coiled down her neck in a resplendent wreath, she appeared to be an empress playing at chef. But this woman's culinary skill was mesmerizing.

I ate at her counter every day for a month, exhausting an entire repertoire of omelet fillings before she finally spoke to me. Leaning over a bowl of eggs, she lowered her voice discreetly so I alone would hear.

"Have you managed the secret yet, young man?" she inquired.

"I am not sure."

"Oh. I suspected utter proficiency. Very well, I shall instruct you today! Observe the steps carefully. The pan must be very, *very* hot. The eggs beaten to a fare-thee-well. Never with milk or cream, mind, but water alone! Butter? The size of a thumbnail and melted quickly before the eggs are poured on." She performed the glittering exercise even as she held forth. "Now the mixture must be scrambled madly. *Mad-ly*—until the omelet refuses to budge!" Her eyebrows raised a bit more imperiously. "But, see here, come round and do it yourself!"

The hour was late. Only a few struggling lunchers dawdled over coffee. My instinct was to flee, but I did as I was bidden instead.

Dione Lucas watched my tentative stove debut with a critical frown.

"Not bad," she allowed, as my omelet was folded onto a waiting plate. "Not good either. You hesitated a moment before scrambling; that leathers the egg's surface. But . . . definitely not bad! You must come to my classes."

"What classes?" I queried timidly.

"My school. Here. Tonight. But (pointing to a fresh spot on my necktie) you are obviously a slipshod boy. Purchase an apron first!"

I never had time to demur.

Dione's tenure in my life far exceeded the several months' tutelage I undertook at her elbow. And, though I still bear a small pinkish scar on my wrist where she cracked me with a wooden spoon for "punishing" a delicate sauce, I truly learned to *think* in the kitchen from this astute and totally irresistible mentor.

I loved her as one adores an autocratic (and sometimes totally outrageous) parent. But never, I must confess, praised her sufficiently for the legacy of good cooking she bestowed. Not just to me, but all the chefs of my generation who profited by her awe-inspiring expertise.

Dione Lucas was the first person to suggest that the kitchen might provide a haven for my undisciplined talents. Although she chided me occasionally for my lack of culinary deportment (dropping eggs or spilling sugar), she sensed that I possessed, even then, what she termed "the true cook's tongue."

I was extremely flattered by her commendation, but never for a moment seriously considered cookery as a career. For one thing, I had my youthful mind set on success in the theater (as a playwright) and no amount of well-meant advice could dissuade me from that appointed goal.

For another, cooking for a living frankly seemed declassé. When I was a child, my grandparents briefly owned a hotel in Saratoga Springs, and the memory of that noisy, hot, often ill-tempered kitchen still set my teeth on edge.

Dione understood my reluctance perfectly. She had spent her adolescence in that very same environment. But she was a lady unswerving in her conviction.

"A true tongue is a rare gift in the kitchen," she admonished gently, ". . . like true pitch in a musician. Don't waste it!"

I am chastened to admit, I did not take the advice to heart.

Over the years whenever we would meet, Dione would somehow manage to bring up the subject of my latent kitchen prowess with sincere regret.

She even offered to write the Cordon Bleu Cooking School (in France) for a scholarship on my behalf, but I stubbornly declined the honor.

At the close of her life, Dione Lucas's career foundered somewhat. Never a very good business woman, she had made serious financial miscalculations. When her cooking school proved insolvent, she turned to television and eventually product endorsements as a source of income—often with dispiriting results. A widely respected teacher and writer, she practiced neither craft and ended her days as a restaurant food-stylist and nominal head of a cookware shop.

As the possessor of "the truest tongue on earth," Dione Lucas's triumphs seem now to have been regrettably short-lived.

The best tribute I can offer her at this late date is one of her own dazzling bequests. For years (as a professional chef-and-teacher myself), I have hungered after the memory of a golden layer cake. I tasted this prodigious confection twice in my lifetime. Once in childhood, at my mother's elbow, when she indulged in a rare but successful bout of bakery, and on another occasion at college in Virginia, when the mother of one of my school friends sent it as a dormitory treat.

Moist-crumbly, light to the fork, and the color of sweet butter, the special property of this particular cake was its staying power.

As my mother pointed out, "It always gets better on the second day!"

I know Dione Lucas is an unlikely source for such a basically all-American sweet, but this surely *is* her handiwork.

Searching for a like enough formula for the cake of my dreams for this book, I weeded through hundreds of printed recipes. On sheer impulse, at the last moment I randomly picked up a copy of Dione's long-out-of-print *Gourmet Cooking School Cookbook* from my bookcase. The page opened to the precept below, *et voilà*, the most exquisite layer cake I have ever tasted.

Consume a slice with a glass of champagne (or simply a cup of coffee) as an overdue toast to the creator.

DIONE LUCAS'S MAPLE LAYER CAKE

FOR THE CAKE:
1 *cup vegetable shortening (I use Crisco)*
1 *cup granulated sugar*

1 *egg*
3 *egg yolks*
1½ *cups sifted cake flour*
2 *teaspoons baking powder*
Pinch of salt
½ *cup milk*
3 *egg whites*

FOR THE ICING:
3 *cups maple syrup*
¾ *cup egg whites (about 5 large eggs)*

I.   Heat oven to 350°. To make the cake: Beat vegetable shortening in a large bowl until light. Slowly beat in sugar. Add the egg and egg yolks, one at a time, beating thoroughly after each addition.

II.   Sift the flour with baking powder and salt. Add to the batter in three parts, alternating with three parts milk.

III.   Beat the egg whites until stiff. Fold into batter. Pour batter into two buttered and floured 8-inch round cake pans.

IV.   Bake cake until a toothpick inserted in center comes out clean, about 25 minutes. Cool on a wire rack.

V.   To make the icing: Heat the maple syrup to boiling in a medium saucepan. Boil 5 minutes. Beat the egg whites in the large bowl of an electric mixer until soft peaks form. On high speed, slowly pour on the boiled syrup in a thin trickle. Continue beating until of spreading consistency. Spread icing generously over bottom layer. Spread thickly over top and sides. (Dione's cake was liberally mounded with icing.)

Serves 8 to 10.

Pining in public after yellow cake has had its dividends. Some while back, I wrote a column for the *New York Daily News* about my yen for such remembered sweets. The result was a foot-high stack of mail, which eventually produced the following recipe, plus a handful of also-rans! The cake (not like my mother's prescription in the least) is a beatific inheritance nonetheless: a dense yellow coffee cake of super-moist texture. And it pleases me to reprint it (with the sender's permission). Mrs. Eckstein's bounty was first made by her own mother fifty years ago and obviously stands the test of time.

SARAH ECKSTEIN'S CINNAMON CAKE

½ cup unsalted butter, softened
½ cup plus 2 tablespoons granulated sugar
2 eggs
2¼ cups sifted all-purpose flour
3½ teaspoons baking powder
⅛ teaspoon salt
1 cup milk
1 teaspoon vanilla
½ teaspoon ground cinnamon

I. Heat oven to 350°. Beat butter in a large bowl until light and fluffy. Slowly beat in ½ cup sugar. Beat in eggs, one at a time, beating thoroughly after each addition.

II. Sift the flour with baking powder and salt in medium bowl. Combine milk and vanilla. Add flour mixture to butter mixture in three parts, alternating with three parts milk mixture. Pour batter into a buttered and floured 9-inch springform pan.

III. Combine remaining 2 tablespoons sugar and cinnamon. Sprinkle over cake. Bake until a toothpick inserted in

center comes out clean, about 45 minutes. Cool on a
wire rack.

Serves 8 to 10.

More Proustian pastry!

When I was a late adolescent and our family finances had
improved somewhat, my working mother decided to hire a
cleaning woman to tidy our living quarters once a week. The
practitioner she chose for this detail (recommended by my
grandmother) turned out to be a needy widow with four children
and a sad family history. Her husband had been murdered
during a robbery attempt on his grocery shop some years before.

One would never have suspected such a note of tragedy from
Mrs. Pendleberry's mien—for she was a doggedly cheerful soul.
Large, red-faced, of considerable girth, and endowed with ill-
fitting dentures, she loved to talk as she worked. Or, to be
accurate, she loved to talk *rather* than work!

Most of her stories centered about her childhood as a poor
girl in England and her migration to North Carolina where she
met her future husband. But these anecdotes always required
some response. If a tale was told and pointedly ignored, Mrs.
Pendleberry would repeat it again (and again) until the listener
gave some form of acknowledgment and the conversation was
bridged.

By nature, she was, I suppose, ill-equipped to be a house
worker—with water on the knee and a bad left arm. As a result
her cleaning abilities left much to be desired. But she loved to
cook and bake and would take any excuse to quit the dust mop
for a stint at our stove.

On one occasion that I recall, when she was washing down
venetian blinds according to my mother's injunction, Mrs. Pendleberry became so enraptured over coconut cake (the fresh-
grated variety she had learned to bake in North Carolina) that
she stopped working altogether. Abandoning her sponge and
cleanser in midsentence, then producing a quarter from her

shoe, she sent me to the market for a coconut. Together we spent the whole, sweet-scented afternoon, paring, grating, separating eggs, measuring flour and sugar, and ultimately whipping up the most extravagant cake in the world.

Fully four inches high, the cake was crusted with snowy frosting and blanketed with drifts of tender coconut. My family was awe-struck at the sight of this dazzling creation when they returned home that night.

Truthfully, I have never forgotten my consummate delight when I first tasted it. Nor my mother's acrimony (the venetian blinds still unwashed) when Mrs. Pendleberry, dutifully counting out her wages, reminded her that she had laid out twenty-five cents for the coconut!

Mrs. Pendleberry's tenure was of brief duration, but her cake will live forever!

MRS. PENDLEBERRY'S UNFORGETTABLE COCONUT CAKE

FOR THE CAKE:
1 *small coconut*
⅓ *cup unsalted butter, softened*
⅓ *cup vegetable shortening*
1⅔ *cups granulated sugar*
3 *eggs*
2½ *cups sifted cake flour*
3½ *teaspoons baking powder*
¼ *teaspoon salt*
¾ *cup whipping cream (approximately)*
1 *teaspoon vanilla*

FOR THE ICING:
½ *cup water*
⅓ *cup light corn syrup*
2½ *cups granulated sugar*
⅛ *teaspoon salt*
3 *egg whites*

1 *teaspoon orange juice*
1½ *teaspoons vanilla*
2½ *cups grated fresh coconut (see step I)*

I.   To make the cake: Poke an ice pick through the eye of the coconut. Drain coconut milk into a glass. Strain milk through cheesecloth; reserve. Break the coconut shell with a hammer. Pare the coconut. Shred in a food processor; reserve.

II. Heat oven to 350°. Beat the butter and shortening in a large bowl until light and fluffy. Slowly beat in sugar. Beat in eggs, one at a time, beating thoroughly after each addition.

III. Sift the flour with baking powder and salt. Combine reserved coconut milk with enough whipping cream to make 1¼ cups liquid. Add both mixtures, in alternating thirds, to the batter. Stir in vanilla. Spoon into two buttered and floured 9-inch round cake pans.

IV. Bake cake until a toothpick inserted in center comes out clean, about 30 minutes. Cool on a wire rack.

V.   To make the icing: Combine water, corn syrup, sugar, and salt in a medium saucepan. Heat to boiling; reduce heat. Simmer until mixture forms a firm ball when dropped into cold water, or registers 242° on a candy thermometer. Beat the egg whites in the large bowl of an electric mixer until soft peaks form. On high speed, slowly pour on boiled syrup in a thin trickle. Continue beating until of spreading consistency. Beat in orange juice and vanilla. Spread one-fourth of the icing over bottom layer. Sprinkle with some reserved grated coconut. Spread remaining icing over top and sides of cake. Press remaining coconut into icing.

Serves 8 to 10.

If the foregoing is the whitest cake in the world, the following is obviously the blackest. Dubbed Mississippi Mud by some misplaced Cape Cod confederate, this recipe is fudgy to a fault! The devise comes to us from the bill of fare of the benevolent Front Street Restaurant in Provincetown, Massachusetts.

MISSISSIPPI MUD

Unsweetened cocoa
1¼ cups strong black coffee
¼ cup bourbon
5 ounces unsweetened chocolate
1 cup unsalted butter, cut into pieces
2 cups granulated sugar
2 cups all-purpose flour
1 teaspoon baking soda
⅛ teaspoon salt
2 eggs, lightly beaten
1 teaspoon vanilla
Confectioners' sugar
Sweetened whipped cream flavored with white crème de cacao
　　(optional)

I.　　　　Heat oven to 275°. Butter a tube pan (9 inches across, 3½ inches deep) and dust bottom and sides with cocoa. Set aside.

II.　　　Heat the coffee and bourbon in a medium-size, heavy saucepan over low heat. Add the chocolate and butter. Cook, stirring constantly, until smooth. Remove from heat; stir in granulated sugar. Let stand 5 minutes. Transfer to the large bowl of an electric mixer.

III.　　Sift the flour with baking soda and salt. Add to the chocolate mixture (on low speed) in four parts. Add eggs and vanilla. Beat until smooth. Pour into the tube pan.

IV.   Bake cake until a toothpick inserted in center comes out clean, about 1½ hours. Cool completely in pan on a wire rack before unmolding. Sprinkle with confectioners' sugar; serve with whipped cream if desired.

Serves 10.

Adrienne Hovsepian is a mere twenty-six years old and the brightest star of the bakery at New York's famed Dean & DeLuca gourmet food shop. When she was twenty, Mrs. Hovsepian lived in Arcosanti, Arizona, where the idea for this most unusual green-gold pound cake sprang full blown into her pretty head—or so she claims. Can her husband's Middle Eastern forebears take any credit for the unusual flavoring of poppy seeds plus lemon and orange peel? Not a bit! Adrienne Hovsepian (a native of Cambridge, Massachusetts) is strictly Welsh/Scotch-Irish . . . and self-trained.

Obviously all-American know-how.

ADRIENNE HOVSEPIAN'S
POPPY SEED POUND CAKE

⅔ *cup gray (or blue) poppy seeds*
⅓ *cup milk*
1 *cup unsalted butter, softened*
½ *cup vegetable shortening*
2 *cups granulated sugar*
6 *eggs*
Peel of 3 lemons, finely grated
Peel of 1 orange, finely grated
1 *teaspoon vanilla*
2 *cups sifted all-purpose flour*

2 teaspoons baking powder
¾ teaspoon salt
½ cup milk
¼ cup orange juice
½ cup lemon juice
⅓ cup superfine sugar

I.   Soak the poppy seeds in ⅓ cup milk overnight. Rinse in cold water. Drain thoroughly. Reserve.

II.   Heat oven to 350°. Beat the butter and shortening in a large bowl until light and fluffy. Slowly beat in granulated sugar. Add the eggs, one at a time, beating thoroughly after each addition. Beat in lemon peel, orange peel, and vanilla. Stir in poppy seeds.

III.   Sift the flour with the baking powder and salt two times. Add to the batter in three parts, alternating with three parts of the ½ cup milk. Spoon into a buttered and floured 10-inch Bundt pan.

IV.   Bake cake until a toothpick inserted in center comes out clean, about 1 hour. Immediately turn out onto a wire rack.

V.   Combine orange juice, lemon juice, and superfine sugar. Spoon over the cake until cake seems moist, but is not soggy.

Serves 10 to 12.

A pound cake of yet another color and flavor, this circle of honest old-time goodness hails from Mobile, Alabama. I first tasted this confection in a transplanted Alabamian's kitchen some time ago and begged for the recipe (an old family secret) long into the night. No soap!

On another occasion (when pound cake was not on the menu) I merely hinted how deprived this book would appear without that truly Southern dessert to round off the cake chapter. No takers!

Last fall when I had settled on a lesser recipe (in hand), I reported that to my baking friend. Still no comment!

But the following formula arrived shortly after in the mail. As a Yuletide greeting.

Merry Christmas, one and all . . .

MOBILE'S MOUND OF POUND

1 *cup cold unsalted butter*
1⅔ *cups granulated sugar*
¼ *teaspoon salt*
5 *eggs*
2 *cups sifted all-purpose flour*
2 *tablespoons vanilla*
2 *teaspoons orange juice*

I. Heat oven to 300°. Work the butter with a large wooden spoon in a large bowl 5 minutes. Add sugar and salt; continue to work until well mixed.

II. Beat in the eggs, one at a time, beating thoroughly after each addition. Add the flour, 2 tablespoons at a time. Beat in vanilla and orange juice.

III. Spoon batter into a buttered and floured 9-inch tube pan. Bake 40 minutes. Increase oven temperature to 325°; continue to bake until a toothpick inserted in center comes out clean, about 20 minutes. Cool 15 minutes in pan on a wire rack. Turn out onto rack; cover with a tea towel. Cool completely.

Serves 10 to 12.

Justly renowned in SoHo, FOOD is the antithesis of a New York stylish *boîte*, yet it is equally hard to penetrate. Open from early morning till late afternoon, this unadorned cafeteria is the hub of Manhattan's art-and-bohemian worlds. A gigantic bulletin board just inside the door is always filled with personal messages and is acknowledged to be the central intelligence agency of SoHo. Bikes lean against the window walls, sandwiched by baby carriages and shopping carts. On a recent outing, an enormous St. Bernard was parked there, too, guarding a pair of disco roller skates.

What is so special about FOOD besides its raffish clientele? The food! The next cake is a neighborhood *pièce de résistance*. Perfected by Lynda Farmer, it is a buttery union of sugar, cinnamon, coffee, and cocoa, studded with raisins and walnuts. Invariably referred to as "The Cake," its reputation has been won in part by its miraculously crumbly texture, due to the yogurt in the batter.

FOOD'S COFFEE MARBLE

FOR THE CAKE:
½ cup dark brown sugar
1 tablespoon ground cinnamon
2 teaspoons instant coffee powder
2 tablespoons unsweetened cocoa
½ cup raisins
½ cup walnuts
¾ cup unsalted butter, softened
1½ cups granulated sugar
2 teaspoons vanilla
3 eggs
3 cups sifted all-purpose flour
1½ teaspoons baking powder
1½ teaspoons baking soda
½ teaspoon salt
2 cups unflavored yogurt

FOR THE ICING:
2 teaspoons instant coffee powder
2 tablespoons hot water
1 package (8 ounces) cream cheese, softened
¾ cup unsalted butter, softened
1¼ cups confectioners' sugar
1 teaspoon vanilla
1 teaspoon orange juice
Chopped walnuts
Raisins

I.   Heat oven to 350°. To make the cake: Combine the brown sugar, cinnamon, instant coffee powder, cocoa, raisins, and walnuts. Mix thoroughly; set aside.

II.   Beat the butter in a large bowl until light and fluffy. Slowly beat in granulated sugar. Beat in vanilla and eggs, one at a time, beating thoroughly after each addition.

III.   Sift the flour with the baking powder, baking soda, and salt two times. Add flour mixture to the batter in three parts, alternating with three parts yogurt. Do not overmix; batter will be thick.

IV.   Butter and flour a 10-inch Bundt pan. Spoon a fourth of the batter into pan. Sprinkle with a third of the raisin-nut mixture. Repeat layering twice; top with remaining batter.

V.   Bake cake until a toothpick inserted in center comes out clean, about 1 hour. Cool in pan on wire rack before removing.

VI.   To make the icing: Mix the coffee powder and hot water; cool to room temperature.

VII.   Beat the cream cheese and butter in the medium bowl of an electric mixer until light and fluffy. Slowly beat in confectioners' sugar. Beat in vanilla, orange juice, and cooled coffee mixture. Beat until almost doubled in volume, about 4 minutes. Spread over sides and top of cake. Sprinkle with walnuts and raisins.

Serves 8 to 10.

Yogurt is the *serious* ingredient in the lemony ring of golden air that follows. I found this recipe in Delaware—*The Armenian Woman's Cookbook*, published in 1946—and was so delighted by its elegant texture and unique savor I marked it down at once.

LEMON YOGURT CAKE

1 *cup unsalted butter, softened*
1½ *cups granulated sugar*
4 *eggs*
1 *tablespoon grated lemon rind*
1 *teaspoon vanilla*
2½ *cups sifted all-purpose flour*
1 *teaspoon baking powder*
1 *teaspoon baking soda*
½ *teaspoon salt*
½ *pint unflavored yogurt*
¾ *cup finely ground almonds*
½ *cup lemon juice*

I.   Heat oven to 350°. Beat the butter in a large bowl until light and fluffy. Slowly beat in 1 cup sugar. Beat in eggs, one at a time, beating thoroughly after each addition. Beat in lemon rind and vanilla.

II.   Sift the flour with baking powder, baking soda, and salt. Add flour mixture to the batter in three parts, alternating with three parts yogurt. Fold in ground almonds. Pour into a buttered and floured 9-inch tube pan.

III.   Bake cake until a toothpick inserted in center comes out clean, about 1 hour. Cool on a wire rack 5 minutes.

IV.   Meanwhile heat remaining ½ cup sugar with lemon juice in a small saucepan until sugar dissolves. Slowly pour over cake allowing mixture to soak in. Cool cake completely in pan before unmolding.

Serves 8 to 10.

I always look for unusual combinations in cookery, yet I abhor *nouvelle cuisine.* Figure it out!

A recent cookery tour (teaching in Indiana and Oregon) provided me with a duet of unusual chocolate cakes both sluiced with decidedly unconventional ingredients. Are you ready for Coca-Cola and mayonnaise? Before you suspect I have taken leave of my sensibilities entirely, look over the next two recipes carefully.

The first is a family prescription (from Indianapolis) for a deep-dyed chocolate confection flavored with a spot of "the real thing." The second (presented to me by a student in Portland on the back of a very ancient Hellmann's Mayonnaise label) is a food of sheer deviltry and more than thirty years old in the bargain!

Either will turn even a reluctant kitchen debutante into a drop-dead chef.

INDIANA CHOCOLATE COKE CAKE

FOR THE CAKE:
1 *cup unsalted butter*
½ *cup miniature marshmallows*
¼ *cup unsweetened cocoa*

1 *cup Coca-Cola*
2 *cups granulated sugar*
2 *cups all-purpose flour*
1 *teaspoon baking soda*
2 *eggs, lightly beaten*
½ *cup buttermilk*

FOR THE ICING:
6 *ounces semisweet chocolate, coarsely chopped*
⅓ *cup Coca-Cola*
1 *cup plus 2 tablespoons unsalted butter, softened*
3 *egg yolks*
⅔ *cup confectioners' sugar*

I. Heat oven to 350°. To make the cake: Combine butter and marshmallows in a medium saucepan over low heat. Cook, stirring occasionally, until marshmallows melt, about 7 minutes. Stir in cocoa and Coca-Cola. Remove from heat.

II. Sift the sugar, flour, and baking soda together into the large bowl of an electric mixer. Beat in chocolate-cola mixture on low speed. Add eggs and buttermilk. Beat on low speed until smooth. Pour into two buttered and floured 9-inch round cake pans.

III. Bake cake until a toothpick inserted in the center comes out clean, about 40 minutes. Cool on a wire rack.

IV. To make the icing: Place the chocolate and Coca-Cola in a small saucepan. Cook over low heat, stirring constantly, until smooth. Remove from heat; let stand to cool. Refrigerate until cold.

V. Beat the butter until light and fluffy in a large bowl. Beat in egg yolks, one at a time, beating thoroughly after each addition. Gradually add chocolate mixture. Beat in confectioners' sugar. Spread icing on bottom layer, top, and sides of cake. Store in a cool place until serving.

Serves 8 to 10.

CHOCOLATE MAYO CAKE

FOR THE CAKE:
3 *eggs*
1⅔ *cups granulated sugar*
1 *teaspoon vanilla*
1 *cup Hellmann's mayonnaise*
2 *cups sifted all-purpose flour*
1¼ *teaspoons baking soda*
¼ *teaspoon baking powder*
⅔ *cup unsweetened cocoa*
1⅓ *cups water*

FOR THE ICING:
1½ *cups light brown sugar*
⅓ *cup water*
1 *tablespoon light corn syrup*
2 *egg whites*
3 *tablespoons white crème de cacao*

I. Heat oven to 350°. To make the cake: Beat eggs with sugar in a large bowl until light and lemony in color. Add vanilla and mayonnaise.

II. Sift the flour with baking soda, baking powder, and cocoa in a large bowl. Add to batter in three parts, alternating with three parts water.

III. Pour batter into two buttered and floured 9-inch round cake pans. Bake until a toothpick inserted in center comes out clean, about 25 minutes. Cool on a wire rack.

IV.   To make the icing: Combine brown sugar, water, corn syrup, and egg whites in the top of a double boiler. Beat with an electric hand mixer over simmering water until of spreading consistency, about 7 minutes. Beat in crème de cacao. Spread icing over bottom layer, top, and sides of cake.

Serves 10.

One more idiosyncratic (albeit superdelectable) treat is an anomalous breakfast coffee cake, dubbed "a brake"! Compounded of baby zucchini and ripe tomatoes, the recipe stems from the garden state of New Jersey, where both viands literally bloom in red and green profusion.

This "brake" is one that every brunch table deserves.

ZUCCHINI-TOMATO BRAKE

1 *cup unsalted butter, softened*
1½ *cups granulated sugar*
½ *cup light brown sugar*
3 *eggs*
1 *teaspoon ground cinnamon*
⅛ *teaspoon freshly grated nutmeg*
4 *large plum tomatoes (about ½ pound) peeled, seeded, finely chopped, drained*
2 *medium zucchini (about ½ pound), grated*
½ *cup chopped walnuts*
½ *cup dried currants*
1 *tablespoon grated orange peel*
3 *cups sifted all-purpose flour*
1 *teaspoon baking soda*

½ *teaspoon baking powder*
1 *teaspoon salt*
½ *cup milk*
2 *teaspoons vanilla*
Confectioners' sugar
Sweetened whipped cream (optional)

I.   Heat oven to 350°. Beat the butter in a large bowl until light and fluffy. Slowly beat in granulated sugar and brown sugar. Beat in eggs, one at a time, beating thoroughly after each addition. Add the cinnamon and nutmeg. Stir in the chopped tomatoes, zucchini, walnuts, currants, and orange peel.

II.   Sift the flour with baking soda, baking powder, and salt in a large bowl. Combine the milk and vanilla. Add both mixtures, in alternating thirds, to the batter. Stir until smooth. Spoon batter into a buttered and floured 10-inch Bundt pan.

III.   Bake cake until a toothpick inserted in center comes out clean, about 1 hour and 20 to 25 minutes. Cool completely in pan on a wire rack before unmolding. Dust with confectioners' sugar; serve with whipped cream if desired.

Serves 8 to 10.

I went to Ohio recently to conduct cooking lessons as a fund-raising event for Cincinnati's Playhouse in the Park.

Only half-joking, I confided to my hostess-chauffeur that I considered every trip away from home a dismal failure if I did not return with at least one "dynamite" recipe.

Without ado, Lorrie Laskey presented me to her cooking husband, Dick, who promptly opened up his kitchen file for his mother's estimable version of applesauce cake.

"Mother comes from Marblehead, Massachusetts, and while she's been living here and there, making this cake for fifty years, things have a way of subtly changing," he noted.

Here then is the *MassOhioan* canon. It is well worth your culinary attention wherever you live in the U.S.A.

EDITH PAINE LASKEY'S APPLESAUCE WINNER

FOR THE CAKE:
½ *cup raisins*
½ *cup currants*
½ *cup chopped walnuts*
1½ *cups sifted all-purpose flour (approximately)*
½ *cup unsalted butter, softened*
1 *cup granulated sugar*
1 *egg*
1 *teaspoon baking soda*
½ *teaspoon baking powder*
½ *teaspoon ground nutmeg*
½ *teaspoon ground cloves*
1 *teaspoon ground cinnamon*
1¼ *cups thick applesauce (recipe follows)*

FOR THE ICING:
4 *tablespoons unsalted butter, softened*
1½ *teaspoons vanilla*
3 *cups confectioners' sugar*
3 to 4 *tablespoons whipping cream*

I.   Heat oven to 350°. To make the cake: Combine raisins, currants, and walnuts in a small bowl. Add ¼ cup flour. Mix well. Set aside.

II.   Beat the butter in a large bowl until light and fluffy. Slowly beat in sugar. Beat in egg.

III.   Sift 1¼ cups flour with baking soda, baking powder, nutmeg, cloves, and cinnamon in a large bowl. Add to the batter in three parts, alternating with three parts applesauce. (If using commercial applesauce, add ¼ to ½ cup more flour to thicken the batter.) Stir in raisin-nut mixture. Spoon batter into a buttered and floured 8- to 9-inch springform pan.

IV.   Bake cake until a toothpick inserted in center comes out clean, about 50 minutes. Cool in pan on a wire rack.

V.   To make the icing: Beat the butter with vanilla in the large bowl of an electric mixer. Slowly add confectioners' sugar. Continue to beat until light and mealy. Beat in just enough cream to make icing of spreading consistency. Spread icing over sides and top of cake.

Serves 8 to 10.

Not having Mrs. Laskey's applesauce formula (her original recipe did not include one), I added my own. Look at it this way—it's another "dynamite" bonus for the chef!

HOMEMADE APPLESAUCE

3 pounds tart green apples
½ teaspoon grated lemon peel
1 cup dark brown sugar
2 teaspoons lemon juice
3 tablespoons dark rum
2 tablespoons unsalted butter

I.   Pare and core apples; cut into ⅛-inch-thick slices. Place apples and lemon peel in a large, heavy saucepan. Cook, covered, over low heat, stirring occasionally, until very tender, about 30 minutes.

II.   Mash apples with a potato masher. Add sugar, lemon juice, rum, and butter. Cook, partially covered, over low heat, 10 minutes. Increase heat slightly if mixture seems too thin. Refrigerate covered until ready to use.

Makes about 2 pints.

Some cooks collect recipes for cheesecake and potato pancakes. Others fancy *quenelle de brochet*. I am hooked on "brownie" prescriptions. I have 100 or so recipes on hand, yet I rarely make a panful; they are so unreasonably caloric!

The best of my best brownies comes from Jackson, Mississippi. I will not divulge the donor's name (she is very famous), but I will allow the taste differential: a dab of good buttermilk stirred into the fudgy sludge!

BUTTERMILK BROWNIES

2 *ounces unsweetened chocolate*
½ *cup unsalted butter*
1 *teaspoon vanilla*
3 *eggs*
1¼ *cups granulated sugar*
½ *cup all-purpose flour, sifted*
3 *tablespoons buttermilk*
½ *cup walnuts, chopped*

I.   Heat oven to 350°. Melt the chocolate with butter in the top of a double boiler over hot water. Stir in vanilla. Cool slightly.

II.   Beat the eggs and the sugar in a large bowl until light and lemon colored. Slowly beat in the chocolate mixture. Add flour, 2 tablespoons at a time. Stir in buttermilk and walnuts. Pour into a buttered 8-inch square cake pan.

III.   Bake brownies until a toothpick inserted in center comes out fairly clean (about 25 minutes). Center should be slightly cakey. Cool in pan on a wire rack; cut into squares.

Makes about 20 brownies.

From across the Continental Divide (Rawlins, Wyoming) comes another brownie worthy of endorsement. This device, sans chocolate, is a rich, chewy, brown sugar-and-pecan rendering. And it's incredibly hard to keep on hand (in my house, anyway!).

BROWN SUGAR BROWNIES

2½ *cups all-purpose flour*
1 *pound light brown sugar*
1 *cup unsalted butter*
2 *eggs*
1 *teaspoon vanilla*
1½ *teaspoons baking powder*
Pinch of salt
1 *cup pecans, chopped*

I.   Heat oven to 350°. Combine 1¼ cups flour with ⅓ cup sugar in a medium bowl. Cut in ½ cup butter; blend with a pastry blender until the texture of coarse crumbs. Press mixture on the bottom of a lightly buttered 9- × 13-inch baking sheet. Bake 15 minutes.

II.   Meanwhile, combine remaining brown sugar and remaining butter in a medium saucepan. Heat on low heat, just until sugar dissolves.

III.   Beat the eggs in a large bowl until light. Slowly beat in brown sugar mixture. Beat in vanilla.

IV.   Sift remaining flour with the baking powder and salt. Stir into brown sugar mixture. Stir in pecans.

V.   Spread mixture over prebaked crust. Return to oven; bake 25 minutes. Cool in pan on a wire rack; cut into small squares.

Makes about 3 dozen brownies.

Black cooks contributed most of the wondrous seasoning in Southern cuisine. In North Carolina, they claim that benne (sesame seeds) were originally brought to the territory on slave ships for good luck. Be that as it may, benne certainly found a home in the Carolinian diet. Note these signal brown sugar and sesame cookies.

BENNE WAFERS

1 *egg*
½ *teaspoon vanilla*
6 *tablespoons unsalted butter, melted*
¾ *cup light brown sugar*
¼ *cup all-purpose flour*
½ *cup pecans, chopped*
½ *cup toasted sesame seeds*

I.   Heat oven to 400°. Beat egg and vanilla in the medium bowl of an electric mixer. Slowly beat in butter. Add sugar; beat until smooth.

II.   Beat in flour on low speed in three parts. Stir in pecans and sesame seeds.

III.   Lightly butter an aluminum foil-lined baking sheet. Drop teaspoonfuls of cookie batter onto foil, placing far apart. There should be only six cookies on each baking sheet, as they spread quite a bit. Bake cookies until golden brown, 5 to 7 minutes. Remove foil from baking sheet. Let cookies cool completely on a wire rack before peeling off foil. Repeat procedure until all batter is used.

Makes about 2 dozen cookies.

The next two cookie recipes are from the original repertoire of The Store in Amagansett. They were made for us by a most unusual and talented lady, Pat Powell, who generously annotated them for inclusion here.

Pat first appeared at The Store as a customer (a good one). So good, in fact, that she soon ran up a staggeringly high bill, and then happily bartered it off with manifold services and some of the best cookies I have ever been permitted to crunch.

Originally from Philadelphia, Pat Powell now resides in Saddle River, New Jersey, where she bakes the very best breads, cookies, and cakes to be found in the state!

Cape Fear Lace (a delicate oatmeal and walnut conceit) was always one of Pat Powell's most prodigious confections. But not until recently, when Pat sent me the recipe, did I realize that the formula was not hers.

"You were always nagging me to come up with some lacy cookie," she reminded me. "I didn't know any such recipe. But Rosalie Gwathmey [wife of painter Robert Gwathmey and another Store supporter] did! She brought the recipe from North Carolina ages and ages ago! I *made* them for The Store—but they really belong to her."

They *are* wonderful treats, no matter the lineage.

CAPE FEAR LACE

1 *egg*
½ *teaspoon vanilla*
½ *cup unsalted butter, melted*
1 *cup light brown sugar*
2 *cups uncooked rolled oats*
½ *cup walnuts, chopped*

I.   Heat oven to 375°. Beat egg and vanilla in the medium bowl of an electric mixer. Slowly beat in butter. Add sugar; beat until smooth.

II.   Beat in rolled oats on low speed. Stir in walnuts.

III. Lightly butter an aluminum foil-lined baking sheet. Drop batter by generous teaspoonfuls onto foil, placing far apart. There should be only six cookies on each baking sheet. Spread cookie batter flat on tray; do not mound. Bake cookies until golden brown, about 8 minutes. Remove foil from baking sheet. Let cookies cool completely before peeling off foil. Repeat procedure until all batter is used.

Makes about 2 dozen cookies.

A genuine Pat Powell donation is the following receipt for lemon coconut wafers. This treasured recipe was passed down from her grandmother Hornor (who lived in Mount Holly, New Jersey) to Pat's mother who passed it to Pat, who passed it to me—who is now passing it to the world. *Bon appétit!*

PAT POWELL'S LEMON COCONUT WAFERS

½ *cup unsalted butter, melted*
1 *cup granulated sugar*
1 *egg*

1 *cup sifted all-purpose flour*
1 *teaspoon baking powder*
⅓ *cup evaporated milk*
1 *can (3½ ounces) shredded coconut*
½ *teaspoon finely grated lemon rind*
¾ *teaspoon lemon juice*

I.   Heat oven to 350°. Beat melted butter with sugar in a large bowl until well mixed. Beat in egg.

II.   Sift the flour with baking powder. Add to batter in three parts, alternating with three parts evaporated milk. Stir in coconut, lemon rind, and lemon juice.

III.   Drop batter by small teaspoonfuls on a lightly buttered baking sheet. Bake cookies until done, about 7 minutes. Cool completely in pan before removing.
                          Makes about 6 dozen cookies.

Years and years ago, I knew a very funny lady who cooked. One of her favorite remarks was:

"A good man may be hard to find but a good gingersnap is a sheer impossibility!"

For Hazel Berrien, I offer the best gingersnap I have ever found (in Hibbing, Minnesota, of all places!).

OLD-FASHIONED GINGERSNAPS

½ *cup unsalted butter, softened*
½ *cup granulated sugar*
¼ *cup molasses*
1½ *teaspoons ground ginger*
1 *teaspoon ground cinnamon*
½ *teaspoon ground cloves*

½ *teaspoon baking soda*
⅛ *teaspoon salt*
1¾ *cups all-purpose flour*

I.   Beat the butter in a large bowl until light. Slowly add
       sugar. Beat in molasses, ginger, cinnamon, cloves, bak-
       ing soda, and salt. Add flour ¼ cup at a time. Mix
       thoroughly; chill dough 4 hours.

II.   Heat oven to 325°. Divide cookie dough in half. Shape
       each half into 1½-inch-thick rolls. Cut dough crosswise
       with a sharp knife into ⅛-inch-thick slices. Place on a
       lightly buttered baking sheet. Bake cookies until
       golden, about 8 minutes.

Makes about 5 dozen cookies.

My taste in sweet endings is monumental.

The best in this collection come from the broadest spectrum
of America's larder, North and South, East and West. Some are
clearly old childhood favorites, but a few came into my possession as recently as weeks before this book went to press. The last
recipe named was also part of The Store in Amagansett legacy.
Two rounds of sweet vanilla wafers pressed about a windfall of
orange-tinctured preserves, the cookie was one of the most
popular on our counter. The recipe was given to us by a
delightful motherly lady, whose name I have long forgotten. This
customer made her way to the very end of Long Island from Salt
Lake City, Utah, one summer as a culinary pilgrimage. She
airily promised us her prizewinning cookie recipe and, by golly,
sent it when she returned home.

No throwaway dessert, these cookies require a certain
amount of kitchen diligence (and a small round cutter as well—
we used a small whisky glass for the chore) but the results are
eminently satisfying.

My donor called her confit "raspberry jammies." I do the
same.

RASPBERRY JAMMIES

1 *cup unsalted butter, softened*
½ *cup granulated sugar*
2 *egg yolks*
Rind of 1 lemon, finely grated
1 *teaspoon vanilla*
Pinch of salt
2½ *cups plus 3 tablespoons all-purpose flour*
½ *cup raspberry preserves*
2 *tablespoons orange juice*
1 *tablespoon orange liqueur*
½ *teaspoon finely grated orange peel*

I.   Beat the butter in a large bowl until light and fluffy. Slowly add sugar. Beat in egg yolks, one at a time, beating thoroughly after each addition. Beat in lemon rind, vanilla, and salt.

II.   With a wooden spoon, stir 2 cups flour into cookie dough. Transfer to a lightly floured board; knead in remaining flour until smooth. Chill dough 1 hour.

III. Heat oven to 375°. Roll out dough ¼-inch thick. Cut into 1½-inch rounds. Place on lightly buttered baking sheets; bake cookies until lightly browned, about 12 minutes. Cool on a wire rack.

IV.   Combine raspberry preserves, orange juice, orange liqueur, and orange peel in a small saucepan. Cook over medium heat until slightly thickened, about 5 minutes.

V.   Turn half the cookies bottom side up. Coat each piece with about ¾ teaspoon of the preserve mixture. Cover with remaining cookies bottom side down.

Makes about 3 dozen filled cookies.

AN AFTER-THOUGHT ABOUT MENUS

Chapter Eleven

Wherever I travel in America, readers ask me the same questions regarding the dishes I write about and teach:

"What will it go with?" they ask. "And when can I serve it?"

As an aid for uninitiated cooks, I have therefore tried to organize some of the recipes in this book into sample menus. But be advised that these are guidelines *only* for possible dinners, luncheons and suppers, brunches, and buffet parties.

Food preferences are a very personal prerogative—and a territory I have no wish to tread. I know that I have stated my feelings about first courses earlier on, but at the risk of boring the reader, I will repeat that vegetables are usually my option for meal openers. I say this because they agree with the contemporary (lightened) diet, for one thing, and because I love garden greenery more than anything else at the table—with the possible exception of gooey desserts.

I would hope that the assiduous cookbook reader (like myself) first will browse through this collection of honest American foods, folding down pages when and wherever some recipe strikes a prandial chord. Later, when the chef is searching for something different for dinner (or a last-moment brunch), all the dog-ears should happily come home to roost!

The fact that one dish at a meal hails from Minnesota, another from Nevada, and yet another from Florida or Puerto Rico only heightens the pleasure of our unique and varied native cuisine. Mix and match it as you will!

DINNERS

Grits Soufflé
San Francisco Bay Cioppino
Puerto Rico Chocolate Flan

Smack Good Peppers
Kentucky Burgoo or Shaker Chicken in Cider and Cream
Pennsylvania Dutch Potato Dumplings
New York Strawberry Ice
Cape Fear Lace

Cold Dilled Carrots
Apple Butter Roasted Pork
Georgia Green Beans with New Potatoes or South Philadelphia
        Sauerkraut
Ginger Ice

Arizona Grapefruit Slaw
Hot Pepper Jelly Duckling with Breaded Dumplings
Hot Red Cabbage Slaw
Lemon Tart

Blanched Okra in the Cajun Style with Mustard Sauce
Virginia Fried Chicken with Cream Gravy
Steamed Rice
Kate Almand's Biscuits
Green Salad
Key Lime Mousse

Frazzled Green Onions
Garlicky Gardiners Bay Scallops or Provincetown Broiled
        Swordfish
Steamed Rice
Wilted Green Salad
Mississippi Mud

Onion Bread Pudding
Cheyenne Buttermilk Roasted Lamb
South Dakota Svenska Ärter
Pan-Fried Pears with Clabbered Cream
Benne Wafers

Zelje
Texas Short Ribs: Sabine River Style
Louisiana Maquechoux
Lemon Yogurt Cake

Farmer's Soup or Puerto Rico Black Bean Soup
Bacon-Streaked Roast Chicken
Dandelion Green Bake
Dione Lucas's Maple Layer Cake

Carrot Fritters with Lemon Cream Gravy
Roast Turkey with Jambalaya Dressing
Cranberry Shrub
Green Salad
Funeral Pie

LUNCHES OR SUPPERS

Chicken Püt Pie
Pickled Beets
Prospector's Sourdough Bread
Peach and Almond Grunt

Ohio's Swedish Meatballs or North Dakota Lamb Stew
Pennsylvania Dutch Potato Dumplings
Green Salad
All-American Apple Pie

Tamale Pie or Deep-Dish Pizza
Wilted Green Salad
Williamsburg Plum Ice Cream
Pat Powell's Lemon Coconut Wafers

Jersey Fennel Loaf
Rosy Scalloped Potatoes

Green Salad
Mrs. Pendleberry's Unforgettable Coconut Cake

BRUNCHES

Bloody Marys
Cornmeal Cleats
Huevos Rancheros
Montgomery Pie

Pfaumeniis
Country Fried Ham
Poached Eggs
Virginia Spoon Bread
Buttermilk Brownies

Screwdrivers
Newport Fish Shortcake with Helen Johnson's Buttermilk
    Biscuits
Tuscaloosa Chicken Custard
Poppy Seed Pound Cake or Edith Paine Laskey's Applesauce
    Winner

Whiskey Sours
Hot Spud Salad with Summer Sausage or Angie Earle's Roast
    Beef Hash
Green Salad
Chocolate Mayo Cake

BUFFETS—PARTY FOODS

Pompey's Head
Quiffle
Cajun Eggplant Lagniappe
Green Salad

Mobile's Mound of Pound
Indiana Chocolate Coke Cake

Spanish Harlem Chicken
Beer Baked Ham with Berry Mustard Sauce
Louisiana Maquechoux
Green Salad
"Shredded Treat" Apple Pie
Brown Sugar Brownies

Burmese Eggs Arkansas Style or Tourtière
Chicken and Oyster Gumbo
Moosup Boiled and Baked Tongue
Carolina Cracklin' Bread
Fresh Fruit Compote
Zucchini-Tomato Brake

A Note about Ingredients!

In every instance, each of the recipes in this book was tested with ingredients readily available at supermarkets across the country. No self-respecting cookbook writer, however, can spend half a lifetime in the kitchen without acquiring some brand preferences. So have a few of mine.

Listed alphabetically below are my first choices from the grocery shelf, along with some limited mail-order resources for hard-to-find items.

BOUILLON POWDER

Most often I use G. Washington Broth (in two varieties: Golden or Rich Brown) manufactured by American Home Foods, New York City, NY. Be advised that these packaged flavorings do contain salt and a modicum of MSG, however.

CHEESE

Swiss: I prefer imported Gruyére or the currently popular *Jarlsberg* cheese that is widely distributed in this country.

Parmesan: The best grade is unquestionably *parmigiano-reggiano* imported from Italy. However, I often make do with Stella brand Parmesan cheese distributed by Universal Foods, Milwaukee, WI, without irreparable harm to the dish I am preparing.

CHOCOLATE

Unsweetened or Semi-Sweet: I use Baker's chocolate in every case.

Sweet Cooking Chocolate: I have a penchant for imported varieties like Maillard Eagle Sweet, Lanvin, or Tobler. But Baker's German Sweet will certainly do, in a pinch!

CHORIZOS (Spanish sausage)

These may be found at most Hispanic groceries across the country. Chorizos are also sold by mail order from: Casa Moneo, 210 West 14th Street, New York City, NY 10011.

COCOA

My first preference is Droste's Cocoa (imported from Holland). If you use a domestic brand like Hershey's (with higher acidity than Dutch cocoa) simply add a jot of sugar and a dash of cream to neutralize the flavor.

HOT PEPPER SAUCE

Though there are myriad brands on the market, Tabasco is most definitely my first choice.

MASA HARINA (corn flour)

This may be found at most Hispanic groceries. It is also sold mail order by Casa Moneo (see address above) in New York City; La Casa del Pueblo, 1810 Blue Island, Chicago, IL 60608; or El

Mercado, First Avenue and Lorenza, East Los Angeles, CA 90063.

MUSHROOMS (dried boletus type)

These may be found in packets imported from Italy. I buy Bruschi Borgotaro brand, available by mail order from: Todaro Brothers, 555 Second Avenue, New York City, NY 10016 or Balducci's, 424 Avenue of the Americas, New York City, NY 10011.

MUSTARD (Dijon variety)

I consistently use Grey Poupon (white wine) mustard made in the U.S.

OILS

Olive Oil: My first choice is Lucca Extra No. 1 or Sasso brand (both extra-virgin olive oils imported from Italy) but recently I have had the good fortune to taste some wonderful and comparably priced, 100% virgin olive oils, cold pressed from Mission olives in northern California. For mail-order information on this product write: Nick Sciabica & Sons, P.O. Box 1246, Modesto, CA 95353.

Vegetable Oil: Wesson is the hands-down favorite.

SHALLOTS

I am able to purchase shallots at most supermarket produce

counters these days. However, they may also be mail ordered from: Rocky Hollow Herb Farm, Sussex, NJ 07461; Hilltop Herb Farm, P.O. Box 866, Cleveland, TX 77327; or Magic Garden Herbs, Box 332, Fairfax, CA 94930.

SOY SAUCE

There are lots of different varieties on the shelf but Kikkoman is my choice.

TOMATOES (canned plum variety)

I choose the Progresso brand, imported from Italy.

TOMATOES MIXED WITH GREEN CHILES

I always use Ortega brand. This product is manufactured by Heublein, Inc. For shopping information write: Box 508, Dept. 2053, Farmington, CT 06032.

VINEGAR

I prefer Dessaux Fils, imported from France. Available at most good grocers or fancy food shops. (Dessaux exports a red wine vinegar and a tarragon-flavored white wine vinegar.)

YEAST

My favored brand for baking is El Molino (active dry yeast). Available at most health-food shops or write to: A.C.G. Company, City of Industry, CA 91746.

Index

Vanilla Extract

quarter vanilla beans, split —
put in w/ vodka — wait 4 weeks then
filter thru coffee paper thru a funnel

Marinated Mushrooms   1 qt.

6 cups water
2 T kosher salt (coarse)
1½ lbs small, white mushrooms, trimmed
        & rinsed
(a) ⌈ 3/4 cup mild white wine vinegar
    │ 1 T coriander seeds
    │ 2 bay leaves
    │ 1 teas sugar
    │ ½ small cinnamon stick
    │ ½ teas whole black peppercorns
    └ ½ teas dried thyme
        1 clove garlic, peeled & halved
        3/4 cup olive oil, approx

1. Combine water + 1 T. salt in
   saucepan + bring to boil. Add the
   mushrooms + boil for 2 min., then
   drain → reserving 3/4 cup of the liquid
2. In enameled / stainless steel
   saucepan, combine reserved
   mushroom liquid, (a) ingred.
        & remaining 1 T. salt. Boil
   for 5 min.